The Secret Art

The Secret Art

A Brief History of Radionic Technology for the Creative Individual

by Duncan Laurie

Anomalist Books
San Antonio * New York

Table of Contents

To Richard "Josh" Reynolds III, Patron Saint of Outlaw Technology.

It has been said that to obtain a small grant from Josh,
it was only necessary to be refused everywhere else.

INTRODUCTION

Having worked as an artist most of my adult life, I became aware early on that there were fundamentally different approaches to making art. Some art forms are bought and sold like commodities. Other art is deemed "priceless" and resides in museums. Music and film compete as entertainment venues and massive sculptural commissions provide ornamentation for architecture and parks.

These familiar forms are only the surface of the art we know and enjoy. Behind the business and institutional world of art, other creative individuals struggle to know themselves through deep introspection, often at the expense of acclaim or financial reward, only seeking to project meaning and inspiration into the culture through their work.

There is an even more remote type of creativity that is all but forgotten by the contemporary art world: The ability that ancient and indigenous artists had to interact with Nature and Spirit to heal, promote agriculture, and articulate the sacred dimension of life.

To accomplish these tasks, the artist/shaman had to be able to understand and tap into natural forces. This process requires a unique capacity of consciousness, one able to manipulate energy and matter toward a desired end.

Today, we call this capacity directed intent. We understand how directed intent can be used to control machinery, computers, systems and organizations, but we do not understand much about how it can be used by our consciousness to mitigate the progression of a disease or the growth rate of a crop, or a host of other activities that fall under the rubric of shamanic processes.

The shamanic process required artistic embellishment through dance, fetish making, costuming, and ceremony. What is not so well understood is the energetic components that the shamanic rituals sought to influence.

Today we tend to look at the shamanic process in the same light as religious ceremony: as an elaborate metaphor for appealing to a higher power to intercede on our behalf. By

1

contrast, as we will examine throughout this book, it is far more likely that shamanic individuals used artistic and technical methodologies employing intent to move energy and accomplish their objectives.

We can only guess how the various ancient peoples accomplished shamanic tasks. But we can look at our technical/industrial society and see if, within our own explorations, we may have uncovered similar techniques or approaches.

In fact, a robust process of creative adaptation employing both art and technology coupled with applied intent does appear on the radar of modern developments. It goes by different names: Occult Technology, Radiesthesia, Dowsing, Psychotronics, and Radionics, to name a few. For our purposes, we will use Radionics as a catchall phrase for any art/technology system that employs consciousness through tools or art to move energy and do work. We will implore the reader to suspend judgment on their viability despite the fact that modern intellectuals consider these techniques non-scientific and spurious. What also must be considered is that little is known about what consciousness actually is and how it functions.

Empirical science has not given us the answers to fundamental questions like who we are, where we come from, what happens after death, or why some people spontaneously recover from a disease while others die. There are far too many unknowns when it comes to the power and potential of consciousness and directed intent in Nature to discard potential opportunities just because they are not understood or condoned by science.

This book will review tools and techniques that have been swept under the rug by a mechanistic and deterministic worldview. We will briefly look at the history of these tools and techniques with the notion of adding them to those already available to the creative process. My objective is to set forth and explain Radionic technology as a platform for understanding and artistically working with Nature in a novel and creative way.

There have been numerous problems in writing this book, one of which is a technical component to the discussion that doesn't square with orthodox science. There is also a very long and complex history of individuals working in the area of what is referred to as "subtle energy" technology. Many valid contributions to understanding "subtle energy" and the tools that influence it are regrettably omitted. I have reduced the field mainly to a study of what is called Radionics. What follows is a historical definition of radionics as it is used for our purposes.

The basic assumption of radionics can be stated in three parts:
1. All matter emits radiations
2. The human body can be used to detect them
3. The mind can influence these radiations in extraordinary ways.

We are taught by our materialistic sciences that disciplines like radionics are both simplistic and impossible. To help overcome skepticism and to support and enhance an understanding of radionics, selective historical, technical, and procedural details are presented in a convincing but simplified manner.

This task also involves translating antiquated or cryptic terminology into modern, coherent language. The story of how mind-based devices have been evolving, like a lingering shadow for the last one hundred years in parallel with our familiar electromagnetic technology, is fascinating. Reading about it however, demands a degree of suspended disbelief from even the most generous reader.

Details of radionic design and construction will readily reveal their artistic and life-affirmative potential to the open-minded readers who consider their merit and potential.

While much of the focus will be on how these devices were invented and work, the underlying discussion is more about what they imply. Radionics is being used today not only to heal people, but also in veterinary medicine, to replace pesticides and fertilizers in agriculture, and for environmental detoxification and re-certification.

My hope is that the use of radionics will soon expand into music, art, and design. Radionic tools and techniques are deeply empowering. Understanding their use and application can be personally and professionally liberating. There are also dangers and responsibilities inherent in developing these skills. They can and probably are being misused. There are no laws currently governing the application of mind based technologies, though the danger is sufficiently recognized that initial legislation defining and limiting their use has been put forth before Congress.

More than anything else, the writer on radionics confronts the issue of believability. Does such a technology even exist, given the dominance of rational, mechanistic thought and the inevitable skepticism when contrasted with the scientific worldview? History abounds with fraudulent products with similar claims. Many of the most credible radionics inventors faced persecution and legal jeopardy. How does one explain why it works? When it does work, it is not always consistent. When successful, there is the impression more of art or luck at work than careful methodology.

Common forms of radionics exist that everyone can understand. We use them daily without realizing it. Everyone understands that the good cook imparts something into the food, which goes beyond the ingredients and mechanics of cooking. Whether we call it love or an extreme aesthetic sensitivity, the food takes on the character of the cook's invested energy. We feel it immediately when we put it into our mouth. I would call this a radionic enhancement.

Can that quality be quantified? In a way,

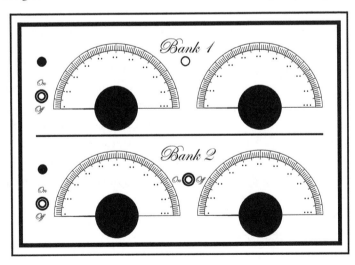

Fig i-1. Radiation Laboratories Model 4 dials

it can. People sitting around the table arrive at a consensus that the food is delicious. There is no empirical yardstick to measure how that food is actually better because subjective, aesthetic criteria are involved. We can agree that the qualities of the food, how they impact our senses, are wonderful. The evaluation is, in part, self-referential; subjectively we know the cook is brilliant. The proof lies in the consciousness of eating. Radionics works best when the mind is applied to a task of balancing ingredients to obtain a desired outcome.

Whether we are discussing a fine cook or artist, an expert gardener or someone else with a subtle gift, it goes without saying that each brings to their skill something beyond the ordinary, a capacity to insert a personal energy into the product of their labor. Radionics is a way to detect, describe and replicate that type of subtle emanation. Much arises from the world around us that eludes mechanistic, scientific interpretation. We don't call love, pain or happiness illusions just because they are subjective impressions. They are all energetic and very real. They can't be measured on instruments, but we do know they are calibrated; there is more or less of each in every instance. Radionics can also be generally understood as a way to calibrate and apply what cannot be otherwise measured, experiences that are often labeled as being composed of subtle energy.

The commonality that cooking, gardening, creative pursuits and other tasks share with radionics lies in how intent, directed through tools or instruments, produces an enhanced end product. In the same general sense, we can see that love and caring in any situation has the potential to improve the outcome. Radionics also benefits from the care, concern, and experience of the operator. In ordinary tasks, discrimination becomes a tuning mechanism to guide decision-making. Mental energy and careful reflection must be invested in improving the outcome. Radionics employs techniques to re-establish natural balance, allowing Nature to heal while we learn. The applications are endless.

I do not approach the task of writing about radionics particularly well equipped. Most of my career has been spent working in glass as an artist/businessman. Until recently, I had little knowledge of electricity or electronic design. I approached radionics as an art, and that is how I perceive and write about it here.

Radionics began life within the confines of the bizarre world of early Medical Electronics. It soon morphed into a completely non-scientific and self-referential methodology based upon the more empirical art of dowsing.

Today, quantum physics has scientifically demonstrated that the perception of events at the sub-atomic level can alter the outcome of those events. This discovery begs the obvious question, "What about here, at our perceptual level of reality?" For some researchers, the quantum field metaphor has thrown open a door into mind/matter dynamics. Such speculation has resulted in radionics undergoing a quasi-scientific revival in certain quarters. In the digital age, the field of radionics has acquired a whole new generation of instruments and potentialities. A more open minded and technologically savvy public has set the stage for a reappraisal of radionic technology.

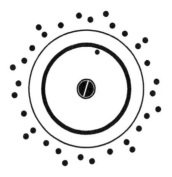

CHAPTER 1
ANCIENT RADIONICS

If one can accept the possibility that a substrate to physical reality exists that can be deterministically altered and influenced by human intention, then much of the mysterious and irrational design objectives of the prehistoric world become more comprehensible.

Lines that go nowhere, like those on the Nazca plain in Peru, or the New England stone walls that go half way up a hill and end suddenly, become viewed as something more than landing fields or sheep pens. Rather they are seen as an incisive design technology seeking to alter an energy pattern binding some aspect of reality. It could be a simple exercise of control. Is this not what all ritual burials propose to effect by their elaborate architecture and symbolism? It is not outrageous to think that a culture that believes it can influence the outcome of events following death would apply the same techniques to living systems.

For many artists who have functioned outside the commercial art world, with ancestors working in a similar way for thousands of years past, the task of art-making involved moving invisible forces. Healing, changing weather, restoring harmony, divination, accessing and making the sacred comprehensible to culture, all were tasks taken on by the shamanic artist. Since the beginning of self-reflection, artistic activity has been a bridge to the invisible world, embodying emotion, spirit, meaning, and transcendence.

By examining the methodology of radionics, I will attempt to introduce the reader to tools and ideas that explain how ancient, traditional art forms worked with nature energies. Anthropologists tell us that pre-historical and aboriginal peoples viewed the relationship between aesthetics and the forces of the natural world far differently than we do today. Even now, many native peoples employ the creative process for accessing subtle energy for healing and other work.

Some researchers tend to dismiss this functional and energetic component of native art as pure mythology. Only New Age true believers with frivolous, self-deceptive agendas could consider such energies as being real and immanent. Worse, many improbable and fraudulent healing devices have been sold to a gullible public for generations. No doubt there are many legitimate complaints made with respect to subtle energy technology, and with good reason. Nevertheless, even valid criticisms obscure important truths.

Despite the punishing weight of science, it remains my conviction that the ideas, tools and techniques outlined in this book will shed light on the ancient energetic approach to art. Take, for example, the drawings of what is described as a Babylonian geomantic device, designed and built by Muhammad Ibn Khutlukh Al-mawsili somewhere in Iraq or Syria in the 13th Century. The device, of extremely sophisticated design and construction, made of brass and copper with moving dials calibrated in dots, was used for interpreting and manipulating telluric energy. Currently on display in the British Museum, the device's fine crafts-manship suggests an ancient heritage of similar designs. This modern looking precursor of a radionics box also shares design elements with a 1950s Hallicrafter shortwave radio.

In many radionic devices, dot matrixes and other purely symbolic notations play a functional role in the operation of the device. Oddly enough, the artistic invocations of dot matrixes for unknown purposes appear in the earliest Paleoart as well.

Archeologist Robert G. Bednarik has documented the worldwide existence of numerous carved cupules in rock, visually forming abstract dot patterns that are dated in some cases, thousands of years before the better-known figurative traditions of the European cave art of the Upper Paleolithic. Cupules are carved circular indentions in the surface of the stone that resemble dots from a distance. The earliest European cupules (40,000 to 70,000 years ago) were found in Neanderthal burial No.6, in the French caves at La Ferrassie. The cupules at this site were discovered on the un-

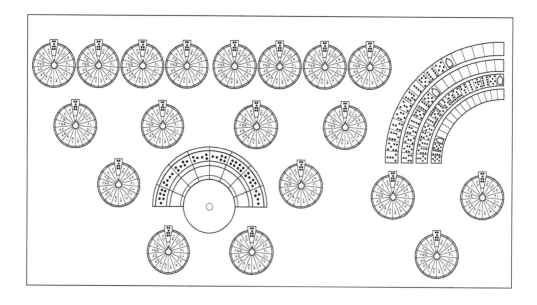

Fig 1-1. 13th Century Geomantic Device

Fig 1-2. 13th Century Geomantic Device

derside of a large limestone slab, in such a way as they faced the corpse of a child underneath. Sixteen of the cupules are arranged in pairs, suggesting a high degree of cultural complexity.

By comparison, Bednarik concludes that the oldest surviving rock art, in the sense of a symbolic activity (usually represented by linear grooves and cupules), first appeared in the Lower and Middle Paleolithic (150,000 to 300,000 years ago) in Asia, not Europe. Of these ancient cupule carvings, he points to the Acheulian Cave petroglyphs of central India, carved into very hard quartzite, generally considered in excess of 290,000 years old. The more ancient

art, being composed of complex geometric or abstract designs, are deemed culturally more enigmatic and difficult to decipher than the naturalistic, figurative forms made much later and commonly seen in European caves.

Bednarik points out that in Australia, it is widely agreed among rock art scientists that cupules are among the oldest carvings on the continent. In northern Australia in particular, they occur at hundreds of sites, "in incredible numbers and concentrations." Their presence seems to have prompted the development of later art forms and traditions at the same sites, especially rock painting.

1 — Ancient Radionics

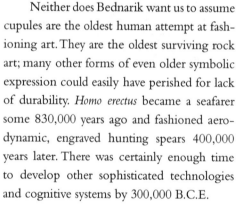

Fig 1-3. The Makapansgat jasperite cobble
2.5 - 3 million years old

Fig 1-4. Abrams' Micro-Oscilloclast

Neither does Bednarik want us to assume cupules are the oldest human attempt at fashioning art. They are the oldest surviving rock art; many other forms of even older symbolic expression could easily have perished for lack of durability. *Homo erectus* became a seafarer some 830,000 years ago and fashioned aerodynamic, engraved hunting spears 400,000 years later. There was certainly enough time to develop other sophisticated technologies and cognitive systems by 300,000 B.C.E.

One wonders what the thematic connection of dot matrixes across such a vast expanse of geography, time, and people – yet with surprising consistency of symbolism and execution – might be. We ponder what shared response in daily experience could have provided such a common denominator in the abstract pattern selection of dot forms. Could these dot forms have been a symbolic way of establishing a relationship with raw natural force? Bednarik notes that a researcher studying cupule-making in central Australia in the 1940s reported their function as an increase ritual for the pink cockatoo. The rock that the cupules were hammered into was believed to contain the life energy of the birds. The dust produced from the carving was believed to fertilize the female birds, thus increasing the yield of eggs, a valued Aboriginal food source.

Dot patterns in modern radionic design are either a function of early electronic component design or become purely symbolic in later devices that require no electricity. They connotate a means by which energy is calibrated or otherwise manipulated.

In this sense, as an artistic motif, radionic design may in fact be terribly ancient, to the point of becoming an archetypal component of the psyche, with the dot serving as the interface between man and nature. Entertaining this possibility allows for an additional crossover between mind, art and the energetic manipulation of mysterious natural forces, be they within an ancient or modern context.

The essence of our argument revolves around such a possibility. Select individuals, utilizing alternative technologies are presently altering the way we approach our lives. They are evolving a creative approach to changing consciousness itself, knowing that it will be easier to disengage from the destructive aspects of our technology today, if we design systems for tomorrow based upon a deeper understanding of nature. By employing the ideas and appliances covered in this book, future artist-inventors may conceivably do just that.

Granted this might sound impossible or improbable. Certainly many of the contemporary technological marvels we enjoy today would have seemed equally improbable a few generations back. Here is the rub. We have been educated and conditioned to believe the

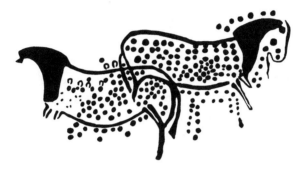

Fig 1-5. The Dappled Horses of Pech-Merle - 25,000 BCE

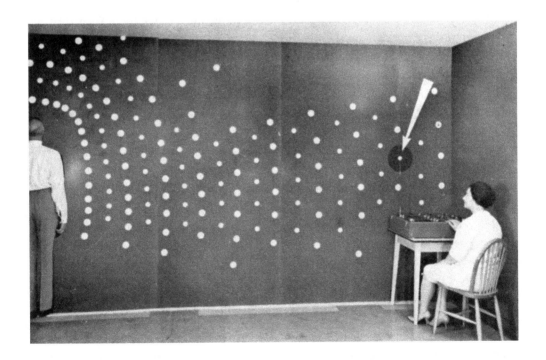

Fig 1-6. Portable de la Warr Multi-Oscillator used as detector

1 — Ancient Radionics

9

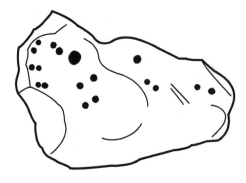

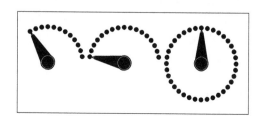

Fig 1-7. "La Ferassie Cave" cupules - 60,000 BCE

Fig 1-8. First Abrams Radionics Oscilloclast

magic of nature cannot ever exist. We are told consciousness is only the byproduct of chemical and electrical reactions in the brain. We can understand our consciousness mechanically and electrically, but basically we are alone with it in ourselves. Everything in our scientific worldview today stands against any truly magical technology: free energy, mind over matter, telepathy, spontaneous remission of disease, antigravity, and life beyond death. Yet in all instances, independent researchers report that such phenomena do exist and are a matter of record, some accompanied with patents and appliances.

The simple fact is that most of our science and technology comes from a study of the world around us, from matter and natural forces, and not from anything to do with consciousness. When we evolved to the point that we needed machines that compute, only then did we really begin to study how the brain and the mind works processing signals and information.

Science has been unable to study consciousness effectively for at least two very good reasons. First, consciousness is not part of the physical, material reality that lends itself so well to the tools of scientific investigation. Second, in matters of consciousness, it is difficult to separate the observer from the observed, which is a primary requirement of

scientific objectivity and repeatability.

Art on the other hand, has always been a discipline that is intertwined with consciousness. To render even the most direct simulation of nature, say a line drawing of a tree, the artist must grapple with some basic problems of consciousness. Determining how the view of the tree is selected, and then rendered, involves an ability to transfer a signal from the eye to the mind to the hand. Then, there are the qualitative issues surrounding the drawing of the tree, such as how representational or abstract the image should be and its aesthetics. Without due consideration to consciousness at every juncture, no human art can be made.

It would seem that artists are well qualified by virtue of the inherent demands of the profession to evaluate, design, and use technology that requires consciousness to work. Under examination here are a number of technologies that utilize consciousness, in the form of directed intent, as the active operating force in the radionic circuit. Ultimately, as with art, the only proof available to sanctify the methodology is the results. Through artistic results, radionic techniques may yet become mainstream and benefit the world with a natural, inexpensive technology to augment agriculture and heal.

The Secret Art

CHAPTER 2
DEFINING RADIONICS IN ART

Radionics is the name given to a largely forgotten medical technology that employs directed intention to cure illness. Radionics is based upon the supposition that all matter gives off radiation, in frequencies particular to the object or substance under observation. By devising a methodology to identify and measure these radiations in both healthy and unhealthy tissue, the operator of a radionics device can assist in restoring balance to the patient. This is accomplished both by neutralizing the frequencies of the disease and by importing healing frequencies, called "rates," into the patient. The device used for this process, of whatever design, is called a Radionics Box.

In the context of this book, I have chosen to expand the notion of radionics beyond the purely medical context. I look at it more as a metaphor for how human intent can be employed to transfer energy and perform work. In the simplest sense, radionics is a methodology by which Information can be used to move Energy, abbreviated as I > E.

The existence of technologies that employ consciousness to move energy have been explored in numerous contexts, mostly outside of science. In examining how the observer may affect the outcome of any observation, there is an implied contamination of objectivity. How does one objectively examine consciousness and its effect upon the world?

The design and application of any radionic technology operates on the premise that by changing the nature of the information our consciousness utilizes to affect an outcome, we marshal the forces necessary to determine that outcome. So far, what appears to be changed by radionic treatment exists deep within the semiotics of the body/mind/nature connection. Radionics practitioners believe that directed intent alters an outcome at the level of physical systems that have become patterns of information and energy. Imagine a disease as a specific geometry, a semiotic of itself; alter the geometry by intent and the outcome of the diseased pattern changes. By doing a

Fig 2-1. Tomb of a friend — Duncan Laurie 1972

series of diagnostics on the vitality of the individual, then boosting the weakened areas with applied intent, the disease is weakened using an inversion of the same process. This is how radionics is designed to work, whatever apparatus or tool is involved.

Due to the growth of media based technology we have adapted to the rapid rate by which one type of Information changes into another type of Information, abbreviated here as I > I. In this sense, a picture of the ocean becomes pixels re-assembled on your TV screen, and a song becomes bits and bytes on the hard drive of your computer. Information is in a fluid process of constant transformation, before and after it reaches the brain of the observer. Certain types of information can cause huge energetic changes within us. We watch our online bank account collapse from a bad investment and the numbers on the screen cause us to fall into suicidal despair. The person we love says one word, "Yes," to marriage;

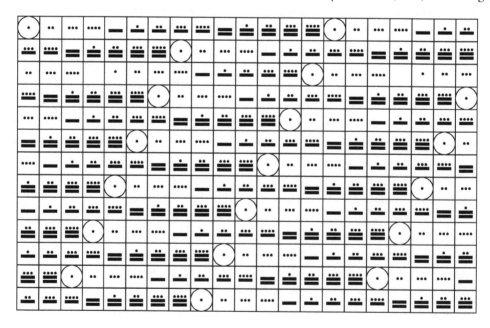

Fig 2-2. Mayan calendar

The Secret Art

Fig 2-3. CARLY PTAK performance at NO FUN FEST 2005 with de la Warr device

our heart roars and our brain swoons. Information moves Energy. I > E is a common fact of everyday life. Yet, when we say that we can design a piece of technology to effectively optimize I > E, it sounds like magic.

The magic we all know that routinely does change information into energy is art. Many people have experienced a life transformative moment (I > E) as a result of being impacted by the power of a work of art.

This then is the purpose of this book. It is a manual on how to understand and apply the way I>E works in nature. One method is radionic technology. To its credit, radionics has survived more than one hundred years of being ostracized and persecuted by mainstream medicine and science. It is still widely used throughout the world to cure people and animals. Recently, radionic technology has become computerized, and with the increase in processing speeds, it has also been successfully applied to healing large tracks of land decertified by environmental contamination. Other inspired uses await the creative practitioner.

Artists, reluctant to make products, could use radionic technology as an alternative artistic venue. We see this in traditional societies. The Hopi Indians routinely perform a ritual dance to invoke rain. I personally witnessed such an occurrence. Within half an hour of the dance, on a sweltering dry day, in a land with only six to eight inches of rainfall per year, huge thunderheads rolled in and soaked the fields.

Native healing traditions invoke a relationship with Nature that has been perfected over many generations. In our culture, the closest analogy to a nature methodology we employ is dowsing. Traditionally, dowsing was a way of finding water holding a "Y" shaped branch of a tree in two hands, while walking the land. When the open end moved dramatically up or down, water was said to be underneath. Today, dowsing instruments come in all forms, from wands, to "L" shaped copper rods, to pendulums. Health systems like kinesiology, which focuses on how the body functions and moves, have also developed a form of dowsing that employs the muscle systems of the body, no tools necessary.

Dowsing has also expanded its applications, ranging from revealing underground tunnels in warfare, to oil exploration, to finding lost persons (via map dowsing), to all types of yes/no question and answer methodologies.

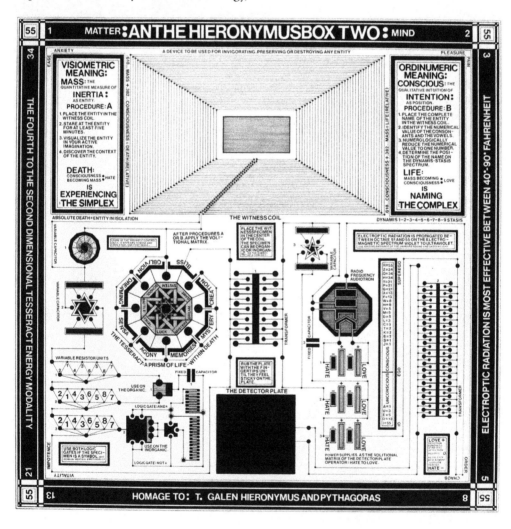

Fig 2-4. ANTHE HIERONYMUSBOX TWO - Paul Laffoley 1991

The Secret Art

CHAPTER 3
THE ORIGINS OF
RADIONICS IN DOWSING

Arguments arise from time to time about the meaning of the terms Radionic and Psychotronic. I have loosely defined them as mind/matter or subtle energy interface technologies in order to apply them in as broad a metaphorical fashion as possible. By doing so, it is possible to understand many ordinary events that focus mind into matter to produce a singular outcome.

Radionics is also a way to detect and describe emanations that arise from the world around us that elude a strictly mechanistic interpretation. The most familiar method of radionic detection is dowsing.

Christopher Bird, in an article on dowsing entitled "Applications of Dowsing, An Ancient Biophysical Art," defined it as: "a word for the art of searching, with a hand held instrument such as a Y-shaped rod, a pair of L-shaped rods, a wand or a pendulum – for anything. In all probability it comes from the German word: *deuten*, which has the following meanings: to explain, to expound, to interpret,

to point at, to signify, to bode, to auger – depending upon exactly how it is being used."

Bird's definition of dowsing includes signification. The understanding is that the dowser uses a simple device to locate a signal emanating from a source that he determines through focus of mind. Dowsing is therefore a semiotic process, whereby invisible signals are represented in the movement of a dowsing instrument and interpreted by the mind of the dowser. This procedure is identical to the way a radionics instrument is used today. The difference is mainly in the capacity of the radionic devices to finely calibrate the emanations under observation into numerical rates.

Noted etymologist and author Philip S. Callahan contributes the following insights into the art of dowsing: "The scope of low level energies is difficult to comprehend by those not schooled in the grammar of the subject. The ruby throated hummingbird – all of three inches long – trips from Panama to the east coast of the United States and back again.

Fig 3-1. 18th Century Dowser

The Pacific golden plover makes a seasonal non-stop flight of 3,000 miles from Alaska to the Hawaiian Islands with no landmarks whatsoever. Solid science has established that birds can detect minute radiant changes in the earth's magnetic field that may well help their orientation during migration."

"Dowsing is the art of detecting low-level energy. Focusing intent is a primal attribute. Arthur Middleton Young, the inventor of the Bell Helicopter, felt that one of the most amazing examples of animal behavior is the motion of an amoeba, which devoid of any musculature can reach out by extending a pseudo pod from any place in the body. Bird quoted Young as posing the question: *What causes the projection if it is not attention and intent?*"

"Dowsers also project an intent to find or a request for the location of a given object or target. One could say that it is a mental or psychic pseudo pod of possibly infinite length. An answer to the request seems to be fed back via their bodies in the form of molecular movements, which – because they are usually not consciously perceived – are called involuntary. The muscles cause the dowsing rod or pendulum to move, thereby objectifying the muscular action that, self-generated by the re-

quester, cannot really be termed automatic."

Callahan discusses the work of Juan Merta, a Czech-born physiologist, psychologist, gifted psychic, and professional deep-sea diver working on oil rigs in the North Sea. Merta, who conducted his experimental work at McGill University in Montreal, became interested in the water dowser's art as it related to map dowsing – a way of searching for missing objects or people. His findings caused him to suspect that muscle contractions in the arms or hands determined the movement of the dowsing device. By building an apparatus that could record both the movement of the dowsing device and any muscular contraction simultaneously, he was able to determine which impulse came first, the contraction or the movement of the device.

Merta, writes Callahan, "electrically wired the carpi radialis flexor in the wrist area of the forearm. The instrument translated what was happening to ink and paper. After the several tests were finished, Merta concluded that the dowsing devices react only after the human beings operating them pick up the signal, which then stimulates a physiological reaction. He further concluded that if the dowsing device were only an amplifier magnifying a sensation, then dowsers should be able to teach themselves to pick up such sensations without recourse to any dowsing device whatsoever."

Merta's idea was that in dowsing a projected request for information, focused intent is analogous to the mind reacting like dialing a telephone number into the vast telephone switching system of the body. The final muscular twitching on the other end of the line was a neural response to the ring of an appropriate telephone connection. Importantly, a successful search depends chiefly on accurate formulation of the requests. Garbage in, garbage out, is the recipe for failure.

The Secret Art

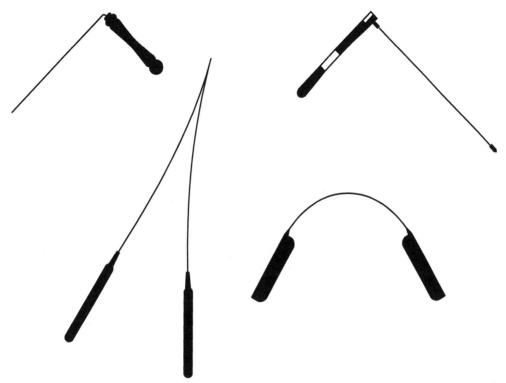

Fig 3-2. Dowsing Rods

As dowsing became more universally practiced and accepted, it acquired a formal name: Radiesthesia. Bird defined radiesthesia as "a word coined in the 1930s by the Abbe Bouly in France. It is taken from a Latin root for 'radiation' and a Greek root for 'perception' and thus means literally the 'perception of radiations.' At one time the *Journal of the British Society of Dowsers* was called RADIO-PER-CEPTION. The word has been adopted all over the European continent with the exception of the so-called 'socialist' countries, which have adopted a newly coined Russian word, Biofizicheskii Metod or 'biophysical method.'"

Bird and the radiesthesiologists leave us with no conclusions regarding the exact nature of the radiations themselves. He refers those frustrated with the lack of scientific explanation to Thomas Edison. When asked what electricity was Edison replied, "I don't know, but it works."

Whatever future explanation arises for dowsing and radiesthesia will also resolve the mysteries of radionics. The fact remains that these tools can be learned and employed without the benefit of an adequate scientific explanation. The basic techniques of dowsing are simple enough for a child to learn. Many people learn them every June in Vermont at the American School of Dowsing. The attraction of dowsing is its practical application. One need do nothing more than learn the basic theory and technique, and begin to practice. Whether one wants to locate water or missing objects, or go deeper into the metaphysical possibilities opened by this training, the very experience of successful dowsing is wondrous to many.

Within the arts, dowsing and radiesthesia are generally not recognized for the intrinsic role they play in developing artistic discipline. In creativity, one is constantly searching for an impulse, idea, tone, melody, color, context, or a myriad of other experiences necessary to develop a theme. The creative process employs a form of internal dowsing, a self-referential technique for locating the next component of the work in hand. Intuitively, this "divining" impulse is nurtured and developed throughout the artist's career. Few people would even consider the fact that the practice of ordinary dowsing or similar techniques like radionics could augment the artistic impulse.

Dowsing and radiesthesia are often pos-

"The meaning (of) Manitou...is more simply stated by placing a small dot into the graphic form. The dot signifies: Manitou. The 'dot' communicates that the creation of life, the earth, and the universe is not considered to be an accident. The 'living observer' of Manitou is often translated as spirit, but this has confused Western culture into a mistaken assumpion of pan-theism or superstition."

— *Mishibinijima and E. C. Lewis, writing about Anishnaabe-Cree artist Norval Morriseau, who in 1962 deliberately broke the ancient taboo of revealing the symbols outside of the secret societies within his own culture. http://mahdezemin.blogspot.com*

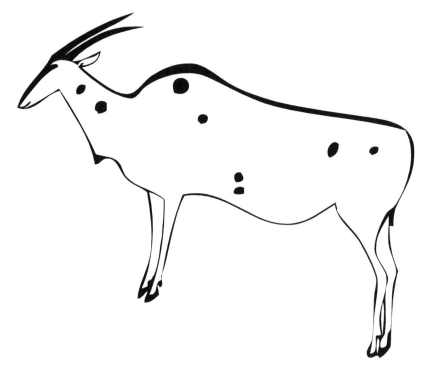

Fig 3-3. Cupule Petroglyph (antelope)

The Secret Art

tulated as proceeding from the psychokinetic (read: psychic or psi) energy of the mind, resulting in an involuntary muscle reflex. When examining the various approaches to subtle energy, one encounters a position that the operator's mind primarily determines the dowsing effects. Psi researchers do not generally accept the position of the dowsers, who feel that these radiations are external to the mind and imbedded in nature. Under the latter scenario, nature provides a signal, while the dowser interprets by muscular reflex, the mind/body response.

Psychokinetic effects (also termed PK) were widely studied in the former Soviet Union. Many individuals of great PK ability required little or nothing in the way of supporting appliances. The study of their psychic ability, with or without the help of a device, has been generally referred to as psychotronics. This loose definition, however, has not stopped psychotronic inventors from pro-

ducing impressive mechanical and electronic devices. The difference in meaning between psychotronic and radionic is still a gray area for many familiar with this field.

Radionics is a specific type of technology with both a founder and an historical line of progression into the current era. Most notably, radionics grew from the application of diagnostic dowsing techniques to medicine, and it is still in practice by that name today.

The origin of radionic diagnosis no doubt dovetailed closely with observations of the physiology of the body. Much of that analysis evolved with the common medical practice of "percussing" the abdomen. Percussive techniques in everyday diagnostic medicine require the doctor to tap parts of the skin primarily over the major organs. The health of the organ can then be determined according to the sound produced by the tapping. Differences in sounds demonstrate a healthy or diseased frequency pattern and gray areas in between. An assessment is then made, drawing on both experience and medical training. Good doctors bring all their abilities, both learned and intuitive, to the service of patients. Despite every tool at their disposal, a force from within must stimulate the body to truly promote healing.

It is my opinion that radionic sensitivity is acquired from nature on a primary, nonverbal level. It may be innate in all of us, but the degree of development varies significantly from individual to individual, as does the area of application. Of foremost importance is that the skill can be developed with training and practice and applied in a multitude of ways.

In the scenario I favor, the radionics practitioner learns how to recognize and interpret signals from an intelligent, guiding source beyond his or her own personality or ego. I refer to this source as "Nature" because it seems to be part of our environment and is entirely natural. It could just as easily be called a "higher power" or by any familiar name conveying the same impression.

Either way, the practitioner's consciousness becomes linked to this source during a successful radionic transaction and functions like a transceiver. Due to the delicate nature of the communications, it is always possible that information passing from nature intelligence to the human mind can be distorted or otherwise corrupted by the manner in which it is interpreted.

Distortion, a very real problem, can arise when practitioners believe their own ego to be the actual source of the healing information. The special nature of this linkage is also vulnerable to pressure from outside observers and circumstances and must be cultivated carefully. Like love and the other subtle gifts of nature that we are familiar with, success in practice requires patience, openness, and a suspension of disbelief.

Radionics devices have been constructed utilizing many different methodologies. Some radionics operators give much more importance to the design and engineering of the instrument than others. Many radionic practitioners value the tuning capacity and calibration of the instrument. They also want their instruments to be incorporated into mainstream medicine.

As a consequence, more emphasis tends to be placed upon the instrument than the mind operating it or the role of Nature in the cure. The design efforts of the early radionic inventors contain fascinating insight into how these priorities were assigned. For the artist interested in using radionics, each invention will seem like a new phase in a developing field of art.

CHAPTER 4
SCIENCE AND SCIENTISM

It is important to understand the reasons why alternative health methodologies like radionics have failed to survive or prosper, and why science is so hostile to their approach.

Part of the problem is what anthropologist Steve Mizrach calls "scientism," which is the belief that science is the ultimate authority to which all problems and questions must be directed. Since science is the be all and end all, scientists themselves must be a de facto intellectual "ruling elite." With science and scientists forming a super ordinate role over the affairs of lesser mortals, their position in society is dominant, and must be protected.

Mizrach describes the history of the problem: "The origins of (Western) science lie in the Scientific Revolution of the 17th and 18th centuries. This event was connected in many ways with other ongoing 'revolutions' – the Protestant Reformation, the rise of mercantile capitalism, the Enlightenment and the dawning of the Industrial Revolution. During the Enlightenment, there developed a sincere belief that reason would now come to govern human affairs, thereby replacing 'superstition and sentiment.' This led people to think that perhaps rational scientific authority would come to supplant 'arbitrary' religious and political authority, and that all that was needed to achieve human liberation was to conquer 'irrationality,' ignorance, and lack of education. This doctrine is what Foucault calls the *episteme* of the Enlightenment."

There is no doubt that science has been extremely successful in many areas of human activity. The broad base of scientific achievements led many to believe it could solve most of humanity's problems. Since World War II, the influence of science on political, military, and industrial activity has grown increasingly dominant. There is no area of our lives in which technology has not provided significant benefit. The astounding success of science in solving problems has definitely given it a privileged status among all types of human knowledge.

"Under the doctrine of scientism," writes Mizrach, "science is the ultimate authority for answering questions, and such things as rationality, reality, and truth are thought to be singular and singularly possessed by scientific inquiry - any deviation being clearly 'irrational' rather than exemplifying a different rationality." Following science's anarchistic fight against dogmatic religious belief early in its ascendancy, we find that it has now adapted an authoritarian structure all of its own.

Scientism according to Mizrach, "utilizes a discursive space (scientific journals, symposia and conferences, scientific honors organizations, etc.) which maintains the boundaries between establishment 'insiders' and 'outsiders' who are the scientists on the outside. Outsiders seek to imitate this space in order to try and 'borrow' some of the 'symbolic capital' and prestige commanded by science." All disciplines outside this discursive space are forced to seek approval from science to be considered legitimate.

Big science, formerly a challenge to religious authority, has today replaced much of that authority with its own set of assumptions and structures. Like the Church, it has its own language and jargon that reinforces its technical expertise and competence, its own complex support system in industry and government, its own media apparatuses, and its own system of reward and punishment. As such, scientism guarantees the power and authority of science, while maintaining the ability to neutralize competition from outside its hegemony that could challenge its authority.

In approaching the notion of "alternative science" and its resulting technology, it is important to differentiate between the initial goals of true science and the cultural imperatives dictated by scientism.

One must ask if the pursuit of empirical inquiry into areas deemed irrational by scientism automatically becomes pseudoscience in a negative sense of the word, or whether scientific inquiry can remain impartial in an unfamiliar intellectual terrain, even one void of a familiar rationality. One needs only rationale. Just follow scientific rationalism into the world of quantum reality and modern astrophysics to determine just how far this slender thread can be stretched.

At every step into the world of alternative science one encounters what is said to be an "appropriation" of scientific method and terminology into what would otherwise be a scientifically unsupported inquiry or discussion. Instead of posing a direct challenge to the ideology of science, many of these inquiries appear only to mimic scientific discourse in furthering what appear to be irrational objectives. To the naive, this appropriation of scientific terminology adds credence to the argument they are bogus. More cynically minded observers would see in this appropriation of scientific terminology an unfulfilled desire for the approval of science, or a crass appropriation of the prestige afforded science in the public mind.

That alternative medicine in general, with radionics being a prime example, should ultimately be found lacking in substance or efficacy by careful thinkers like Steve Mizrach is not too surprising. His primary criticism of alternative medicine lies in the need these methodologies have for mimicking scientific procedure and instrumentation, seeking in form, an implied approval from the orthodoxy, without any of the careful testing and peer review of the scientific method.

Instead, he recommends a revolt against what he calls "the Dictatorship of Reason,"

The Secret Art

pointing out that when science has met anomalies it cannot explain, the ensuing crisis should provoke a revision of cherished paradigms. For many scientists today, environmental awareness, particularly the hysteria around global warming, has revealed that widely divergent viewpoints exist within the tightly bound monolith of orthodoxy.

Other forms of alternative science, particularly areas like research into consciousness, suffer from the limitations of scientific method as it is applied today, particularly observer independence. I argue within these pages that alternative technologies like radionics may better be represented as an art form. Other healing modalities, like shamanism go completely beyond art and science altogether into pure mystical experience. How do you quantify something like that?

Whatever the proclivity for self-delusion, not all alternative science is without scientific merit. Consider the fate of the Princeton Engineering Anomalies Research (PEAR) laboratory. For over three decades, PEAR strove to prove that thoughts could alter the outcome of physical events. Since 1979, the laboratory's founder, Robert G. Jahn, former dean of Princeton's engineering school and professor emeritus, outraged Nobel Laureates, found money to continue research, and eluded academic censure – well almost.

"It's been an embarrassment to science, and I think an embarrassment for Princeton," said Robert L. Park, a University of Maryland physicist and the author of *Voodoo Science: The Road from Foolishness to Fraud*, to *The New York Times* upon the closing of the lab. "Science has a substantial amount of credibility, but this is

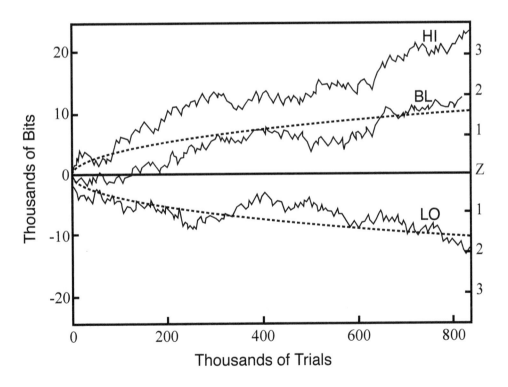

Fig 4-1. Cumulative derivations - 12 years of PEAR data

the kind of thing that squanders it."

In response, Jahn countered, "For 28 years, we've done what we wanted to do, and there's no reason to stay and generate more of the same data. If people don't believe us after all the results we've produced, then they never will."

Princeton University did not comment.

Jahn, a Ph.D. and world-class expert on jet propulsion, defied the system by virtue of private donations, particularly those from James S. McDonnell, a founder of McDonnell Douglas Corporation. Jahn researched telekinesis and related phenomena. By employing random event generators, which average out thousands of events like the toss of a coin to zero, Jahn could ask a subject to try and skew the results by using their mind to favor one result over another. Thousands of "coin flips" later, the machine data could be mined for statistical deviations beyond chance.

The results demonstrated that thought could alter the machines' random behavior every 2 or 3 times out of 10,000, not very much one can argue, but statistically significant. Certainly, when a physics Ph.D., an electrical engineer, and a developmental psychologist all joined the project, one would think the data would command some peer review. No one, however, would review it. Without peer review, they could not expect academic funding. Expert panels convened over the years could find no flaws in their approach. The students and the public were more charitable. Today, people the world over regard, with deserved admiration, this effort from within academia to bring scientific attention to the power of thought.

In many areas of alternative science, only a hostile intellectual climate, not faulty reasoning or distorted facts prevent serious in depth study of important topics that concern us all. Rejection of knowledge is as much a social and political process as its acquisition. Scientific and academic taboos can be created where popular culture weights in heavily upon the topic of study, trivializing it in the minds of serious researchers. Research on psychedelic drugs and UFOs have suffered similar fates. Were this not the case, alternative research could better inform our lives and stimulate our intellectual curiosity.

Radionics was conceived as a diagnostic and treatment technology at a time when modern electronic theory and biomedicine had not become the dominant sciences they are today. Early radionic devices incorporated the new discoveries of radio and electronics into their design. During that period, the functional assumptions of radionic technology did not seem as implausible as it does today. However, it wasn't long before radionics became outmoded and completely non-scientific. As Mizrach has noted, radionics continued to appropriate the methods of orthodox science into its design and terminology, making the probability of understanding what it could accomplish even more difficult to assess.

I will examine this appropriation in a spirit of tolerance, given the state of electronics and medicine circa 1910, when radionics was first discovered. I will do so in order to shift the focus of this interesting technology from the scientific to the metaphysical, where the reader not limited by a need for scientific approval can evaluate it. My aim is to provide a reasonable means of evaluating radionic technology as an artistic methodology.

CHAPTER 5
THE DIVIDED LEGACY OF MEDICINE

The invention and refinement of radionics in the early decades of the 20th century by Albert Abrams, A.M., LLD, M.D. was considered by some to be one of the most important medical discoveries of that time. Before revisiting this fascinating period and the circumstances surrounding the origin of radionics, it is important to have some concept of the intellectual climate surrounding this discovery.

In 1897, Sir J.J. Thompson had just discovered the electron. A few years later, Sir Ernest Rutherford had shown that all atoms consisted of a central nucleus surrounded by the constant movement of electrons. The study of electronics was in its infancy, but already Electron Theory had demonstrated the electrical nature of matter. By the early 1910s, Marconi was stating, "We are just entering what may be called the field of vibrations, a field in which we may find more wonders than the mind can now conceive."

Einstein was immersed in formulating the theory of relativity. Cezanne was laying the foundations for abstract art. Automobiles were appearing on roads and airplanes were staying in the air. "Heroic" medicine, the forefather of modern allopathic biomedicine as formulated by Benjamin Rush and others, had practitioners who were busy lancing, leeching, bloodletting, and poisoning their way to the forefront of contemporary healing.

At the center of the medical controversy of this time was a conflict going back to the Hermetic Tradition of Paracelsus, generally recognized as the founder of modern scientific medicine. Should disease be treated through the introduction of chemical substances, or was the patient to be restored to a state of harmony, whereby the life force, unimpeded by blockage, would allow the body to heal by itself?

Heroic medicine prevailed, by adapting itself to and incorporating new scientific discoveries. Significantly, germ theory, which relied upon a plethora of new technology arising from the study of optics and electronics, came to the forefront of medical thinking. By contrast, competing medical approaches like radionics appeared to resemble sympathetic magic.

Returning to Steve Mizrach's thesis from "Medicine on the Fringe," consider the origins of the conflict facing medicine around 1910. He points to what historian Harris L. Coulter called a "Divided Legacy" in medicine. For perhaps 2000 years, dueling approaches to healing have been utilized, what Coulter calls the Empirical and the Rational. Empirical medicine is based on direct observation and experimentation, while the Rationalist approach is deductive, employing logic derived from abstract, a priori methods for approaching disease.

In this analysis, radionics would fall into the Empirical category. Radionics requires careful consideration of the patient's overall history, medical and circumstantial. The doctor then diagnoses and treats in large part from his own experience. A case can be made that that radionics goes even beyond empiricism into what scientific historian Gerry Vassilatos has called "qualitative science."

Qualitative science is a term Vassilatos employs for the deductive process that we all use to measure the felt or intuitive aspects of nature, over and above the purely quantitative measurements. Qualitative science seeks to understand not only what can be perceived and measured, but also how we perceive and know.

In painting, for instance, what the artist knows is only comprehensible to others through the means by which the artist expresses it. The quantities of paint, the size of the canvas, the colors and forms in and of themselves do not add up to a painting. It is only by the artist employing a structured methodology of qualitative decision making that we come to experience what a work of art is or means. Likewise, self-referential methodologies like radionics may follow empiri-

cal procedures, but the results derive from the qualitative skill of the practitioner.

By contrast, biomedicine today is a rationalist method. The doctor approaches treatment by virtue of logic, following the procedural methodology learned in medical school. Coulter's observation is that as medicine becomes more corporate and professional, the empirical gives way to the rationalist approach. He suggests that early on, allopathic medicine was more of an Empirical system, but the need to become ever more professional soon resulted in adopting standards – in education and through the formation of the American Medical Association – which led to adopting a more Rationalist approach. When alternative medical systems like radionics tried to emulate the success of allopathic medicine, they eventually compromised their empirical foundations.

The schism in the philosophy of medicine for the last 2000 years, the Rationalist versus the Empirical, was very much in play during the early 1900s when radionics was first discovered. In fact, the resulting controversy over radionics presents a vivid mirror of the transition modern medicine was making at that time from empirical to rationalist.

An immediate conflict appeared as radionics sought to use electronics to transmit an unknown biological energy. Radionic technique required the practitioner to be something of an artist, projecting the doctor's considerable healing skills into a subtle, mind sensitive instrument. To make these techniques palatable to others, radionic devices had to mimic machines rooted in a procedural method, explainable in the scientific terminology of the day. In that development we find the seeds of much future controversy.

CHAPTER 6
THE FATHER OF RADIONICS

Dr. Albert Abrams was born in San Francisco in 1863 and is largely credited with discovering radionics. Abrams qualified for admission to a medical college before he was old enough to receive a diploma. Learning German, he went to Europe to continue his medical studies, graduating with the highest honors in medicine from the University of Heidelberg. He continued post-graduate work in Heidelberg, Paris, Berlin, Vienna, and London under some of the most famous teachers of the time.

One of these was the eminent 19th century physician, mathematician, physiologist, physicist and philosopher of science, Hermann Von Helmholtz. It was through Von Helmholtz that Abrams learned physics and became passionate about finding a correlation between its laws and biology.

Upon returning to the U.S. Abrams began teaching at Stanford University where he eventually became Director of Clinical Medicine. By age 30, he was President of the San Francisco Medico-Chirurgical Society and a fellow of the AMA. With twelve books on the shelves of the Library of Congress, he was regarded as one of the foremost neurologists of the day. His book *Spondylotherapy*, published in 1910, was popular enough to run into six printings and was translated into French and Japanese. Sir James Barr, a former President of the British Medical Association, in writing a foreword to a book on Abrams' radionic discoveries, described him as the perhaps the greatest medical genius of the previous half century.

In Barr's own words, "I have often said that if Abrams had done nothing more than discover the cardiac and pulmonic reflexes, he was worthy of a prominent niche in the temple of fame. In America and France, Abrams' cardiac reflexes must have saved thousands of lives. Had Abrams not been possessed of both an overwhelming curiosity and a substantial inherited fortune, he may well have never got around to arousing the controversy and vilifi-

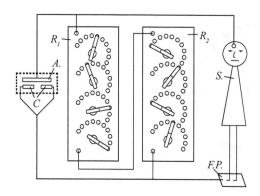

Fig 6-1. Abrams' Dual Circuit Device

cation stemming from his discovery of Radionics."

Using Abrams' radionic therapy is still a criminal offence in most states in America. Why? The answer lies in the very peculiar strain it has continuously put upon scientific procedure. One problem was that radionics and similar diagnostic techniques employed dowsing-like methodologies that worked in practice but were not thoroughly understood scientifically. One such empirical technique that Abrams and many other doctors of that time relied upon was percussion of the abdomen. Regarding percussion, it was assumed that a better knowledge of the physics involved would eventually follow to explain

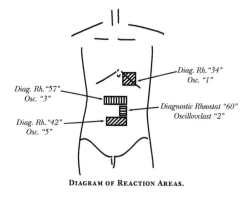

DIAGRAM OF REACTION AREAS.

Fig 6-2. Abdominal percussing diagram

the experimental results. This assumption has not been realized to date. As a result, medical dowsing has been largely dismissed as quackery by orthodoxy.

In percussion, the human abdomen was used as a diagnostic medical instrument. The doctor tapped the patient's abdomen in an attempt to feel and hear the stomach and other organs. If he found an area of several square inches that, instead of sounding hollow like a drum, was flat and dull, it could indicate a particular illness.

The art of percussion consists of tapping with the middle finger of the right hand on the middle finger of the left hand, which is held against the abdominal wall. It was a diagnostic technique Abrams had used for many years. From experience he knew instinctively that a dull sound above the naval could signify that the patient was in the early stages of cancer. A similar sound along the inner border of the shoulder blade confirmed his suspicions.

His reasoning for the sound was that the cancerous tumor was emanating a specific radiation that was affecting the nerve fibers of those areas, reflexively causing a muscle contraction of the abdomen in that spot. By testing other patients with similar conditions, he could verify that each had a contraction in the same location.

These observations caused him to question whether a cancer tumor removed from a patient would have the same effect in the proximity of a healthy person. To answer this question, Abrams devised a clever experiment. He found an entirely healthy young man (called the "subject") and had him apply to his forehead a vial containing a piece of a malignant tumor just removed from a cancer patient nearby. Within a few seconds the dull areas percussed on the cancer patient sounded dull on the body of the subject, but only when he was facing west. For an unknown reason, when the subject wasn't facing west, or removed the vial from contact with his skin, the cancerous tone disappeared.

This astounding discovery was repeated many times. For the first time, a slice of diseased tissue held against the surface of the skin, in a closed container, produced a clearly observable reflex action in the nervous system of a healthy person that hadn't existed moments before.

Abrams surmised from his knowledge of physics that the molecules of the diseased tissue must have a different atomic or electronic signature than healthy tissue. If the difference between the healthy and diseased tissue were electronic in nature, then perhaps it would travel down a wire and produce the effects at the other end.

The subject was asked again to stand with a wire fastened to a small aluminum disc held by elastic against his forehead. On the other end of the wire, an insulated handle was mounted to a larger aluminum disc. This wire was passed behind a screen, where an assistant who could not be seen, held a cancer specimen. Neither Abrams nor the young man would know when the assistant holding the cancer specimen pointed the disc. In each instance, the same dull tone appeared in the young man's abdomen just as before and every time the wired disc was pointed away, a healthy tone sounded. This tone was audible to the assistant behind the screen, so he knew exactly when the tone matched his pointer.

In later experiments, thousands of varying conditions were tried. Different diseases resulted in dull tones appearing at various locations on the body. However, it was not long before Abrams discovered that certain diseases,

Fig 6-3. Dr. Albert Abrams

like syphilis and cancer, shared locations close to one another on the body.

To overcome this obstacle, Abrams reasoned that if the signal of the diseased tissue would travel down a wire, then perhaps he could distinguish one radiation from another using the methods of electrical calibration. He simply cut the wire going between the assistant and the man being percussed and attached a variable resistance box between the two cut ends and resumed his tests.

Edward W. Russell, a prominent writer on radionics who knew many early radionic inventors, described this box as: "Large and durable, it had three knobs fastened to brass blades that were designed to sweep across three arcs of studs. The studs were attached behind the box to coils of wound wire inside. With three blades able to make contact with a total of sixty-one studs, it was possible to accurately measure resistance in ohms across the two connecting terminals." By using variable resistance, which assigns a numerical rate

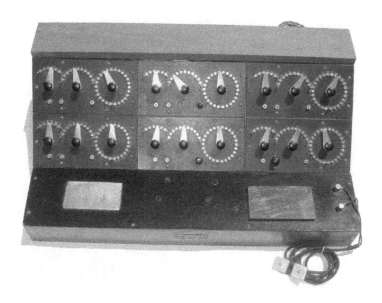

Fig 6-4. Abrams Reflexophone

to the amount of resistance (in Ohms) in the line, Abrams was able to numerically differentiate between the different diseases that he observed in his experiments. The first notorious "Black Box" was nothing more than three old-fashioned dial resistors, but Abrams gave it a complicated name: the Reflexophone.

When testing for cancer, the assistant held the wire pointed to the tumor sample while he twisted the dial of the resistor. When he hit 50 ohms resistance in the circuit, Abrams heard the familiar thud on the abdomen of the subject. At 49 and 51, it disappeared. When he tested for syphilis, the thud appeared at 55 ohms, and so on. With this process of calibration in place, Abrams was able to assign a spot on the body, and a rate in ohms, to thousands of diseased conditions. He published his findings in a book called *The Atlas*.

Abrams' simple experiment was of critical importance for the next hundred years of radionics. The measurements made with the resistance box were called the "Electronic Re-

actions of Abrams" or ERA. Later, the process became known as "radionics."

So far, nothing Abrams had done went beyond what any highly curious and talented researcher might have done under the same circumstances. Given the many unknowns about electricity at that time, Abrams' discovery of a biological radiation that had an electrical component would certainly have merited scientific investigation. Many of his contemporaries duplicated the simple experiments with similar results. The enormous implications of his findings – being able to electrically detect radiations emanating from diseased tissue – were eagerly received by many physicians of his day, though they are all but lost to us now. Yet, this discovery was just the beginning for Abrams and as he began to devise instruments to treat illness based upon these mysterious radiations, Abrams silently crossed over the invisible boundary between science and metaphysics.

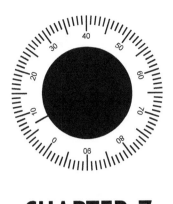

CHAPTER 7
THE OSCILLOCLAST

There are elements of Abrams invention, the Reflexophone, such as the use of simple materials, clear-headed observation, and the willingness to creatively explore possibilities through experimentation, which uncannily parallels the discovery of radio. With regards to radionics, the essence of the discovery was denied scientific confirmation, and to this day, it remains largely in the hands of alternative healers and inventors.

Abrams could have stopped his research at this point. He could have spent much of his fortune and talent moving this knowledge of a strange biological radiation into mainstream science that was not then as thoroughly mechanistic and deterministic as it is today. But this was not to be the case.

Abrams was not only brilliant and endowed with the stamina of an iconoclast, he was also rich. He had the means to pursue his research and discoveries without the need to justify it to anyone. He didn't have a shrewd publicist to constrain his exuberance, or a board of directors to answer to for his pay. His freedom accelerated the work, but also brought with it envy and a cruel and debilitating professional skepticism.

Abrams also made some crucial professional miscalculations that considerably weakened his scientific objectivity. One mistake was in unwisely popularizing the mysterious attributes of the radiation by doing oddball experiments for fun and relaxation. In a book entitled, *New Concepts in Diagnosis and Treatment*, Abrams offered dozens of off-hand and spurious observations that made his discoveries seem more like a parapsychology sideshow than a serious professional undertaking. All the controversy aroused by the extensive publicity cast every person he helped and each new invention he discovered in a surreal light, which certainly did not endear him to his conservative profession.

The next critical turning point occurred when Abrams obtained clear and reliable readings in his resistance box using only a drop of the patient's blood. Abrams realized he had discovered an entirely new way of diagnosing the individual patient. No longer was it even necessary to visit his office in person, as long as a blood sample was on file.

In the early 1900s, scientists and physicians were unaware that a drop of blood contained the blueprint of an individual's entire genetic makeup in the form of DNA. The world was decades away from that discovery. Likewise, they could not have even imagined that cells emit measurable radiation in the form of light. Today, we continue to discover a great deal about our physical make up and about biological radiations that make Abrams' discovery seem ever more palatable.

Unfortunately, the mysterious manner by which blood seemed to yield personal information to a strange instrument had a sinister quality to it. Images of voodoo and the occult came to mind. The more exotic Abrams' pronouncements became, the more dogmatic he was in defending their authenticity. The louder the ridicule became, the more his credibility suffered. A media circus began revolving around radionics that went on for decades. This circus distracted public awareness from the diligent experimentation Abrams had done and the fascinating discoveries that emerged from it.

The truth is that the language Abrams used to refer to the mysterious radiations – "energy provided by thought" – did not serve him well. In other instances, he would make equally cryptic statements like "Psychic energy passes through metal and all other media thus far tried." By leaning towards a psychical interpretation of his data, Abrams was guiding radionics outside mainstream science and into parapsychology. The result was an inevitable conundrum. One could not adequately study the radiation scientifically because it was in part or in whole a product of the consciousness used to study it!

Regardless, Abrams was able to obtain usable medical data by placing the blood sample, now referred to as the "witness" of the patient, into the "well" of a homemade condenser. Again, he chose to give an ordinary electrical component a peculiar name: the Dynamiser.

Writer Edward Russell described its construction: "It was a circular container made of hard rubber about three inches in diameter in the base of which were two electrodes connected to earth. The lid was formed of discs of aluminum with layers of mica between. A wire from the lid was connected to the resistance-box to another wire connected to a pointed electrode with which the patient or an assistant could determine the precise location of the disease."

Abrams soon found that the Dynamiser intensified the reactions, and it was soon supplemented with two grounded aluminum plates on which the patient stood. This discovery proved beneficial in that it eliminated the necessity of having the patient wait while the doctor completed the diagnosis by percussing the subject.

Just how significant was Abram's energetic approach to the diagnosis and treatment of disease?

Consider the words of Dr. Francis Cave, in an article about Abrams written for *Pearson's Magazine* in 1922: "How can vibrations destroy disease? Everything in nature has its natural period or rate of vibration. If one approaches an object with a source of vibration of the same vibratory as itself, the object will also be set in vibration-as shown by the response of the harp to the tuning fork. This forced vibration of the object may attain

Fig 7-1. Abrams' Oscilloclast

such magnitude as to fracture or destroy it… and it makes no difference whatever whether the source be a chemical, a pigment, a ray of light, an electrical current, or some other thing yielding the same vibratory rate. This brief statement contains in concentrated form practically the entire therapeutic philosophy of Abrams. Prolonged demonstration is proving to be absolutely fundamental and the first successful effort to deal with medical problems on a purely mathematical basis. Disease is merely the expression of a vibratory rate. If this vibratory rate can be measured, something can be found with a similar vibratory rate which can be imposed upon it and destroy it, thereby to a large extent proving the correctness of the Hahnemannian principle of 'Simila Similibus Curantur.' If we can make it impossible for the vibratory rate of disease to exist, the disease itself cannot exist. Abrams has shown the world not only how to measure out the vibratory rate of disease, but also how to measure out its virulence, a thing which is not possible with any other method known to me. When these things are ascertained, and the application of his therapeutic reasoning is made, the disappearance of the disease is a practical certainty.

"Here is the basis for all therapeutic systems, whether allopathic, homeopathic, osteopathic, or mental. The vibratory rate of the diseased organ or tissue must be changed or recovery cannot ensue. Just how the different schools of practice successfully make this change could readily be determined by the application of this process of reasoning to their respective problems. The rise and fall of therapeutic systems and schools of the medicine will hereafter be determined by the degree of their acceptance and application of the basic electronic principles and practices first enunciated by that scientist and humanitarian, Dr. Albert Abrams, of San Francisco. He has been the first to supply a definite yardstick by which all other methods can and must eventually be measured."

In the Abrams era, the term "electronic" had much more of a mysterious connotation than it has today; it was much like the term "psychic energy" today. It is important to remember that the vacuum tube had only just been invented, in 1905, and was not turned into an amplifier until much later.

The public mystification of radionics began with the idea that Abrams' "Black Box" alone could heal a person of disease. This distortion of fact was in part due to an interesting discovery Abrams made shortly thereafter, when Abrams tested the blood of a malaria patient together with a few drops of quinine and found no reaction at all on the subject. This discovery suggested to him that the quinine "radiations" were able to cancel out the "radiations" of the malaria.

Abrams was fortunate enough to hire the very best engineers to design his variable resistance instrumentation. He reasoned that since all matter was electrical in nature, the specific radiations of the diseased tissue might be energetically reversed and the disease thereby cancelled out.

Abrams had the most accurate variable-resistance boxes money could buy. The appliances were so sensitive that some critics contended that his measurements must be due to some variable inductance from the resistance coils themselves. It is a shame that more information about how he addressed this criticism is not well documented.

While a great deal of patient research and good fortune enabled Abrams to carry his early diagnostic work forward, it was tragedy that pushed him to develop an instrument to cure. His Radioscope and Dynamiser had allowed him to calculate both the intensity and the location of a disease. He also discovered that he could detect the existence and severity of a disease long before it took on a physical manifestation. For ten years, Abrams watched in growing desperation as his wife developed and ultimately died from an inoperable form of cancer that he had detected long before it ever appeared in her body.

Spurred on by the painful conundrum of having discovered a revolutionary diagnostic technology that could detect disease but not cure it, Abrams was determined to find a solution. To this end, he retained and collaborated with an inventor named Samuel Hoffman. In 1919, the collaboration produced a piece of equipment known as the "Oscilloclast."

The Oscilloclast was basically an electrical device designed to subject the patient to a negative electrical charge with radio-frequency electromagnetic pulses in between. A resistance box with different settings for adjusting and controlling the treatment "rates" of the patient was placed in the circuit between the Oscilloclast and the electrode attached to the forehead of the subject.

A technical writer of the time, whose name is not known, described it this way: "Today's tube Oscilloclast belongs to a class of electrically operated devices known as short-wave treatment instruments. Such instruments are divided broadly into high power and low power devices. The Oscilloclast belongs to the low power class. It differs from the conventional low power devices in that it produces three kinds of energy. One kind is the usual short wave; another kind is an impulse excited damped wave and the third kind is an alternating magnetic energy. All of these energies are of low power and, it is thought, act to help the body overcome pathology and restore normalcy in the tissues by utilizing characteristics of the low power energies themselves rather than to produce heat in the tissues.

"The continuous waves are chopped up into short wave trains without changing the frequency or heights of the waves. This kind of chopping up continuous waves is done to produce dots and dashes in the receivers in radiotelegraphy. The high frequency waves in radiotelephony are not chopped up into short-wave trains as in radiotelegraphy but the

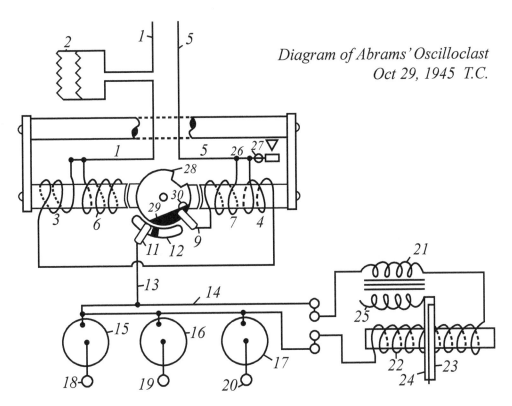

Fig 7-2. Oscilloclast diagram

broadcasting oscillators are so controlled that their high frequency waves have different intensities or heights. If a line is drawn so that it touches the tops of all of the high frequency waves it will describe a waveform with the waves much longer than the high frequency waves. The high frequency waves are called carrier waves and the longer ones are called modulated waves."

Treatment could be up to an hour in duration, during which the patient felt nothing. It is interesting to note the writer's observation about how the wave train of signals generated by the device occurred in a digital dot to dash formation used in electrical communications (Morse code). The electrical waves may in fact be carrier waves for the biological information, dependent upon the intent focused upon it by the operator.

As Abrams progressed with his discoveries, it became more and more apparent to adherents and critics alike that some form of Information to Energy (I > E) conversion was taking place. The doctor solicited the information component of the disease by applying percussion to the patient. That information was energetically transmitted along an electric wire to the instrument, where it became information again, in the more precise form of variable resistance. Likewise, in treatment, the correct healing information was sent back by the Oscilloclast to the patient as radio pulses, triggering the body to heal itself. The whole process was deeply semiotic, a theme we will return to in later chapters.

The Oscilloclast was a very well thought

out and well built medical device. It may have inadvertently taken advantage of a psychic process inherent in healing itself, but any physician trained in its use knew it was designed for reliable, mechanical dependability. Abrams and other physicians cured many people that had given up all hope with the Oscilloclast. Could they have gained such notoriety had these devices not performed as advertised?

It is important to the understanding of radionic technology to see how it progressed from a remarkable medical discovery praised by many scientifically trained men into a system that had more in common with shamanic healing. To understand the artistic and design potential of radionics, this transformation provides intriguing insights.

CHAPTER 8
INSIDE DR. ABRAMS' CLINIC

It is difficult to visualize exactly what is being described in a radionic treatment. Fortunately, an article published in *Pearson's Magazine* in June of 1922, written by Upton Sinclair and entitled "The House of Wonder," helps to clarify what was involved. Thanks to Sinclair, a renowned American writer, we have a first hand glimpse of the Abrams clinic. Following this excerpt is Sinclair's response to the American Medical Association, which had criticized both this article in particular and Abrams' discoveries in general.

"For some fifteen or eighteen years I have had the good fortune to count among my friends one of America's greatest poets and most loveable of men, George Sterling. For ten or twelve years I have been accustomed to read in his letters extravagant statements concerning a certain San Francisco physician. He would say, 'I should never again be afraid of getting any disease. Abrams would cure it in a week or two.' He would say, 'My friend Abrams continues to work new miracles, so rapidly that the medical profession had been frightened away from him.' These statements were so extreme, that I failed to take them as seriously as I should. I wish now to profit by that blunder, and tell what I have to tell as cautiously and conservatively as possible, so as not to frighten the reader away.

"A few months ago I received from George Sterling a letter from which I quote a couple of paragraphs: 'I am glad to see you're interested in Dr. Abrams, and I wish I could orally discuss him with you. He has utterly revolutionized medicine and henceforth nine operations out of ten will be unnecessary, especially where bacilli are concerned. I send you one of his quarterly pamphlets, which he publishes for the many physicians who have taken his course. There are always a lot of them in his laboratory, and they tell me that his diagnoses are 100 per cent correct. In this quarterly read especially the article by Sir James Barr, late president of the British Medical Association; realizing meanwhile what it means for a conservative English physician to make such statements! And Barr is going to be convinced even as to cancer. I know of many cases that Abrams has cured lately, four of them personal friends of mine. And Tuberculosis is nothing to him. To me he seems the greatest man ever born…'

"So I decided to go to San Francisco and investigate. I planned to spend a day or two, but what I found there held me a couple of weeks, and it might have been months or even years, if urgent duties had not called me home. I think the best way to present the work to you, the work of Dr. Albert Abrams, is to take you to his clinic, and let you see what I saw at my first visit, without any preparation or explanation.

"It is a two story building on Sacramento Street, and after I had visited it a few times, I took to calling it 'The House of Wonder', for I saw in it such miracles as I had never dreamed

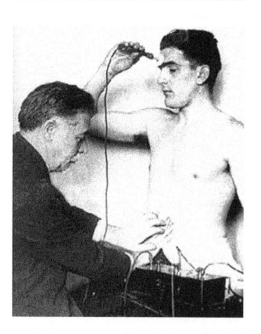

Fig 8-1. Dr. Albert Abrams percussing an abdomen

of in this world.

"You are in a physician's laboratory, with rows of raised chairs on one side of the wall. These chairs are occupied by a score or so of physicians, who have come from all over the country to study Abrams work. In the center of the room there is a long table containing some electrical apparatus. One of the wires from these apparatus ends in an electrode, and in front of the table upon a grounded plate, stands a young man stripped to the waist, and with the electrode pressed to his forehead. Dr Abrams sits on a chair before the young man, and taps with his finger upon the latter's abdomen, a method known to physicians as 'percussion.' To save you any unnecessary bewilderment, I explain at once that this young man is not the patient being examined; this young man is known as the 'subject,' and his body is merely one of the instruments, which Abrams uses in his examination. The patient is in Toronto, or Boston, or Mexico City and all that Dr. Abrams has is half dozen drops of his blood upon a bit of clean white blotting paper.

"'Next specimen,' says Dr. Abrams, and his assistant takes from an envelope a blood specimen which has come in this morning's mail, and cuts it to the right size and puts it in a little box which is connected by a wire with a rheostat, in turn connected with the body of the subject.

"The doctor's assistant hands him a letter which has come with the specimen, and the doctor reads it to his clinic: 'I sent the blood of Mrs. J., age 16 years' that is all. 'No symptoms!' grumbled Abrams. 'They want me to try it out, of course, and I can't blame them, but it is a waste of time to begin at the beginning of each case. All right, gentlemen, we set the instrument at 49 which is the vibratory rate of human blood. I don't happen to know this doctor who sends the specimen, and there are people trying to play tricks on me all the time. If this specimen contains human blood, the vibratory rate will come through on the body of the subject, and we shall have a dull area on this spot, if it is a male.' The doctor indicates a line just below the navel, and about an inch to the left. 'If it is a female, the dull area will be on the corresponding spot on the right. Now listen.'

"He presses the second finger of his left hand against the abdomen of his subject, and with the second finger of his right hand, used as a little hammer, he begins to tap. He starts a couple of inches off from the correct spot and you hear a slightly resonant sound. He moves his finger, and when he comes upon the correct spot you notice a difference in the sound --- at least you come to notice it after you have listened through several sessions of the clinic and your ear has become practiced. The sound is duller, which is the same difference you would notice if you were percussing a table, and changed from the middle of the table to a spot over one of the legs.

"'It is human blood, female,' says Abrams. 'In order to verify it, I set the rheostat at 50, and you notice that the dullness disappears. I set it back at 49, and the dullness returns. I call your attention to the fact that the subject is facing west. I turn his body slightly out of the line, so, and you note the dullness is gone, even at 49. I have to impress upon you again and again the importance of these minute details. I do not know why it is necessary to face west; it must have something to do with magnetic currents of the earth, of course. All I know is that if you face west you get these reactions, and if you face any other way, you don't get them. All this work of mine is empirical, you understand. I experiment and find what happens. I try one way, and then I try another; so

little by little I am groping my way to these secrets of nature…Next specimen.'

"The assistant takes the blood specimen from the little box and throws it into the trash basket. She touches the top and inside and cover of the box with a little horseshoe magnet to destroy the radioactivity of the last specimen, and puts in another specimen. This time it is from a physician in Boston. This specimen is marked 'male, age 62.'

"'Another physician I do not know,' says Abrams. 'And again, no symptoms given. It seems that we have to spend the whole morning doing this a-b-c work; every physician in the country has to be separately convinced – and then they aren't convinced! All right, no help for it. First, is it human blood? We set the dial at 49. Forehead, please.'

"The subject places the electrode upon his forehead, and Dr. Abrams begins to tap. 'Aha!' he says. 'A practical joker. No human blood! You see gentlemen; it is clear and unmistakable. The area for human blood is precisely here. Now listen carefully; there is no difference whatever in the sound. Neither male nor female! About once a week we have someone trying to play this silly joke upon us. Just for fun, let us determine what kind of blood it is.'

"And the doctor sets the rheostat at one figure after another. 'Cows blood? No, dog's blood – no! Monkey, cat, sheep---ah yes, sheep's blood. He has pressed the paper against his Sunday dinner before it went into the oven. All right, we will waste no more time upon that.' The doctor takes the envelope and the vehemence of his pencil as he writes the words 'sheep's blood' ought surely, if there be anything in his theory of radioactivity, to convey a vigorous shock to the doctor in Boston who has played the trick.

"'Next specimen.' And so we proceed. Another sample is put in, and the tapping begins, and we are told that this person has 25 ohms of tuberculosis, located in the spinal cord and left kidney. We are told that the disease is of 12 years standing, also that there is 'strep', that is to say streptococci, or pus infection in the teeth on the lower left hand side. We are told that the next specimen, which comes from a town in Texas, indicates a tumor located on a certain precise spot of the brain. The next specimen comes without any indications whatever, and we are told that it is a woman 52 years of age, and she is suffering from acquired syphilis of 14 years standing, and the lesion will be located on the right fore-finger.

"Some of these findings are made in two or three minutes. None of them take more than ten minutes, and after you have watched the work for an hour, you find yourself with one clear-cut conclusion in your mind. This eager and excitable little Jewish doctor is either one of the greatest geniuses in the history of mankind, or else one of the greatest maniacs. You are not quite sure which and you go on day after day, and still you cannot be sure, because that unveiled to your view is so amazing, you cannot make it real to yourself.

"But one thing becomes quickly clear to you. The hypothesis of fraud must be excluded. This man is passionately, even furiously, convinced of the reality of his phenomena; also he is a reverent scientist, working in the highest traditions of the healing art. He is a much over-worked man, irritable and nervous.

"Things go wrong with his apparatus; the wires get in his way, or his assistants make blunders, and he says, 'Damn it' and has to apologize to the lady doctors. But present him with a new idea, some way to verify or perfect his work and he pounces on it like a cat.

He is a veritable incarnation of Nietzsche's phrase about the human soul which hungers for knowledge like a lion for his food. There is no experiment he will not try: you suggest an idea to him one morning, and discover the next day he has slept only two hours because he was working the rest of the time on that idea. There is hardly any subject of human thought about which he has not read and has not something vivid and vital to say. Incidentally, he is a warm-hearted and loveable man whose work is a personal pleasure to aid.

"He has a marvelous acquaintance with the human body. He calls it the most delicate scientific instrument in existence, and he has not merely that knowledge of its structure and functions which other physicians and surgeons possess for he has gone on to explore the radioactivity it manifests and the infinite variety of reactions resulting therefrom.

"Many years ago this man was known in the medical profession as the discoverer of 'the reflexes of Abrams.' He studied the nervous system of the body, tracing out each minute thread of nerve, and showing exactly where disturbances in the functions and structure would manifest themselves. It is this knowledge about nerve reactions, which he has now turned to use. The nerve threads all carry out different vibrations, and if radioactivity is introduced into the body, they instantly sort it out, and manifest it at a certain area, which can be found.

"You decide that the man is not a fraud, and then you begin to wonder, can it be that he is deceiving himself, and that he only imagines that he is getting these reactions? You talk with the physicians who sit watching. 'Why did you come here?' you ask, and the answer is, 'I sent Abrams some blood specimens, and found his diagnoses were right every time.' You

Fig 8-2. Reflexophone Dials

ask another, and get the same response. You ask a third and he says, 'He diagnosed my cancer while I was in Illinois, and cured it, so I came to learn about it.' Half the physicians here have been cured of something, you find, and several are in the process of a cure…

"I assume that the reader is skeptical concerning these miracles. It is proper that he should be. Some one may point out that the little drama with Dr. So-and-So might easily have been arranged in advance, after a fashion understood in the "medium parlors", where you talk with the spirit of your deceased grandmother for the sum of two dollars. But I sat in this clinic twice a day for a couple of weeks, and in that time I saw several hundred blood specimens examined; and letters and telegrams sent to physicians all over the United States. Abrams has examined to date over 12,000 blood specimens for other physicians, and the fact that letters continue to arrive by special delivery can have only one meaning, that the physicians find his diagnoses correct.

"Also, I saw in this clinic more than a hundred patients who had been treated, or were being treated, by Abrams' methods. He must have been a stage manager of supernatu-ral skill to have taken all this variety of people, men and women from a dozen races and of ages varying from eight to eighty, and taught them to play the strange roles, which they played before the critical audience! Again and again I saw Abrams make a diagnosis from the blood, and then bring in the patient, and invite some physician in the clinic who happened to be a specialist, to make an examination and see if he could find signs of the disease…

"And here comes an actor, who has had a tumor on the brain, and had lost the power to make connected sounds, and was rapidly losing the power to walk. Now, after two month's treatment, he can both talk and walk again, and his stage ambitions have revived. He is a tall, black-coated figure, presenting a weird appearance, because a part of his treatment has consisted of shaving his head and painting it a vivid red, some substance whose vibratory rate corresponds to that of sarcoma.

"'Now show us how you can walk,' says Abrams. 'Can you stand on your toe?'

"'Yes, sir,' says the actor, and he toddles around.

"'You couldn't do that a few weeks ago?'

"'I fell on my face every time I tried it.'

"'And now on your heels. You couldn't do that?'

"'No, sir, if I got up on my heels when I got out of bed, I fell back on the bed helpless.'

"'And your voice is coming back all right?'

"'Well, you can hear it,' says the actor proudly. His voice still falters, but he tells us how in the old days he acted in England, and how some day he is going to act in Richard III. He shows us how he will do it, with many expansive gestures: 'Now is the winter of our discontent Made glorious summer by this sun of York!'

"What is the principle upon which these marvels are based? Let us bear in mind to begin with that all our explanations in this matter are guesses. What Abrams has done is to find out what happens. He has done this by twenty years of minute and painstaking experiment. Having found out he tries to account for the happenings, to rationalize them, but if all his guesses are wrong, that does not alter his facts…

"Every high school boy knows that water consists of two molecules of hydrogen and one of oxygen, and if it varied from that composition, it would be something other than water. In the same way, Abrams has discovered experimentally that every disease has a radioactivity peculiar to itself; uniform and invariable. He calls this the 'vibratory rate' of the disease; but you must bear in mind that this term is purely arbitrary, a name which he gives to certain effects which he has observed and measured, though he does not know what they are or how they came to be. Tubercular tissue, and the tubercle bacillus and every drop of blood from a body which contains the tubercle bacillus — all these substances produce a reaction when the rheostat is set at 42, and

if the reaction does not come through at this point, there is no tuberculosis in that body. That this is amazing and new does not in any way alter the fact that it is so. It has been demonstrated by Abrams in many thousands of cases. It is demonstrated over and over again, scores of times every day in his clinic, and it can be demonstrated by any one who will take the trouble to understand his method.

"It would be impossible to exaggerate the revolutionary nature of this one discovery. It gives us for the first time an infallible method for the diagnosis of disease; it gives us also a means of exploring disease and understanding its real nature."

Upton Sinclair's original article is far longer and fascinating. Likewise, his letter to the American Medical Association extolling the virtues of Dr. Abrams' discovery is compelling as well. Their response was brief and revealing:

May 12, 1922
MR. UPTON SINCLAIR:
Your point of view as to what constitutes scientific evidence is so at variance with that of our readers that it would be a waste of space to publish your letter.
Yours very truly,
THE JOURNAL OF THE AMERICAN MEDICAL ASSOCIATION
(Signed) George H. Simmons.
P. S. We are returning your letter herewith.

CHAPTER 9
PSYCHICAL PHYSICS

It seems peculiar to us today that prominent medical doctors and famous writers like Upton Sinclair would be so supportive of what could only be considered the use of psychic energy in the pursuit of medicine. We cannot readily appreciate how interested many scientists at that time were in the crossover of electrical phenomena with consciousness and psychic phenomena.

In late 2006, *The New York Times* ran an Op Ed entitled, "The Ghost in the Machine," in which Pulitzer Prize winning journalist Deborah Blum wrote:

"The human brain is, in surprising part, an appliance powered by electricity. It constantly generates about 12 watts of energy, enough to keep a flashlight glowing. It works by sending out electrical impulses — bursts of power running along the cellular wires of the nervous system — to stimulate muscles into motion or thought into being…

"The scientific study of the supernatural began in the late 19th century, in synchrony with the age of energy. It's hardly coincidental that as traditional science began to reveal the hidden potential of nature's powers — magnetic fields, radiation, radio waves, electrical currents — paranormal researchers began to suggest that the occult operated in similar ways.

"A fair number of these occult explorers were scientists who studied nature's highly charged circuits. Marie Curie, who did some of the first research into radioactive elements like uranium, attended séances to assess the powers of mediums. So did the British physicist J. J. Thomson, who demonstrated the existence of the electron in 1897. And so did Thomson's colleague, John Strutt, Lord Rayleigh, who won the 1904 Nobel Prize in Physics for his work with atmospheric gases."

With so many respected Victorian scientists taking an active interest in psychic research, blending electrical discoveries with mental processes, it is not surprising that some technology would emerge from this approach.

The possibility that a psychic phenomenon was an energetic manifestation of nature rather than a byproduct of brain chemistry is genuinely exciting. It implies a lot more is going on in the world around us than has been acknowledged so far.

The gradual recasting of radionics as a psychic technology began when Abrams discovered that blood samples allowed him to diagnose a patient from a distance. He also claimed that the mysterious radiations he studied could fill a Leyden jar for about an hour. Likewise, they could charge a condenser or even a piece of paper. The charge present in these materials was often sufficient to cause a stomach reflex several hours later. Abrams also found that colored light could amplify the ERA reflex if shined upon a section of the diagnostic circuit.

Today, Stanford University physicist William A. Tiller, who has spent decades studying the physics of consciousness, points out the plethora of photon radiations given off by living systems: "Ultra-weak photon emission from various living systems is a common phenomenon for all plants and animals with the radiation intensity being on the order of a few thousand photons per second…The spectral range of the photon emission spreads at least over the region from the infrared to the ultraviolet with the mitochondria in cells appearing to be the localization of the radiation source…Cancer cells are intense radiation sources with peak intensities, without spectral shifts, increasing by a factor of 100 after treatment with toxic agents.

"It is interesting that the human photoreceptor, the flavin molecules, are not limited to the retina of the eye but are ubiquitous, being found in virtually every tissue of the body. In addition, flavins are not the only photoactive

molecules in the body: carotenes, melanin and heme molecules are also photoactive."

Given the capacity of the body to produce and receive photonic radiation, which we are beginning to understand today, and its potential role in expanding our knowledge of psychic phenomena, perhaps the rush to judge Abrams mysterious radiations as unscientific was a bit hasty and shortsighted. Decades later, radionics inventors would reassert evidence that some form of electrically stimulated light was the conductor of radionic emissions.

These simple and interesting facets of Abrams' basic experiments may hold unrecognized potential today. What if the hard drive of a computer were also capable of holding this radiation? Could it be sent along computer circuits to do its bidding? Would the color on the screen amplify the process? Could it be sent across the internet and be downloaded into a viewers mind as a subconscious semiotic command?

Abrams tried many techniques for long distance diagnosis. First, he measured the Earth for conduction, a method he called "radiogeodiagnosis," which was only reliable for short distances. He tried the telephone, asking the patient to place the witness (blood sample, etc.) near the receiver while he searched for the appropriate stomach reflex in his clinic. This technique, which he called "telediagnosis," was good for about 500 miles. When he tried for direct communication through the air, the best he could do with any accuracy was one mile.

There was one other very serious obstacle to advancing the ERA reflex into a fully electronic technology. Abrams was not able to escape the constraint of having a living, healthy stomach nearby for determining the appropriate reflex. At one point he became so

THE AUTOCLAST

IMPROVED, NEW MODEL

Office Machine in Cabinet. Highest Mahagony Finish. The Most Beautiful
Electronic Treatment Machine in Existence. Finest engraved Bakelite
Panel, Testing Telephone built in, Nickelplated Handle on Top, etc.

Complete with all necessary Electrodes Cords;
Lamps, Vacuum Tubes, etc. Ready for Treatments: $ 150.00

T E R M S : $ 50.00 with Order; Balance on Delivery C. O. D.
(We also make a Portable Autoclast described on the next Page)

E. R. A. ELECTRIC CO. 1947 Broadway NEW YORK CITY
Tel. Trafalgar 3150   Cables: Erarays, New York

Fig 9-1. E. R. A. Electric Co. Autoclast advertisement

desperate to create a substitute for this human component that he offered $10,000, a small fortune in those days, to anyone who could engineer a suitable instrumental replacement for percussing the human abdomen. It was becoming increasingly hard to find young men willing to stand the long hours necessary for compounded diagnostics.

The next technical advancement Abrams accomplished was to circumvent the necessity to learn the percussive techniques. For some physicians, this skill had not been easy to acquire. In its place, he substituted a glass rod held firmly over the abdomen to be stroked back and forth over the abdomen. When the rod appeared to drag or catch over the reaction area, which puckered from the reflex, one could thereby diagnose the condition.

It was becoming more than obvious that something beyond electricity was at work. Abrams had found that radiations from drugs like quinine had cancelled the radiations of malaria, as mercury had with syphilis. Can you imagine the damage to the drug industry today if only a small portion of a medicine's radiations directed at a disease could promote the same curative effects?

Abrams had also discovered the peculiar fact that any of these mysterious radiations could be neutralized by the magnetic fields of the earth. For some unknown reason, no reflex reactions were possible unless the subject faced west. The capacity for cancelling the radiations of a disease by counter radiation became a major component in the development of his Oscilloclast instrument. Ironically today, with magnetic resonant imaging (MRI), we are able to see a magnetic image of all the organs of the body. The image is constructed of the particular magnetic characteristics of that organ. Should a tumor appear on the im-

age screen, is it so far fetched to imagine that those precise frequency characteristics could be inverted to cancel out the disease? A Bose headset uses inverted frequencies to cancel out disturbing noise. Can inverting the frequency characteristics of a disease do the same?

At the time of Abram's discovery of radionics, chemistry was at the beginning of its long march to take control of modern medicine. One can see as we view Abrams' discovery through the eyes of his longtime friend, author Upton Sinclair, that with more institutional support, radionics might well have become part of the modern roster of diagnostic tools. One can only wonder as to the health benefits had these discoveries of Abrams and his followers not been effectively squelched in their infancy.

Today, the current public fascination with alternative healing modalities and the increased investigation of psychic powers in the scientific and defense community have all set the stage for a reconsideration of Abrams' work. Experimentation with these techniques, especially in the arts, could foster greater public awareness of the potential of tools like radionics.

After Abrams death, much of the early scientific excitement behind radionics research was eclipsed by a more occult approach to obtaining results. Where Abrams upheld high standards of training and manufacturing, refusing to sell his instruments to unqualified individuals, soon they became available to anyone. The blurring of technology and psychic healing accelerated. Ironically, while these developments created utter consternation with medical authorities, the popular culture surrounding their miraculous cures and improbable technology continued unabated.

CHAPTER 10
FROM AGRICULTURAL RADIONICS
TO PREHISTORIC ART

Curtis P. Upton, the son of an associate of Thomas Edison, was an engineer who graduated from Princeton University in 1904. Some years later, upon learning of Abrams' work, Upton began to wonder if similar techniques could be applied to diseases in plants. With the help of an electronics engineer, William J. Knuth, he set about modifying radionic equipment for agricultural experimentation.

Upton, following other researchers, substituted a rubbing plate on top of an electrical condenser for the human abdomen. Next, he began using a continuous higher frequency radio wave for transmitting the radionic signal rather than Abrams' pulsed negative charge. Finally, on the input end of the device, he attached a copper plate or screen to the device to hold a plant specimen or photographic negative, and on the output side was a small antenna. The idea was that a leaf or photographic negative placed on this screen would serve as a "witness" to the entire plant or field.

This technique enabled entire fields to be treated through aerial photographs. To enhance growth, all that was necessary was for the operator to link their intent mentally with the broadcast, which would occur for five or ten minutes once a week. This would result in a signal being sent to the witnessed plants to stimulate growth. The radionic command operated like a feedback loop until the plant was again healthy and strong.

To treat for infestation, a "reagent" that was noxious to the pest (natural poisons worked best) would be added to the leaf or to a photograph of the crops, and the process repeated. Upton found that even from a distance, 80 to 90 percent of the pests treated in this manner would be dead or gone in 48 hours. In control experiments, Upton would black out or destroy certain rows on the negatives, while treating adjoining rows by his methods, in order to demonstrate the precision and effectiveness of his invention.

"One of Upton's most fascinating experiments," wrote Edward W. Russell, "was to

EXAMPLES OF JAPANESE BEETLE CONTROL
1952

County—York
Crop Treated—Sweet Corn
Owner—Bittinger Cannery
Procedure—By U.S.D.A. Method

Radionically Treated Area			Untreated Area (Check)		
	No. Silks Examined	No. Silks Damaged by Japanese Beetles		No. Silks Examined	No. Silks Damaged by Japanese Beetles
Row No. 1	100	37	Row No. 1	100	90
Row No. 2	100	17	Row No. 2	100	81
Row No. 3	100	7	Row No. 3	100	87
Row No. 4	100	34	Row No. 4	100	88
Totals	400	63		400	346

Results—81% Japanese Beetle Control based on damaged silks
Surveyors: Dr. E. H. Sigler—U.S.D.A.
Warren Maines—U.S.D.A.

Fig 10-1. UKACO Results

chase the worms off a tree with the flower of a geranium. He would take a leaf from the infested tree and lay it on the collector-plate alongside a geranium flower. When he switched on the transmitter, the radiation from the geranium would be 'keyed' to the distant tree and would give the latter some kind of 'taste' or radiation which the worms disliked and which would cause them to hurry to the nearest exit and fall to the ground. This usually happened in five minutes and, at close range was almost instantaneous. But the sturdier the growth, the longer it took."

Upton's device greatly simplified radionic applications. It invoked a seemingly magical response in a timely way. It was so good in fact, that the Pennsylvania Farm Federation (PFF) ordered their research department to initiate an investigation of his methods in 1949. Russell states that one year later, after successfully reproducing his experiments, the PFF asked for exclusive use of his product in Pennsylvania. By 1952, better results were forthcoming, adding much needed revenue to the research effort.

In California, partner William Kunth initiated a No Results/No Pay system that didn't

obligate a farmer to pay for a treatment unless they were satisfied with the results, the costs of which were a fraction of spraying.

In his book, *Report on Radionics*, Russell documents many of the actual experiments and their results, including those performed by fertilizer and pesticide companies, who were alarmed by these developments. Russell describes the UKACO Corporation, which was formed in 1947 with the help of Upton's Princeton roommate, Howard H. Armstrong, a metallurgist and chemical engineer who was also the son of an inventor. Through Armstrong's influence, retired Brigadier General Henry M. Gross, a powerful and well-liked personality in Pennsylvania (who also had training in mechanical engineering), was brought in to guide the fledgling enterprise. Through this collaboration, both a non-profit and a for-profit corporation were formed to advance agricultural radionics.

Further independent research by the Pennsylvania Farm Bureau Co-operative Association in 1948 confirmed earlier successes, with the director, B. A. Rockwell, recommending "a comprehensive experimental program during 1949, to further determine the possibilities of insect control by Radionic processes."

Following such enthusiastic support from government farm agencies and farmers alike, Upton and his associates were soon attacked for their success. The first attack was regulatory, and came in 1951 when the Beltsville U.S. Agricultural Research Center decided to investigate the UKACO device. Scientists both pro and con were asked to monitor a series of radionically treated fields during the summer of 1952. By August, all agreed the report on the results would be favorable. Yet when a letter arrived on November 5th, the Beltsville officers claimed the counts in the fields "did not provide an adequate basis for estimating the 'U.K.A.C.O. Process.'" Their conclusion and other pertinent data were clearly at odds with the summer's events.

Director Rockwell was then warned not to publish his data. Rockwell also discovered that the Beltsville agency had begun a campaign to ridicule the radionics methods of UKACO and vilify Armstrong, while appearing willing to continue research at a later date. Private inquiries by General Gross convinced the group that the chemical lobbies had been behind the fix. Due to the prestige of the Beltsville center, important corporations and farmers groups were discouraged from expressing further interest in UKACO.

Beyond his interest in agriculture, Upton was known to occasionally use radionics to treat the sick free-of-charge. In 1960, his wife was tricked into accepting some money in marked bills from a person who had convinced him to provide a medical radionics treatment. For this Upton was prosecuted and spent a few days in jail, but he ultimately obtained a suspended sentence. Of course, these complications affected his, and his company's, reputation. He died a few years later in 1966 and Armstrong six years later in 1972.

One other interesting facet of Upton's work concerns his discovery regarding pencil marks. Pencil marks, according to Upton, could provide an equally effective witness or "key" for radionics diagnosis or treatment as a blood spot, a photograph, or a leaf. This technique required holding a graphite pencil sharpened at both ends over a piece of paper. The paper and pencil were first "cleaned of all radiation" by passing a bar magnet over them. Then the pencil was held with a thumb over the upraised point while the other end

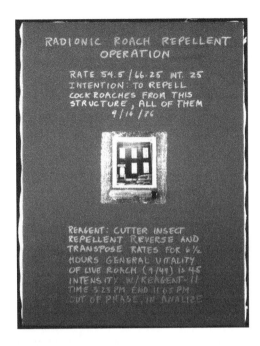

Fig 10-2. Radionic Roach Repellent Operation - D. Lauire 1986

marked the paper or wrote a signature or instructions.

When finished, Upton would pick up the paper with rubber gloves and place the paper on his device and begin the analysis. This unusual discovery has significance in the discussion of the relationship between radionics and art, particularly shamanic art. Taken at face value, the discovery that inscriptions can conduct radionic energy provides a clue to prehistoric cave painting and petroglyph art. Can these powerful inscriptions and paintings be interpreted as an expression of a functional psi-based semiotic system of applied intent?

From the perspective of Upton's agricultural radionic experiments, petroglyphs carved repeatedly over long periods of time in remote and inaccessible locations (not likely a decorative decision) take on a more decidedly functional significance. Are the images we find carved on rocks all over the world merely graffiti, or are they part of an ancient system of radionic technology? If only graffiti, then why are the images often found on sacred locations on the landscape known for their telluric power?

Did cave paintings made with spit and blood charge the imagery with subtle energy? Should we choose to interpret their functioning as radionic witnesses, employing a tellurian energy to expedite a pre-conceived goal, then their existence has a pragmatic explanation over and above their ceremonial or decorative purposes. To look at these paintings today, after 10,000 to 40,000 years, is to be reminded of how well they have preserved the intensity of their creator's intent. Perhaps those early painters, unhindered by artistic preconceptions, were more conversant with using imagery and energy to accomplish a task than we give them credit for.

Upton's idea that a personal "signature" conveys something essential of that person is universally accepted. It remains established at the core of our legal and financial institutions. The idea can be taken one step further by postulating the signature as containing an energetic version of DNA that expresses fundamental properties of that individual.

When the individual achieves command of an art medium and its distribution, those properties become broadcast into the environment. One can envision the point where art moves beyond employing metaphor alone and becomes a form of energetic technology that can be used to heal or do other forms of work. What takes an occult technology beyond pure functionalism and back into high art is the power, beauty, and breadth of the intention that is given expression.

Like many artists, the radionic innovators were not concerned that their work was not understood by the world at large. What was important to each researcher was the empirical process and whether or not it led to meritorious and important results. Imagine if the agricultural radionics pioneers of the 1940s and 1950s had had the support and resources of the environmental movement of today? Their insights provided a profound sense of ecology before it even became a popularly recognized field of study. Among their contributions would have been an ecological alternative to fertilizers and pesticides. Their model may have evolved into understanding the landscape as an energetic whole, supported by intelligent life energy. Environmental Radionics today would be decades along in innovation, instead of just beginning. Curtis P. Upton's radionic work would now be legendary instead of lost.

CHAPTER 11
PRANA, KUNDALINI
AND OCCULT TECHNOLOGY

As Abrams was building his first device, many occult schools were becoming aware of energetic concepts that had their origins in India, China, and the Middle East. Prominent among Eastern religion are the Indian terms for subtle energy, prana and kundalini. In the simplest interpretation, prana is the life energy circulating throughout our body, a living fluid at the core of our physical and mental being. Kundalini is a concentration of prana, the evolutionary force of nature, embedded in the physical body with the express purpose of effecting biological and cognitive transformation.

The importance of Eastern energetic concepts to the occultists of Europe and America cannot be overstated. Essentially, they offered a competing worldview to scientific materialism. The success of science in harnessing invisible forces like electro-magnetism had pushed the occult believers into looking for parallel technologies from prana and kundalini. The quest turned to the manifestation and

demonstration of subtle biological energy and how it can be turned into a physical force that can do work.

No writer has had more direct experience with kundalini and prana than Gopi Krishna, whose direct experience with kundalini was spontaneous, unexpected, utterly transformative, and irreversible. The actual experience of kundalini arising in his body and his awareness of it was also very difficult for him to cope with when it occurred. His experiences are well documented in his own works. Consider how he observed and defined these energies:

"Kundalini is the ancient Sanskrit word for a form of bioenergy, the life force in humans which drives evolution and leads the race to a higher state of consciousness…In its cosmic form prana is a highly diffused intelligent energy spread everywhere. But in the individual it takes a specific form as the bioplasma or individual prana composed of an extremely subtle organic essence drawn from the elements and compounds forming the body. It is this essence, which, transformed into psychic energy, becomes the fuel for thought. The bioplasma, sustained by the cosmic ocean of prana, permeates each and every cell of an organism. In fact, it is the life of the cells as also of the organism itself. The nervous system with its countless extremely fine threads floats like a serpent on this pool of bioenergy, which is itself surrounded and permeated by the boundless ocean of universal life."

Gopi Krishna is adamant about the difference between how bioenergy is perceived in the West versus the East. For the West, "this energy, whatever the manifestation by which it can be identified, assumes the same position as other material energies in the universe. The underlying idea in the minds of the investigators is often the same as that which influences their study of physical energies, namely to understand their nature and laws to harness them for pragmatic purposes.

"But for the ancient (or contemporary) Indian adept, bioenergy or prana is the super intelligent cosmic life energy to which he owes his own existence and the existence of the world around him. He considers himself to be no more than a transient bubble, blown up by the action of this almighty force, which continues to work day and night through all the period of his life, to maintain the ego-bound flicker of consciousness that he knows as himself.

"Research on bioenergy implies entry into the realm of the spirit, into the subtle plane housing the energies and forces of life."

Prana exerts a type of radiation on the brain that alters consciousness. This is the essence of the traditional, mystical view of subtle energy as experienced by Gopi Krishna and others. Prana is perceived as a form of "vital fuel," which is stored in every organic cell of the body and whose function it is to sustain the activity of life and consciousness.

Said Gopi Krishna: "The extremely dim glimmer of sentience that regulates the conduct of a single cell, when combined and magnified with the marvelous mechanism of the human cerebrospinal system, gives rise to the wonderful world of awareness present in us. The pattern and volume of the mental activity exhibited by a human being or an animal depends solely on the pattern and volume of the bioenergy supplied to the brain. When this supply fails, the connecting link between the organism and the world of life is cut off and death ensues."

Gopi Krishna believed that bioplasma is the energy drawn from every cell of the organism by the nerves up to the brain and fosters the growth of intellect, talent and genius in an individual. It is likened to milk, or semen in the body in yogic metaphor, and is identical to the reproductive substances but with a different function.

"The whole cellular structure of the human body has the genetic principles present in it," said Gopi Krishna. "From the point of view of the bioplasma also, every cell is a radial center of this energy. The activation of the kundalini merely makes use of a potential already present in the body. The evolutionary mechanism is constructed in a way that, by stimulation through certain disciplines or of its own accord when ripe for the experience, it can be activated in a manner that makes the human body a virtual dynamo of live electricity or psychic energy which can stream into the brain with shattering effect.

"In fact, it is this transition of the human organism from the normal condition to the state of a powerful generating plant of high-grade bioplasma which is designated as the arousal of kundalini. Every neuron in the brain, every nerve, and every nerve filament becomes a participant in this whirlwind activity that starts in the body on the awakening of the serpent power."

Many occult practices and traditions in the East were designed to strengthen prana or arouse kundalini. Though prana and kundalini have physical manifestations, they are generally discernable only as an aspect of consciousness. In any discussion of subtle energy, it is of paramount importance to distinguish whether the energy under discussion is perceived through the senses in the external world or apprehended internally by the mind. Of those practices that invoke kundalini, change in perception is most often the desired outcome, not alterations in the physical world.

Kundalini-like effects are widely experienced today via plant hallucinogens and psychedelic drugs. A theoretical argument can be made that a synthetic chemical compound like LSD is a form of occult technology. Although the resulting inebriation is predictable, the subjective outcome of the experience is not. For better or worse, in terms of widespread reliability and results, laboratory spawned hallucinogenic compounds are probably the most pervasive occult technology ever designed by man.

Just how significant hallucinogens are to the discussion of the occult and its technology will not be resolved here. There is little doubt that these and other drugs often play a substantial role in occult ceremony, but there is no evidence connecting them to practical methodologies like radionics.

Different manifestations of subtle energy demand their own respective language and tools. Many cognitive subtle energy disciplines

Fig 11-1. Diagram of the Spheres - Jonathan Koons

have evolved aesthetic technologies, like yantra drawings and mandala paintings. Adherents consider almost all shamanistic ceremony a form of technology.

Tantra, which includes the manipulation of sexual energy, can be used to expand consciousness or to develop occult power. Both disciplines have resulted in the creation of artworks that are considered tools for the manipulation of consciousness toward predetermined ends. These art forms are used for directing energy, much as in radionics, but their goal is primarily metaphysical, not physical. However, they can be and have been used for pragmatic ends, like healing and for environmental purification. Many writers describe sacred architecture as an aesthetic technology used in part to restore people and the land into a harmonious relationship with nature. Megalithic monuments and chambers were designed for both practical and metaphysical purposes, ceremonially impregnating the earth with light to insure fertility, as well as marking celestial events.

When it comes to altering consciousness, a wider range of tools and methodologies are available. These tools don't have to change anything in the external world, so it is more difficult to describe them as technology that does work. One intriguing crossover is psychokinetics (PK). PK consists of mental action directed upon the physical world, such as telekinesis (control of objects), aero kinesis (control of wind & weather), pyrokinesis (control of fire), electro kinesis (control of electricity and magnetism) and microtelekinesis (control of molecules). PK likely plays a substantial role in radionics and other occult technology.

In the West, PK is not considered in the same category as consciousness technologies utilizing prana or kundalini. Rather, PK is thought to resemble electricity, magnetism, light, and the sub-atomic forces. The notion that PK might be something to engineer, or to detect with an instrument, came to the forefront as modern science began investigating paranormal forces.

A comprehensive 534-page textbook by geologist S. W. Tromp, entitled *Psychical Physics*, was published in 1949. It thoroughly and scientifically examined every aspect of divining phenomena. Tromp's exhaustive study discusses every aspect of electrical, magnetic, geophysical, biological, electrostatic, and psychical activity that he could imagine impacting dowsing and radiesthesia, and therefore, by implication, radionics. Wherever possible, Tromp and his associates devised experiments

to test their hypotheses and developed the theory of the dowsing reflex. The results were faithfully recorded, complete with graphs, diagrams, and photographs in his book, which despite the empirical approach was derided and neglected by scientists.

In the concluding paragraphs of his text, Tromp had this to say about his research efforts: "We have endeavored to demonstrate that an enormous number of fundamentally unknown phenomena occur in the living world that should be united into an independent science, the science of divining phenomena. This should be the sphere of interest of the Laboratories of Psychical Physics all over the world. It is a sign of narrow-mindedness that these experiments are often rejected by scientists because the explanation sounds unscientific and might be completely wrong. It is not the interpretation that is important, but the facts. Interpretations given by even the most prominent scientists often had to be changed during the history of mankind, but the facts remain. Most scientists of the 20th century seem to lack the courage and the romantic feeling to tackle problems which at first sight seem incredible and without any practical prospects. It is the unconventional scientist who enables the work to progress more rapidly."

Like Tromp, Abrams and subsequent radionic inventors would be inclined to argue that PK was a "force of nature" detected by their instruments from muscular reflexes. They would argue that the psi hypothesis would eventually be reconciled scientifically, in a quantitative, measurable fashion like any other physical force.

For the time being, it is practically impossible to state in unequivocal scientific terms how any technology that incorporates subtle energy of the mind or biological energy of the body actually functions. Both mind and body, joined through consciousness, are uniquely dependent upon the influence and characteristics of whatever tools and techniques are used to describe them, be it the limitations of scientific instruments or the mindset of the observer. What can be examined is how an occult technology like radionics evolved and was perceived by the people who designed and applied these unique and novel tools.

Radionic practitioners, however, were not alone in claiming to have found a previously undiscovered energy capable of doing work. The 19th century brought the advent of Theosophy, Anthroposophy, the Ordo Templi Orientis (OTO) and numerous other groups oriented to occult and magical knowledge. At the same time, the industrial revolution was taking hold in Europe and America. Perhaps the shadow of capitalism created a milieu in which the germination of occult technology was not only favored by many but also expected. John Jacob Astor (1864-1912), one of the richest men on earth, was willing to invest heavily in occult technology. He was also an inventor in his own right with a visionary mind. In the course of his life, he sponsored many of the most occult inventors of his era, including John Worrell Keely (1837-1898).

Keely's inventions preceded the widespread use of electricity. They were, in fact, more noticeably pneumatic or hydraulic, even sonic, in the sense that the strange force he employed moved pistons and went down pipes and through valves as though it were steam or oil. Keely's inventions are by today's standards 100 percent occult technology. This apparent liability did not prevent him from obtaining millions of mid-19th century dollars in funding and extraordinary notoriety

Fig 11-2. Keely Compound Disintegrator interior

during his life.

A completely unknown vibratory force, withstanding repeated public demonstration, powered Keely's beautifully crafted machines. As a result, Keely was able to attract not only John Jacob Astor but also William K. Vanderbilt and numerous other New York millionaires to invest in his technology. Unlike radionics, Keely's devices were all designed to do

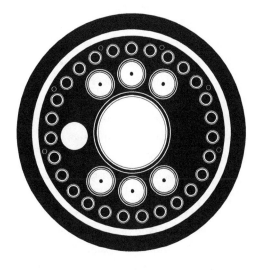

Fig 11-3. Keely Compound Disintegrator exterior

labor intensive work, albeit with a very other-worldly type of physics.

One such device, called the Liberator, extracted an "etheric vapor" or "inter-atomic force" that could then be stored for various tasks. This force was said to "furnish power to the extent of ten tons to the square inch." One observer labeled it a "sympathetic etheric force" that could best be described as "coming nearer to the primal force of the willpower of nature than any force yet liberated from her storehouse."

Keely's force was applied pneumatically and harmonically to a host of inventions: a cannon, a means of disintegrating minerals for mining purposes, a locomotive force, and a suspension of gravity capable of propagating air ships – even space flight. By many reports, Keely's demonstrations were more than convincing. They were repeated before thousands of visitors and as his notoriety grew, the stock in his various companies was publicly tendered.

Not everyone was convinced. Many famous contemporary inventors, including Nikola Tesla, claimed there was nothing truly scientific in any of Keely's work. Others claimed outright fraud, and at one point Keely was jailed briefly. Various institutions and scientific publications were deeply skeptical, as his results could not be independently verified outside his own lab. No patents were ever issued, though many were promised; a few applications were filed.

Regardless, enough satisfactory demonstrations with working devices were produced to convince numerous skeptics, including many engineers who began working with Keely. The possibility that any of these devices worked as claimed seems preposterous to us today. In Keely's era, however, mid-way through the 19th century with the Civil War behind them, Americans felt a great deal of exuberance and confidence, with technological progress tantamount to Manifest Destiny.

Given an almost divine prerogative to utilize the unexplored forces of nature like electricity and subtle energy, it was not surprising to see some wild inventions developed. Many credible people believed that these devices worked as claimed. One must wonder whether an esoteric energy like prana or kundalini was inadvertently evoked by Keely and ran through his machines. To this day it is disputed whether some truly unknown force was at work in his technology. What is beyond dispute, as researchers like Gerry Vassilatos have confirmed, is that many inventors of the Victorian era developed, demonstrated, and even patented working technology that drew upon energy in nature. But much of this technology has now been lost or discarded.

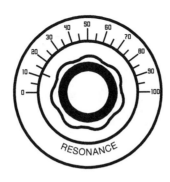

CHAPTER 12
RADIONICS: OCCULT OR ELECTRONIC?

World transforming innovations are not always welcomed with jubilation. A 1926 report on Abrams' techniques by the International Hahnemanian Committee had this to say about innovation: "In 1878 a London newspaper called the telephone a great American humbug, and said it was far inferior to the old and well established system of speaking tubes. Daguerre was put in jail because he said he could reproduce the face of a man upon a tin plate, and Marconi was considered an idle dreamer when he proposed the wireless transmission of sound and speech."

Following the death of Abrams, the world of radionics exploded into a psychedelic panoply of inventors, theories, and devices. Notably, these would include J. W. Wigglesworth of the Pathometric Corporation, who produced a vacuum tube upgrade of Abrams' Oscilloclast called the Pathoclast, and Ruth Drown, who invented Radionic Photography. Other devices from the late 1920s included the Calbro-Magnawave (Caldwell and Bronson),

the Dynamiser (Richards), the Radioclast, the Wilson machine, and most notably some time later, the U.K.A.C.O. (Upton, Knuth, and Armstrong Co.). But T. Galen Hieronymus was the first and only radionics inventor ever to receive a U.S. Patent.

In England, radionics found a much more appreciative audience. Free of persecution, English practitioners – notably Guion Richards, Marjorie and George de la Warr, Langston Day, Malcome Rae, Darrell Butcher, and David Tansley – continued to pursue both the scientific and occult aspects of radionics. In other countries, the study of radionics branched into color therapy (Dinshah and McManus), treatment by direct radiation (Lakhovsky), and pure research (Tromp), with many subsequent developments.

Each researcher had an individual understanding of what was taking place in their work. For every new approach, there was a unique set of tools and practices. New discoveries stimulated the design of more appliances.

Fig 12-1. Wilson Instrument '51'

These devices encouraged different interpretations of the underlying forces involved. Among certain inventors, a sense of scientific rigor was sustained, especially those seeking to have their technology adopted by the medical mainstream.

A contemporary review of important technical developments up through the 1920s was offered in the May 1940 issue of *The Journal of the Universal Society of Pathometrists*: "Dr Albert Abrams (MD) is generally credited with having done the first note worthy research (1915) in the field. This theory was known as E.R.A (Electronic Reactions of Abrams); his instrument was called the Oscilloclast. Although roundly criticized and often condemned by his medical brethren, Abrams achieved considerable success. (When he died in 1924 he left a million dollars in trust for purposes of carrying on with Electronic research.)

"While Dr Abrams was still very actively engaged in developing E.R.A and in teaching his system to doctors, and after a certain amount of progress had been made, other important personalities came into the limelight (1919) principal of which was Dr. J. W. Wigelsworth. With the assistance of his brother, A. E., and together with other associates, Dr. Wigelsworth set about the development of different equipment he hoped would prove superior. Thus was born the first major branch of Electronics (the earlier term for radionics) known as Pathometry, ('patho', meaning disease, 'metry' meaning to measure).

"By 1919-20 the first pathometric instruments were manufactured and sold to doctors. The technique of operation was somewhat simpler than Abrams technique but classes of 30 days duration were taught nevertheless. In these classes doctors qualified themselves to lease instruments.

"In 1924-25 another group developed equipment known as radionics, under the trade name of Calbro-Magnowave. The radionic theory followed more closely the electronic ideas. In 1930, a radionic type of equipment developed by another group took the name of Radioclast ('radio' from radionics and 'clast' from the pathometric instrument called the pathoclast, 'clast' meaning to break). As the E.R.A. suffered at the death of Dr. Abrams, (1924) radionics became quite popular. Pathometry and radionics continued in parallel for a time until becoming unified later under the term 'Radionics.'"

At this pivotal time, the two fields of radionics described above were still co-joined by many researchers seeking a scientific basis for the psychokinetic influence of radionic functioning, believing it to be an integral but unrecognized part of electronic engineering.

In time, there were more disagreements about approach and methodology. Even the

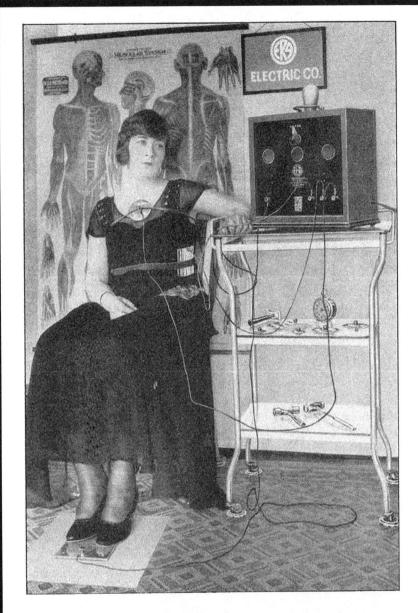

AUTOCLAST TREATMENT

Illustrating Treatment for T.B. in the Lungs. Patients feet rest, with Shoes on, upon Emanation-Plate, Spleen Electrode is connected to Terminal 1, Chest Electrode to Terminal 3 and a third Electrode (not visible) is placed for general treatment upon the Neck, connected as shown to Terminal 2.

Fig 12-2. E. R. A. Electric Co. Autoclast advertisement

Fig 12-3. Micro-Quantumeter

facts were doubted, as radionics became ever-more a self-referential system where observation and interpretation were reduced to completely subjective criteria. Ruth Drown, who entered the stage following Abram's death, began the era of occult radionics. Drown's influence on the course of radionics all but marked the end of radionics as something of scientific interest. However, in spite of being ostracized from medicine and science and soon burdened with legal and institutional persecution, radionics continued to thrive.

The only explanation for the continued pursuit of radionics, outside of pure self-deception or outright fraud, lay in the possibility that as yet unknown and unexplained forces were actually healing people and curing disease. Fraud and self-deception admittedly played a significant role in the development of radionics and other early medical technology. More than a few devices and their inventors were undoubtedly fraudulent, but many more genuine practitioners were also at work, far more than the pure cons. Of course, criminal negligence by opportunistic businesses posing as something benign are not confined to quackery. Open any paper today and you will likely find reference to tobacco or pharmaceu-

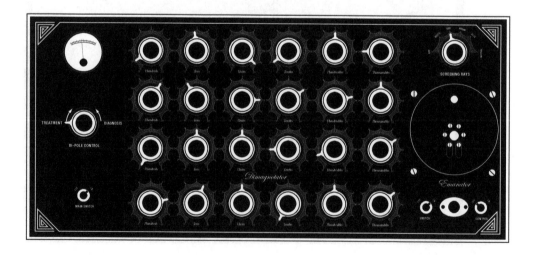

Fig 12-4. Hemodimagnometer

The Secret Art

tical litigation derived in part from false claims and abused medical and research procedures.

Even if placebo effects made a significant contribution to early radionic cures, no one can deny that many individuals were helped or were fully healed by radionics after suffering from debilitating diseases.

It can be construed, given a continued success rate over the ensuing century, that many of the competent radionics inventors and practitioners actually did accomplish what they claimed. What they claimed was that they used their unusual instruments to enable their minds to alter reality outside their body, namely in the healing of their patients. Or perhaps, the device allowed the user to circumvent the assumption that they couldn't heal in this manner. As physicist William Tiller pointed out, while radionics may have served merely as "training wheels for the mind," it is a type of mind we are not yet very familiar with.

By the last quarter of the 20th century, much of radionics was still firmly in the grip of 19th century occult thinking. At that time, an American living in Britain, David Tansley, is credited with introducing Eastern philosophies into radionics. A sculptor and horticulturalist early on in his career, Tansley received a diploma from the Los Angles College of Chiropractic in 1965 and returned to England to begin his practice.

While in California, Tansley studied at the Ananda Ashram where he became aware of the "subtle anatomy of man," an Eastern theory by which disease is said to originate from subtle, etheric bodies nested within the physical. These etheric bodies are thought to contain localized energy vortexes, termed chakras. Once Tansley had learned of radionics through the British Radionics Association, he felt confident that radionic balancing should be ap-

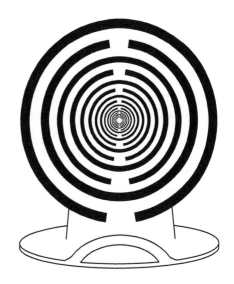

Fig 12-5. Lakhovsky Multi-Wave Oscillator

plied to these pre-physical subtle bodies as well as the physical body. Conveniently, Eastern mystical terminology began to be adopted by energy medicine, providing both a new philosophical basis for the existence of subtle energy and a medical operating platform with a thousand year history of practical success.

This gave birth to what we now refer to as "New Age" healing and metaphysics. Any so-named essence, crystal, talisman, or electromechanical apparatus became, in effect, a de-facto radionics device. But new age culture continued to dilute the original design and purpose of radionic influence. Ironically, in new forms and guises, radionics continued to advance its ideology, as more and more people adopted new age cures and lifestyles. For many people today, new forms of radionics/energetic treatment continue to be both desirable and effective alternatives to drugs and orthodox medicine.

Curiously, while the essence of radionics morphed into many new varieties of "energy medicine," the professional radionic communities largely held onto their occult traditions, with figures like Tansley providing support. Less conflicted and more to the point were the radionics devices themselves, which continued appropriating the appearance of electronic instrumentation and later, computers and software. Then a significant development altered the dependence of radionics on the lethal mixture of occult knowledge and scientific technology. Toward the beginning of the new millennium, a few radionics innovators began to design working radionic devices that resembled art; specifically, miniature color field paintings.

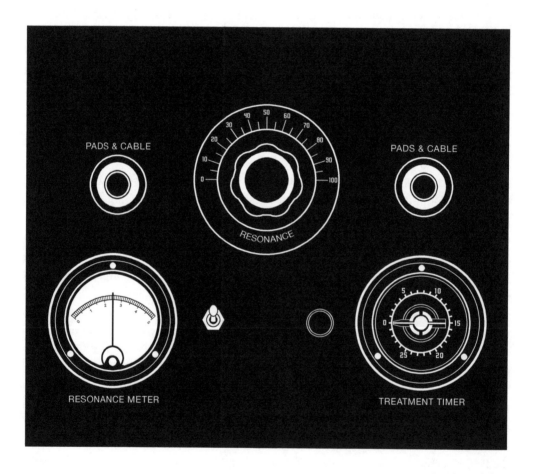

Fig 12-6. Radatherm

The Secret Art

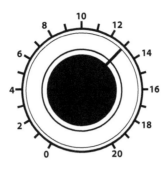

CHAPTER 13
RUTH DROWN

It should come as no surprise that the continued academic and political backlash in radionics after Abrams' demise should fall on someone, and that was Ruth Drown. Various sources describe Ruth Drowns' contact with Abrams either as a chiropractor who became familiar with his work early on or as a secretary working in his clinic in the early 1920s. In spite of her modest medical training, Drown is generally credited with having been a significant figure in the field for the next 25 years.

Drown had no scientific training. Her diagnostic work and her later instrument designs were largely based on exceptional intuition and psychic ability. Radionics historian Edward W. Russell quotes Drowns' friend, Bell Helicopter inventor, Arthur M. Young, as saying: "In conversation with her, one could feel that she was in touch with a tremendously complicated internal system of patterned harmonics, a self-regulating system of 'resonant vibration' of which all I can say is that I was convinced she knew what she was talking about, even though it could not be translated into terms which would pass muster in present science."

Arthur Young was deeply impressed by Ruth Drown, especially her "angelic presence." Nevertheless, when questioned about "rates," her answers only confirmed his suspicion that the radionics instruments only function was as an aid to concentration, even though he accepted that the rates served a rational and useful purpose. What bothered him more was that her comprehension of radio and television seemed completely "deluded," a factor that would cost her dearly later in life.

Young didn't believe that Ruth Drown and other sensitives he knew as friends were delusional or otherwise fraudulent. Instead, he felt the subtle vibrations and other mystical events they encountered were expressions of the way they went about describing what they visualized. In this respect, one could think of what an artist expresses in form, a radionics practitioner expresses in healing. Today, we don't expect an artist to be able to heal, but in aboriginal societies it is not uncommon. The root "vision" can demand any number of outcomes, as a study of modern primitive artists will readily reveal.

The result of Drowns' intuitive approach was to discard any pretext of scientific objectivity in favor of a more occult system of treatment. Her first revision of radionic instrumentation was to remove all electric current from the modified Abrams type devices she designed (except a small light bulb to warm the device). Her second important revision replaced the percussive technique on the human abdomen with a type of dowsing apparatus called a "stick plate."

The patient would stand upon two metal plates connected to the stick plate, which supplied an input to the device. The operators' fingers moved across a flat rubber pad covering a detector until they appeared to stick to the surface. This dowsing technique replaced abdominal percussing. Simultaneously, the operator turned the variable resistor "dials" of the radionics box until the "stick" indicated the appropriate rate to diagnose or treat. This technique is still very much in use today.

Described another way, one would turn the dial to establish a rate, while the other hand moves across the stick pad. As the dial is turned slowly, one waits for the finger to suddenly halt its gliding across the surface and "stick" to the plate. This sticking action is presumed to result from the same dowsing reflex observed by Abrams as causing the abdomen to harden under the glass wand or while percussing. Whatever numerical rate is observed on the turning dial when the sticking occurs provides information on the patient's condition.

Drowns' stick plate effectively discarded the use of ohms and inductance altogether to measure the rate of a disease. It relied solely on the operators' dowsing ability to determine where on a rotary dial a particular rate existed, either to diagnose or to treat.

By using this method, Drown reportedly was also able to correlate her dowsed rates to the actual atomic weights and numbers of the organic and inorganic specimens she examined. By doing so, she hoped to instill her technique with a measure of scientific authenticity. In actuality, radionics adopted a deeper level of mysticism in instrument design, philosophy, and technique.

Ruth Drown should also be considered the first radionic inventor to invent an art form – her discovery of radionic photography. Imagine her excitement and the vindication she must have felt for her techniques upon discovering that the radiations of a diseased organ could be captured on a photographic plate attached to a radionics instrument. This astounding development was obtained by connecting a wire from the radionics device to unexposed film after it was tuned to a patients' condition. When the film was developed the tuned organ or tissue would appear on the film without the benefit of any exposure to light. If the patient were connected directly to the instrument, the outside of the organ would be revealed, but if a blood sample was used instead, the inside of the organ appeared, usually in cross section.

Drown performed many photographic diagnoses in front of audiences of medical doctors, occasionally of their own pathologies. The lack of a clear scientific foundation for her discovery did no stop the British from issuing a patent (#515,866) for her camera on December 15, 1939. She never implied that her camera technology was fully understood scientifically. But problems with the repeatability of this process made it clear that some personal, psychic, or psychokinetic mechanism was involved in the acquisition of the image. After the harrowing inquisition she faced later in life, she was no longer able to take these photographs at all.

The process of obtaining images through psychic means, accidentally or deliberately, is far more common than one would imagine possible. The process whereby a psychic individual is able to affect a photograph has also received some scientific scrutiny under William A. Tiller. In Tiller's laboratory side-by-side film cameras were set up and pictures taken, one sensitized to subtle energy by a psychic, the other not. While the non-sensitized camera operated normally, the sensitized one recorded unusual features and imagery that were not the result of mechanical error.

"From this study," Tiller stated, "I deduce that subtle energies exist for which the camera lens cap and the human body are at least semi-transparent. Further, it seems that photographic film has a layer or layers of subtle substance capable of registering an imprint from a pattern of subtle energy entering the lens. The presence of [a person's psychic] energy field appears to allow interaction between this subtle substance imprint and the silver halide grains of the physical film so that an imprint transfer takes place that is ultimately recorded by the photographic development process."

One interesting facet of Tiller's work was that whenever the unusual energy the psychic projected onto the film took place, the psychic experienced a strange feeling in his back between the 7th cervical and the 4th thoracic vertebra. This involuntary muscle response allowed him to time the precise point at which to take the picture. Like the radionics stick, this reflex action acted as an indicator. It is not

Fig 13-1. Dr. Ruth B. Drown

clear from Tiller's account whether the precise moment described by the muscle reflex acted like a trigger mechanism for an energy release from the subject's body onto the photograph, or whether the moment merely indicated that the correct conditions were in place for a spontaneous occurrence. Either way, Tiller's description of the correlation between intent, subject, and instrument, which required a muscular reflex tuning process, provides a simple confirmation of radionics methodology independent of radionic literature.

What is so unusual about the Drown photographs is that they served a practical, diagnostic purpose and contained useful medical information. Arthur Young, upon visiting Drown, asked if she could photograph his condition (without telling her what it was). He noted that she placed the photographic plate (connected to the radionics box) in a light proof box when the picture was snapped,

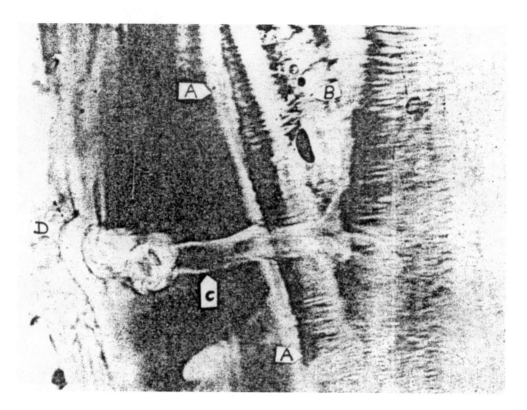

Fig 13-2. Abcessed Tooth

but that the plate was developed in full light. (Normally, this would result in completely overexposed film.)

What she produced was a detailed 8 X 10 print of teeth. Young's condition was, in fact, a toothache. Being skeptical, he asked her to take another picture, this time pressing his jaw with his finger, increasing the pain. The second picture was similar, only larger in scale.

Young was impressed enough by the experience to give a great deal of thought to how radionics worked. Later on, he found a Japanese book on "Thoughtography" which described how thoughts could be transferred to photographic plates. The key ingredient, he felt, was purpose. This hypothesis was later confirmed when a prized chestnut tree on his property became infested with worms. Young

prepared a photograph of the tree and sent it to a radionics practitioner for treatment, but before the letter arrived, a flock of birds landed on the tree and ate all the worms. His purpose, he believed, was enough to activate the radionics command, and nature took care of the rest.

Many radionic practitioners since Abrams have pointed out that while there are similarities to the way radionics works with electronics communications technology, the source energy is not electricity but life energy. The individual provides intent and a well of life energy. Through the tuning process, the instrument simply separates the nested signals into numerically identifiable segments, in accordance with Fourier's Theorem. This entails assigning a number or "rate" to each condi-

The Secret Art

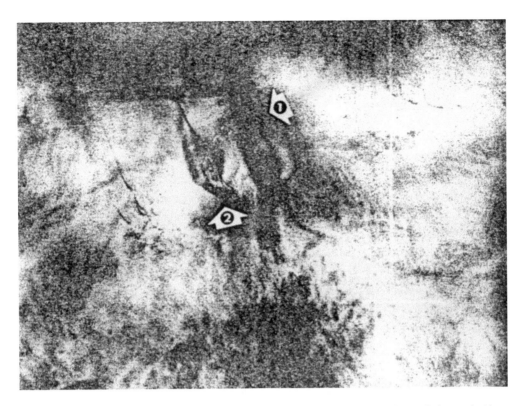

Fig 13-3. Surgical Instruments Photographed Across the Atlantic

tion and particular vibration.

Any compound or mixture of substances can be examined and a rate established. What is essentially being described as a rate could also be called a resonant frequency. It can describe the geometry of the substance or the vibration of its energy. The rate, being either a waveform or a structure, is characterized as a pattern in radionics, tying it visually into the artistic language of abstract geometric form.

On the electronics side, Trevor Constable, a qualified radio engineer and researcher who wrote about Drown in *The Cosmic Pulse of Life*, spoke about the analogy of radio to radionics: "In the case of the radio receiver, the 'carrier wave' of the station being tuned strikes the antenna. On this carrier, the broadcasting station has superimposed the an-nouncer's voice or music. Whatever its nature, this superimposed element of the signal is called the *modulation*. The radio receiver picks up the carrier wave, extracts and amplifies the modulation from the carrier, and reproduces it through a loudspeaker.

"In our analogy, the electrostatic energy of the human body – which remains with it after death – is the carrier wave in the Drown conception of the process. The vital energy (orgone) of the human being, which flows into and through and animates the human tissues, is the *modulation* or intelligence. This energy is not present in the body after death. Absence of this energy turns a living human into a corpse. This vital or orgone energy enables our organs and tissues to maintain their form. The Drown instrument tunes into the histological structure to determine whether or not the 'carrier' in the various organs and glands is receiving the proper amount of intelligence or modulation, i.e. life energy."

Treatment is ultimately performed by the patients upon themselves; it is not due to the electronics of the box, which in Drowns case did not use electrical current. "In therapy," Constable continues, "the patient is placed in a complete circuit with himself. His energy is collected on a plate of block tin placed over the solar plexus. This energy is passed through the instrument and back to the patient via his feet, the latter resting on two plates of German silver. The minute electrical current resulting from the junction, via the patient's body, of the dissimilar metals tin and German silver, acts in the therapy hookup as a carrier for the vital energy.

"The patient's energy normally would be radiated into the ethers to return to him after a world-circling journey. Under this therapeutic system, the energy is passed through the instrument instead. The tuning of the device governs the precise area of the body into which the totality of the patient's energy returns. The focusing of his total energy results in increased cell division in the tissue so treated. New cells come in healthy, and the diseased condition is gradually overcome.

"Over a period, and with systematic and careful monitoring by the doctor, the affected organ or tissue is largely restored. Never should it be forgotten that the energy involved in therapy is possessed inherently of form-giving power. As regeneration begins, the vibratory rate of the area under treatment begins changing back toward a normal, healthy rate of vibration. Regular checking by the doctor is necessary to keep the instrument in tune

Fig 13-4. Drown Homo-Vibra Ray

with the tissue under treatment."

Drown perfected the process of using a patient's drop of blood placed in her instrument to diagnose and treat a patient remotely anywhere in the world. The inevitable result of this assertion was to place her work even more squarely in the realm of the occult. In occult theory, blood is believed to contain portions of an "etheric web," or a "unifying bio-energetic continuum." In other words, blood contains a pattern recognition component that can be used in various ceremonial ways to produce change. Drown's medical successes reinforced this usage and she tried to transpose it into the practical world of medical technology.

We are lucky that several informed, contemporary individuals have provided us with a closer look at her methodologies. In 1930, according to Constable, a friend gave her a copy of MacGregor Mather's book, *The Kabbalah Unveiled*. She is described as being subsequently "overwhelmed" by this treatise of esoteric Jewish tradition with its own mixed and controversial academic foundation.

The Kabbalah is considered an ancient form of Jewish and Babylonian mysticism that is commonly associated with magical practices and occult technology. Drown tied her radionics knowledge into the Kabbalistic "Tree of Life," essentially fusing her new form of radionics with Jewish mysticism. This association with radionics theory has persisted to the present day. As Constable noted so succinctly in 1976, "From the inception of her work, Dr. Drown's instruments were the 20th century concretion of the Qabalah."

Some of Drowns contemporaries claim she refused to relinquish the monopoly she held on her technology to the medical profession, thus arousing their ire. Through the aura of secrecy Drown initially maintained around

Fig 13-5. Drown Mechanical Detector

her discoveries, coupled with her independent attitude and enormous success with her patients, she ultimately attracted the attention of the FDA, which in 1951 moved in for the kill. Knowing that Drown was the most visible of all the radionics practitioners, the rationale was that by toppling her, others would be intimidated.

The result was a vigorous prosecution. One could argue today it was based upon entrapment. The prosecution capitalized on her

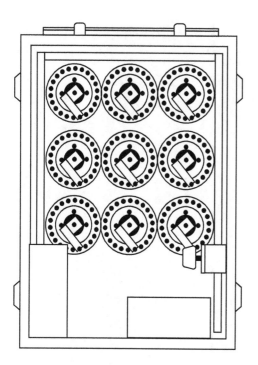

Fig 13-6. Drown circuit

When released, she was emotionally exhausted, broke and professionally ruined, with no way to make a living. Within a few months, she suffered a series of strokes and died.

From this point on, radionics was officially an outlaw technology. The benefits that may have accrued from radionics treatment were no longer considered viable. There was no longer any scientific reason to explore their potential. Soon, any approach to healing that did not meet scientific standards was vigorously persecuted or condemned. As a result, anyone practicing radionics on humans, selling these instruments for medical purposes, or even shipping them across state lines was subject to prosecution in most states.

enthusiastic and over-confident attitude and set her up. Many former patients and friends came to her defense and testified to the cures she provided, but the problem with her credibility came with claiming her technology employed radio and electronics. The jurors were effectively persuaded by the testimony of electronics experts that radionics had nothing technically to do with radio and that her devices couldn't possibly work the way she claimed. Therefore, radionics was essentially fraudulent. None of the numerous testimonies of patients bearing witness to the effectiveness of her treatments persuaded them otherwise. She was convicted of fraud and medical quackery. Her appeals dragged on for years and in the end she served a short time in a California prison. All her instruments were seized and destroyed.

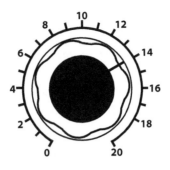

CHAPTER 14
PROFILES IN BRITISH RADIONICS

Dr. Guyon Richards

Before he became interested in radionics, Dr. Guyon Richards had a distinguished career as a surgeon and administrator in the Indian Medical Service and later in World War I. Contemporaries regarded him as an unassuming person of great integrity and common sense. He counted among his friends' doctors and scientists with distinguished careers, such as Sir James Barr.

His book *The Chain of Life* was published in London in 1934, ten years after Abrams' death. With an experimental methodology as rigorours as Abrams' approach, Richards modified the Oscilloclast circuits to amplify short wavelengths. He took the trouble of measuring his subject (stroking the abdomen with a glass rod) while he and his equipment were shielded inside a Faraday cage, which he had modified. The Faraday cage prevented electro-magnetic signal contamination from the environment reaching either Richards or the equipment, a precaution he felt would make for more accuracy and also help determine the nature of what was being detected.

Edward W. Russell, a personal friend of Richards' and writer on radionics, attested to the fact that Richards' equipment did in fact make the reactions on the subjects' abdomen more discernible, however unlikely it seemed that electronics was responsible for it. In retrospect, Russell felt the results seemed to flow not so much from the design of the equipment as from the conviction of the operator.

But his methods also diverged from Abrams in some fundamental ways, though the subject still needed to face West during the procedure. Improvements beyond amplifying the signals from the patient included washing the wires from the subject with colored light in a "color box" composed of four bulbs, red, yellow, green, and blue.

After further refinements made with the assistance of a top instrument maker, Richards was able to obtain radionic measurements down to one one-hundredth of an ohm. In this manner he was able to confirm the accuracy of Abrams' rates. This accuracy became even more important when Richards began measuring elements and substances. What he discovered, as Ruth Drown intuitively sensed, was that the atomic numbers of the element being analyzed corresponded to the figures on his rheostat. For some unknown reason, hydrogen would cause a one-ohm reaction on his subject; oxygen, eight ohms; sodium, 11 ohms; etc. Russell writes that Richards was perfectly aware that ohms were an entirely arbitrary measure applied to quantify the percussive reaction and many observers would believe that was just a figment of his imagination.

Nevertheless, he continued extensive testing over time, which convinced him that the correspondence to atomic number was accurate: "I have used this method now for so many years and with such excellent results that I have in the meantime lost sight of the fact that the correspondence of the ohm and atomic number, atomic weight etc., must sound strange to others, who have always regarded the ohm as a purely arbitrary measure."

To those who criticized Richards' methods as purely imaginary, Russell reported "he could work out a case by employing actual substances in place of numbers; that he had clinical and laboratory support for his results, and that his conclusions were never reached until after many months of laborious experiments." These results were collaborated by a fellow surgeon Dudley Wright, F.R.C.S., and many others who followed his research.

More significantly, by 1930 Richards claimed to have discovered a new form of matter he termed "Biomorphs," which were oddly reminiscent of Wilhelm Reich's "Bions," or individual particles of the life force he termed Orgone. Like Reich, Richards considered biomorphs to be a manifestation of the life force at a very primary level. In examining this substance, he determined that it could be measured in concentric rings, nestled among the atoms and molecules of the specimen. Minerals had one ring, vegetables two, insects and reptiles three, mammals and birds three and four, humans four and five, the fifth being detected on or near the navel.

Richards found that these rings or layers had a corresponding presence outside the human body in what we nowadays would call a field structure or aura. Russell points out that Richards' observations preceded by fifteen years the discovery by Yale scientist Harold Saxton Burr that all living forms (and various forms of matter) are controlled by electrodynamic fields (L-fields, or Fields of Life), measurable by high-impedance voltmeters unavailable in Richards' time and later captured in Kirilian photography.

Due to the increased sensitivity of his instruments, Richards soon realized that thought could impact radionic measurement. He established that radionics could function as an essential tool in the early detecting of disease. Again, these assertions presented an overwhelming problem in establishing a scientific basis for radionics, which by definition must remain independent of the operator and objectively verifiable.

In Richards' work, we again encounter an example of a highly qualified medical doctor conducting serious, in-depth research in a scientific and empirical manner, in harmony with the scientific principles of his time. Ironically, it was his measurable data that ultimately lead away from physics and into parapsychology, a problem that continues to confront radionic researchers today.

Malcolm Rae

To any casual observer, by the last quarter of the 20th century, radionics already had much in common with art. Each inventor had developed a system and a technology that was partially derivative and partially unique from earlier styles. All contained idiosyncratic elements that were self-referential and required a psychic component to work. Many produced results that were based upon measurements of some kind, but exactly what was being measured could not be defined scientifically any more than could aesthetic observations.

In Britain, new systems of radionics developed that were highly artistic in their design and operation. Two will be examined here. The first "design" system, Magneto Geometry, was the brainchild of a businessman and retired British Navy Lieutenant Commander named Malcolm Rae, who was born in Cheshire, England in 1913.

Rae did not become a radionics pioneer until well into mid-life. Introduced to radionics while in the navy, he initially rejected it. Then, later on in life, he began experimenting with instruments that Abrams and Drown had designed. Mention of his work does not appear regularly in radionics discussions until the 1960s. Many of his innovations were characterized by the introduction of mathematical concepts, especially imposing Golden Ratio proportions onto radionically inspired diagrams and devices.

In Rae's designs, the various emanations of substances were coded into numbers. Later, these numbers were transferred to angular relations of the Earth's magnetic field, which he dowsed onto a series of concentric circles with a pendulum. The resulting diagrams took the form of same-sized printed cards, with the angles radially marked on the innermost cir-

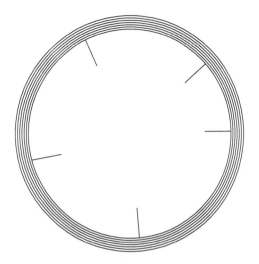

Fig 14-1. Rae Diagram - Agraphis Nutans

cle, resolved to one degree of arc. These cards, called Remedy Simulator Cards, could be inserted or placed upon a radionics device. Rae's collection of diagrams represented all the various structures, diseases, and remedies used for treatment (currently more than 25,000), replacing the dials and electronics of earlier and more traditional radionics design.

Rae designed several different devices to function with the cards. The Rae Analyzer was used to work up an energetic profile of the patient. It was a two-part device connected by wires and utilized a pendulum. The cards would go into slots on a unit, where switches selected the desired function and potency of treatment. This unit was connected by wire to a chart holder, which allowed interchangeable charts for analysis and treatment. The pendulum would be used to indicate what parts of the chart needed to be addressed. Another device, the Simulator, was employed for making remedies or treating patients.

Rae returned to traditional pendulum dowsing over the diagnostic chart or graph to affect his diagnosis. The chart contained

Fig 14-2. Malcolm Rae

condition. His techniques were also the first to embrace aesthetics, through the use of phi, found extensively in nature and also in art and architecture. Aesthetics can be subjective, and that problem needed to be addressed.

To bring potential subjective differences under one common nomenclature, Rae decided that two things were necessary. First, the questions being asked of the pendulum had to be as precise as possible. Second, the best way to quantify the answer to a proper question was through the introduction of ratios (or sometimes shapes). In particular, ratios could be used to describe deviation from optimal potential.

Rae dowsed for the best possible design calibrations for his early dial instruments, a process which led to the Golden Ratio (1:16180337…), or Golden Section. Apparently, at the time, Rae was quite unaware how important this ratio is in nature. The golden section ratio explains the relationship of two parts to a whole, where the ratio of the smaller part to the larger part is the same as the ratio of the larger part to the whole. Phi is also the basis for the Fibonacci numbering system, named for a 13th century Italian mathematician, Leonardo of Pisa (1170 - 1250). Progressing Fibonacci numbers, (each number after the first two is the sum of the previous two numbers, 0, 1, 1, 2, 3, 5, 8, 13, 21, 34, etc.) approach the Golden Ratio, and can be visualized in spiral growth patterns such as those seen in the exquisite nautilus shell.

Artists have often seen in the golden ratio a revelation of mystical content in form. These geometries reflect the inexplicable presence of metaphysical meaning in nature, so fundamental to many radionics inventors. Robert Lawlor, in *Sacred Geometry: Philosophy & Practice*, goes to the heart of the issue of how

enough information that, by asking a question and watching where the pendulum moved, a diagnosis or treatment could be obtained. Often the pendulum was designed to contain a coil of wire wound in a Golden Ratio phi (denoted by the Greek letter φ or phi) to enhance effectiveness. This revised pendulum replaced the stick pad as the primary divinatory tool in Rae's inventions.

The return to dowsing and the introduction of sacred geometry had deeper implications for Rae's approach. He believed that the radiesthesia sense or psi function was just another type of natural sense, like vision and hearing, only subtler. As such, it could account for the discrepancies between different individuals and their radionic perceptions of a

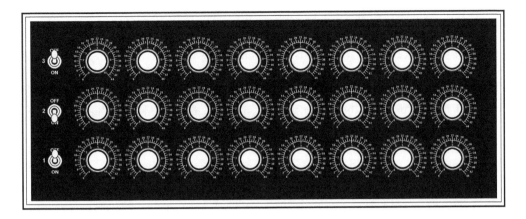

Fig 14-3. Rae 24 dial Base 44 device

sacred science differs from ordinary science when he states: "The relationship between the fixed and the volatile (between proportion and progression) is a key to Sacred geometry: everything which is manifest, be it in the physical world or in the world of mental images and conceptions, belongs to the ever-flowing progressions of constant change: it is only the non-manifest realm of Principles which is immutable. Our science errs in attempting to attach fixed, absolute laws and definitions to the changing world of appearances. The history of science shows us perpetually discarding or revising one world model after another. Because of the disturbingly unstable quality of scientific knowledge, not only our physicists, but also our philosophers, artists, and society as a whole have become relativists. But the unchanging, generative principles remain, and our contemporary rejection of them is taking place only because we have sought for the permanent in the empirical world instead of in its true abode, the metaphysical."

In brief, by incorporating sacred ratios into the design component of his radionic devices, Rae not only bridged the gap to aesthetics but also infused his machines with cos-mic significance. By employing this overlay, Rae aligned optimal health with a mathematical ideal.

Rae soon discovered that representing this proportional relationship on paper as geometric drawings was far easier than engineering them into electronic components, although he used both. Eventually, for simplicity and for accuracy, he substituted a drawing of a ratio for a rate. He would calculate the geometry as a ratio that described how far the patient's condition had deviated from normal, and then he would use it in treatment.

To broadcast a curative geometry to the patient, Rae initially returned to the approach used by Upton in the UKACO design. He used a broadband radio frequency broadcast to blast the intention into the witness. Later, the EM transmission process was replaced with an information signal sent into the body of the patient utilizing thought, via the witness, or sample of hair or blood provided by the patient. Rae believed that the correct answer to any question was inherent within the collective unconscious. All that was required to obtain an answer was that the questions be precise, clear, and unbiased.

To this end he devised an aid in the form of a rubber sheet impregnated with magnetic particles that he placed under the chart being reviewed. The magnetic influence was said to lessen intellectual activity and eliminate pre-conceived ideas. Controlled breathing then acted as a carrier of thought, which was linked to the dials through a magnet housed in the device. Once abstracted, the thought became crystallized, either numerically or geometrically by the selection of a card. The message to the patient ultimately was to restore himself or herself to optimal condition. Physical distance was irrelevant.

By using the standard radionics procedures of analysis and treatment via a representation of the person – the witness, (i.e. drop of blood, hair, etc.) – and by broadcasting them "electronically," Rae maintained an operational protocol very much within the overall definition of radionics. What he added was an aesthetic, in the sense that health was very much an expression of correct balance and proportion within the mind and body of the patient; in the same sense, it was a universal standard of beauty within natural form.

Darrell Butcher

Darrell Butcher, an Englishman, was an elusive figure in radionics who also had a very artistic approach to technology. He is said to have been an aircraft engineer much of his life until he became involved with radionics in the 1950s. His particular "automated" approach to radionics design came about largely due to his inability to use either a stick-pad or a pendulum with any success. Unwittingly, this handicap brought his radionics designs even closer to art.

Undaunted by his inability to obtain the "radionic stick," Butcher spent fourteen years designing instruments that worked either by virtue of the operator's mental concentration or entirely alone. Like artworks, their symbolism was unique to his creative expression. In addition, he made all of the devices himself and his design and craftsmanship were masterful.

Very little information remains in the public record concerning this fascinating individual who completed the bridge between utilitarian and aesthetic radionics begun by Rae and others. Most certainly, developing an artistic form of radionics was not his primary aim. What has been written about him is vague in respect to both his technology and his personal life. But radionics writers R. Murray Denning and Jorge Resines have provided clues that convey something of his aesthetic approach to radionics.

Butcher attempted to design radionics equipment that did not require either psychic ability or self-referential procedures to operate. In his research, Butcher was inspired by the work of a 19th century physicist named Adolphe Ganot (1804-1887). Ganot's work, entitled *Elementary Treatise on Physics* (5th Edition, translated by E. Atkinson, Ph.D., 1872) contained a chapter called "The Principle of Light," which led Butcher to believe in the existence of what he called a "Downpouring" of energy from the cosmos.

Regarding "downpouring," Butcher said: "This is a known force. It has been given many names. I am of the personal opinion that different people are able to attract different amounts of this force, but it is always with us. And that it does come down vertically under normal circumstances and this can only be made use of if we abide by the laws of light, one of which states that: Vibrations of the ether take place, not in the direction of

 The Secret Art

the wave, but in a plane at right angles to it, and the latter are called transversal vibrations (from Ganot's physics)."

The concept of downpouring gave Butcher the idea that a device could be constructed that connected the downpouring energy directly to the individual simply by placing a witness in a properly designed receptacle. These designs began with a series of objects Butcher called "meters" or "comparators." The top of the device was made of a combination of designs and materials, including Archimedean Spirals made of black and white plastic covered with paper elements utilizing the same spiral design. These components were centered on a needle arm protruding from the suspension mechanism and were employed in directing the downpouring energy toward the patient.

Another more evolved design involving the same general idea of the downpouring was called the "Straw Hat," as it had that general appearance. The "straw hat" component was mounted upon a supported needle, allowing it to move freely. An electric lamp, housed underneath, allowed light to pass under the brim of the straw hat and out horizontally. Placed upon and around the brim were Rae rates or George de la Warr's graphic cards for treatment and diagnosis. Just outside the brim was mounted a small input well for the sample representing the patient, termed "witness." Butcher described how this device was designed to work: "The lamp also gives rising heat to the top of the 'straw hat' which because of the flutes revolves it in one direction.

"All things being equal, once the 'straw hat' is revolving in accordance with the rising heat, it should not stop. But it has been found that if a patient's sample is placed close to the rim of this 'straw hat' when it is revolving, and

Fig 14-4. Butcher Upright Treatment Instrument

when the symptom from which the patient is suffering comes by on one of our bits of graph paper, the thing hesitates and stops. Sometimes it goes past and comes back again, but whatever happens it stops.

"This is quite revealing and useful. It is a form of diagnosis over which we have no control, and with which we do not interfere.

"It is especially useful as regards toxins and hormones and we also use colors for treatment in this manner. Here again we have the story of the cones. It is the downpouring. [The cones refer to another design of the "meter."]

"When you get a really good 'stick' the 'straw hat' goes around in the opposite direction, because you get a downpouring from above that sits on the back of the flutes and instead of the air from underneath pushing it one way, the downpouring pushes it the other. It's incredible it should have this amount of power."

Fig 14-5. Butcher — Straw Hat Instrument

Writer Denning referred back to similar comments that Butcher made while describing the effects of the downpouring upon his instruments. Butcher said: "One little instrument was evolved which is rather puzzling and it has bothered a few scientific types, and that is three paper cones freely supported, something like a wind-meter. It has been found they go back-

wards, i.e. that is towards their bases when in a room where there is resonance with a patient, meaning by that, when we have what would be known in ordinary parlance as a stick,' then we find this incredible breeze coming along that blows these things round in the opposite direction to which they should go.

"This puzzled us for years, and after further checking, it was found that when we placed a piece of board above the cones all this stopped, so it rather looks as if this is another example of the Fundamental Force being brought down and accelerated by the fact that we have obtained our objective, and impinging on the outside of the cones, which are at an angle of 45 degrees and pushing them forward towards their bases.

"People have been puzzled because cones have been placed on a window-shelf, near air coming in and have been gaily going round in the normal direction, which is to their apex, blown by the wind. And it is very strange to see them stop, stagger, struggle and eventually go in the opposite direction."

These descriptions of the downpouring in Butcher's own words give some idea about how his instruments were designed to work. Another beautifully designed instrument combined a meter with a pegboard design. In one box were moveable pegs that corresponded in some way with adjustments made to the meter. Named The Pegotty, each peg hole placement corresponded to the "rate" set by the operator. Butcher observed the instrument working long after the operator left the room.

By far the most visually sophisticated of Butcher's instruments was the one described by Denning as the Upright Treatment Instrument. Sadly, there are no existing notes for this device. All we know is that the instrument

Fig 14-6. Butcher — Peggoty Board Instrument

The Secret Art

imitated the more traditional radionics device, particularly the George de la Warr box, with its nine-dial facade. It also had an additional bottom section or box that protruded perpendicular to the top and contained additional dials and input wells.

The entire visual design was a carefully balanced relationship of circle to square, black to white, and ring to ring to dot pattern describing an unknown form of calibration. White dots were painted in an asymmetrical fashion around the dials with no clear indication as to their purpose. This artistic effect adds to the overall design of the box, with its concentric black and white rings and stylish, retro design. Butcher gave the Upright Treatment Instrument a surreal, futuristic quality that is the dominant aesthetic of his work.

Although his designs mimicked more traditional radionic components, there is another important distinction. All of Butcher's instruments transcend the need to impress upon the viewer a concrete relationship to orthodox science and technology. This distinction is particularly noticeable through the lack of electrical components and circuitry. Butcher replaced wires and condensers with plastic and paper cut into spirals, perforated holes, or painted dots and rings.

In many ways, his instruments are more like a talisman or fetish adapted to a concept of instrumentation. Refreshingly, Butcher appeared unconcerned with the acceptance of his discoveries by scientists. Like many an artist, he was absorbed in his own empirical investigation, more concerned with the quality of the results than with outside approval.

This liberating feature of Butcher's work is due in large part to his aesthetic view of radionics interactivity. For Butcher, the connection of light to the downpouring transfers

Fig 14-7. Butcher — Meter I

the design imperative into what Resines calls "spatial interference." This term is also used in the description of how holograms are made.

Both Resines and Denning went to great lengths to make sense out of Butcher's design innovations. Denning's curiosity about Butcher's sources also led him to believe that Huygens' Principle (named for Christian Huygens 1629-1695, a Dutch physicist who proposed an early theory of light) played a role in Butcher's thinking, but he didn't elaborate. Resines gave it a try in his pamphlet, *Automated Detecting Devices*, carrying the Huygens' supposition much further, but I will leave it to the reader to find this pamphlet and draw their own conclusions, as it resisted my comprehension. Let it be said that some unknown scientific theory led Butcher to connect his dot symmetries to a theory of light. The authors' empathy for this conclusion rests largely upon Butcher's own assertion that he spent more than 14 years researching and designing his devices, when coupled with his expertise as an aircraft engineer, led them to believe some unknown technical guidelines prompted his efforts.

More obvious to the uninitiated, the dot patterns, plus a copious use of geometry to evoke non-physical force, draw immediate

Fig 14-8. Duchamp Rotary Demisphere

comparisons to Keely's work a century before. Notably, the Archimedean Spiral design of Butcher's Meter 1 contains a component made of an array of fine lines of nested arrows, which are drawn of thin lines etched onto a curved piece of transparent Plexiglas fitted within the meter. This arrow complex stimulated Resines to analyze the ratios of the descending angles nested in the arrow form.

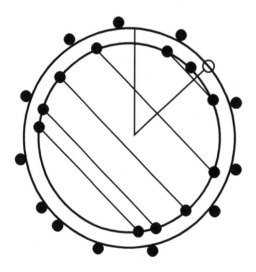

Fig 14-9. Butcher — Rings Diagram

These ratios, according to his calculations, correspond to various "energy harmonics" found in the works of Bruce Cathie's energy grid hypothesis, a complex of interrelating theories involving earth energy and related ideas, that Resines believes supports Butchers observation of a "downpouring."

As to Butcher's extensive use of dots, both on the dials of his instruments and in supplementary drawings and cards with circular holes punched within them, and specifically regarding the holes punched in the cards, Resines made the following observation: "The most extraordinary fact is that Butcher experimentally proved that the patterns punched on the cards corresponded exactly with the etheric energies emanating from samples placed in a moveable holder and which came from sick people. This would be another indication…that from it we can evolve a reliable and fast diagnostic method…the spinning clockwise (motion) can explain its power of amplification."

Resines advanced another notion about the way in which Butcher's radionics ideas relate to art is: "The usage of black and white-colored parts serves again for the dissemination and absorption of light, thus creating an effect similar to a radio-message which possesses waves that undergo compression and expansion (as modulated by human voice) to convey a message from a sender to a receiver."

This idea suggests that the modulation of alternating tones and color act as carrier waves for the subtle energy imbedded within them, placed there through intent. Whatever the rationale, the design conclusions are purely aesthetic, with the added thought that arrangements of form and color are capable of directing the flow of some form of subtle energy.

Any artist seeking to design their own

The Secret Art

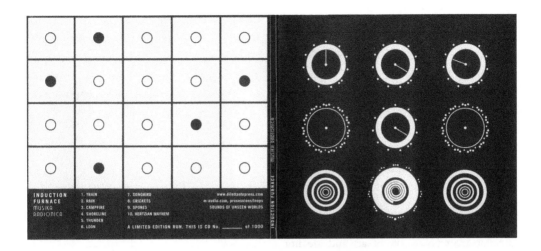

Fig 14-10. Induction Furnace CD jacket

radionics devices will be fascinated by how Butcher's engineering background, coupled with his fastidious design and craftsmanship reconcile with such an aesthetic sense of radionics. It seems plausible to compare his obsessive thematic embellishments to various outsider artists, who often discover a purpose to their efforts and proceed to evolve a lengthy body of work in an effort to bring that purpose into form.

The pegboard motif also shares a high design and functional correlation with Australian aboriginal dot painting, which likewise is said to serve an energetic function. Similarly, the angular geometries and spiral waveforms employed by Butcher have strong corollaries to Navajo sand painting that also serves a curative purpose. Like Darrell Butcher, shamanic artists function successfully without a rational scientific interpretation. Their results alone affirmed their value to the people employing their methods, who found these simple tools could both heal and transform their lives.

Darrell Butcher's thoughts and inventions are largely lost to posterity, but his par-ticular view of radionics has survived in the design of the instruments themselves. They are indeed artistic creations, more so for being rendered irrelevant by science.

For the artist interested in radionics, Darrell Butcher's designs have great significance. They represent an unusually high watermark in their ability to employ radionic ideas in a conceptual fashion, void of cumbersome mechanical and electronic contrivances and free of scientific rationalization.

Visually, Butcher's Upright Treatment Instrument is reminiscent of Marcel Duchamp's 1925 *Rotary Demisphere* and the 1922 *Optophone 1* by Francis Picabias. His meters also have an uncanny resemblance to Duchamp's 1935 *Rotoreliefs* with their spinning spiral motifs.

Another interesting subtle energy to art crossover can be seen in Linda Hendersons' book, *Duchamp In Context*, where in image #172 she displays Sir Oliver Lodge's 1913 *Signaling Across Space Without Wires* diagram, which she points out appears in Duchamp's 1918 glass sculpture *To Be Looked at (from the*

Other Side of the Glass) with One Eye, Close to, for Almost an Hour. Incidentally, an almost identical form appears in Butcher's Upright Treatment Device, where it performs some unknown radionic function. Also noticed in the same text, image #114 titled *Oculist Witnesses* from Duchamp's *Large Glass*, plate 1, figure 76, is a floating concentric ringed form with a broken notch in the outer ring, which bears an uncanny resemblance to the Malcolm Rae rate diagrams.

The radionics devices designed by Butcher are truly works of art and are not merely visual aids for developing psi ability. They encompass a form of lost science derived from the distant past but foreseeable in a post-scientific future where mind more effectively shapes physical reality. As shamanic art-tools, they deserve a respect and consideration not generally afforded fringe technology.

I believe radionics history clearly shows a progression from a mechanical and electrically based technology towards one of aesthetics, information and ultimately spirit. As radionics has become less and less comprehensible in conventional scientific terms, it has become more and more accessible in artistic terms. Given the preponderance of radionics-like themes permeating world culture, especially with respect to understanding the art of indigenous societies, is it not plausible that radionics deserves further reflection?

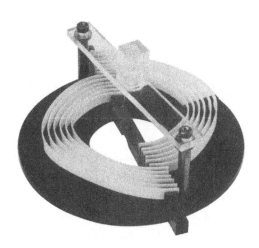

Fig 14-11. Butcher — Meter III

The Secret Art

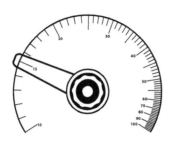

CHAPTER 15
GEORGE & MARJORIE DE LA WARR

In England, as we have noted, radionics took a much different turn than in America. For one, the British radionic inventors moved away from an electronic basis for their devices and into other forms of design. Predominately, English design utilized light, magnetism, diagrams, and sound to effect radionics transactions. As such, they were aligned much more closely to traditional occult technology. The radionic devices also appeared more artistic in the manner in which they were conceived, constructed, and used.

Langston Day, writing with George de la Warr about his instruments, said, "They were effective only if the operator was able to control his thoughts and form a clear picture of the diseased organ, or whatever it might be, with which he was dealing. In fact, these instruments were no more than aids to personal skill, and although the help they afforded was great, de la Warr was not satisfied. His ambition was to invent an automatic device that would eliminate the personal factor. This would not only overcome the difficulties of inept or poorly trained operators, it would lend itself far better to scientific investigation of its merits. But as he was to discover, the invention of such an instrument was a very difficult matter indeed."

Regardless, the revival of radionics in Britain was due in large part to the efforts of this dynamic Oxford couple, George (called "Bill") and Marjorie de la Warr. Bill de la Warr was born in 1904 and was educated as a mechanical engineer. For sixteen years, he was the Chief Engineering Assistant of the Oxfordshire County Council, among other jobs. Marjorie was the daughter of a scientist. Together, around 1940 when Bill was discharged from the Army for asthma and contact with persons outside England was difficult, they received permission from Ruth Drown to copy her instrument.

In light of subsequent developments in radionics, particularly for art, many of their laboratories' discoveries had long ranging effects. In many ways their work foreshadows the current era of radionics sound devices and sonic art installations. De la Warr's fascination with sound began when a friend casually remarked that plants probably emitted their own individual musical notes. At that time, de la Warr had been pursuing a course of study that convinced him that nature held the remedy for most ailments, and that the curative properties of plants and minerals were probably due to the radiations they produced.

De la Warr wondered if sound or ultrasonic radiation could play a role in this process. He attached some galvanometers to plants that could measure tiny electrical reactions, following the work done by Jundigar Bose in India some years before. These tests convinced him that plants emitted a radiation capable of reacting to outside stimuli, namely the static electricity around the cells that was particularly influenced by sound. Further tests showed that the proper tuning of sound waves to individual plants increased their rate of growth.

These experiments, conducted in the early 1940s led de la Warr to evolve a complex theory of resonant relationships that replaced the established notion in radionics of radiations emanating from matter. He believed that subtle resonances, when combined properly in the right harmonic relationships, could produce waveforms in a "primary" state of matter that could be instrumentally detected and interpreted by his devices.

De la Warr's experience and research caused him to believe these resonances, especially in living matter, were extremely complex waveforms corresponding to harmonies and chords. This resonance phenomenon, he believed, established a relationship, "link," or force field that acted as a "carrier" for whatever energy was used with it, such as light or sound. Resonant links of this kind could be established between blood, hair, and photographs – all the normal witnesses found in traditional radionics procedure. Because the resonant link was more information than energy, it did not obey the laws of physics and diminish in intensity with distance. Once the resonance between patient and operator was established, it would respond to influences, such as electrical stress, magnetism, sound, chemical action, or light. This revelation led to the design of devices for manipulating sound and light that were said to improve the therapeutic effect of his radionics equipment.

De la Warr's first experiments set about trying to make antenna arrays that could pick up these waveforms from plants. Ultimately, the operator using a stick plate that covered a hollow resonant cavity inside the detector obtained the best results. The detector linked the operator's sensitivity, expressed by the stick reaction, to the radiations being given off by the plant, which was captured in the resonant cavity and then calibrated in various ways, ultimately by a resistance dial. Visually, it was a familiar form of radionic dowsing but used in a completely different technological sense than earlier techniques.

The operators rubbed the plate while seeking the desired resonance in some numerical or graphic form. When the resonance was found, the finger would stick or drag on the rubber covering the stick plate. In this manner the operators' consciousness acted as a modulator of complex and constantly shifting waveforms emitted by the subject. The skill came in holding one's mind on the object under study long enough to allow one's own bodily radiations to tune to the plant or whatever other object was under study. When these radiations came into a harmonic rela-

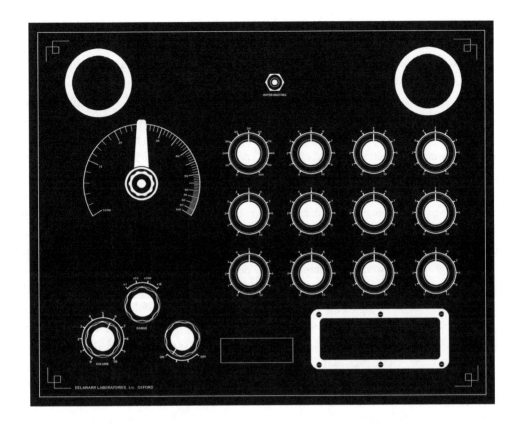

Fig 15-1. De la Warr Diagnostic Instrument with Oscillator

tionship with one another, the effectiveness of the process was augmented and reinforced, objectively perceived by the finger sticking on the plate.

De la Warr's plant experiments led eventually to the design of very sophisticated radionics equipment that incorporated a color and sonic component into their design. Light and sound manipulation were seen as an economical and highly flexible way of directing and rearranging the subtle, pre-physical resonances from the realm of thought and emotion, which he believed were the source of diseased conditions. These treatments were initially performed directly upon the patient, and it came as a surprise that they could be transmitted across space along the resonant link.

What is striking about de la Warr's experimental procedure is the degree to which he allowed an intuitive aesthetic sensitivity, based upon resonance and harmonic coupling, to guide his research and instrument design. It strikes me that the designs of his instruments have far more in common with a violin than they do a radio transceiver. De la Warr's description of energy resonance will perhaps be more comprehensible to those artistically inclined. Paintings, music, art of all kinds give us a sense of meaning, or convey an energy that completely transcends the form and circumstance of the work, including the best scientific description of the medium. What explanations are available usually rely upon terms such as "resonance" to explain what takes place between the viewer and that being viewed.

In addition, de la Warr's approach to the entire field of radionics seems far more intuitively comprehensible than the purely electronic or psionic/occult methodologies developed by earlier inventors. Far from precluding the mind as an active agent in obtaining a radionics diagnosis, he instead applauded the mental faculties employed and the need for concentration in obtaining results. His approach had a deeply artistic approach but one that also explains something about the subsequent growth of advertising techniques employing modulated imagery composed of sound and light.

What struck me about the approach that de la Warr took to radionics was that he seemed to understand the subtle signals he sensed were more akin to values than actual patterns of energy or frequencies. By using the word "values" it is suggested that his technique was more like the resonances a composer or singer uses to dial in a particular emotion or feeling. A great deal of aesthetic subtlety is needed to turn a group of notes or pitches into music that is deeply felt and appreciated. The artist must layer the nuances onto the mechanics of generating a composition, a song, or a theatrical presentation. The de la Warr method of radionics was more about calibrating nuance and using it to shift the modality of a disease, comparable to an artwork that can cause us to see and feel the world in a new way.

De la Warr had a passion for accuracy and a high regard for fine instrumentation. When confronted with the task of reconstructing and improving on the Drown design, he brought in a top instrument maker and a physicist to consult on the project. Together with Marjorie, they began Delawarr Laboratories. Mar-

jorie's efforts were directed toward creating a successful radionics practice while the others concentrated on design innovations.

The Drown instrument was among the first to be run on mental energy, not electricity, although it used electrical components in its design. Drowns' approach was considered occult, involving esoteric concepts from the Kabbalah and elsewhere. By contrast, de la Warr's approach, while equally esoteric, appeared more grounded. For him, the radiations of life and matter were described in terms of resonance and harmonics, an approach that drew them closer to art, music, and geometry. Even more interesting was the fact that his instruments shared commonality with ancient technology, especially geomantic devices and, in the detectors, African rubbing board oracles.

When de la Warr discovered that plant growth and electrical potential could be stimulated by sound waves of certain frequencies, he noticed that their potential seemed to change when the plant was rotated in relation to the magnetic field of the earth. This observation is reminiscent of the Abrams discovery many years before. De la Warr found that when a plant was rotated to a "critical position" vis-à-vis the Earth's magnetic field and then planted, it grew better.

These discoveries impacted his radionics designs. He was able to construct graduated dials of spring metal in a uniform way that allowed for a standardization of rates across all of his instruments. Nine of these tuning elements were first connected in parallel and then to the lower plate of the detector. This detector was a condenser made of rubber mounted over a metal sheet, which was separated from a similar piece of metal below it by a pocket of air (the resonant cavity). The dials were mounted on a Bakelite (plastic) panel and connected to two small "wells" to hold the specimens being analyzed. The small unit did not require electricity and was easily transported in its black carrying case. The enigmatic "Black Box" was thus reborn, British style.

The ease of construction and standardized design allowed the de la Warrs to establish their own set of "rates." In refining this process, they discovered that by adding a rotating magnet to define the instrument's position in the Earth's magnetic field, they were able to stabilize and sharpen the tuning capacity of his device. The tiny bar magnet was placed on a rod attached to a rotating dial. The magnet was mounted between the two input wells, above the panel holding the dials, and connected in parallel to them. In time, more than 8,000 rates corresponding to various conditions and their cures were established and printed as the *Book of Rates and Detail Sheets*.

One can only imagine the contempt, derision, and skepticism such a subjective, self-referential technology met with in scientific circles. But the howls were only beginning.

Upon returning to the sound experiments with plants, the de la Warrs devised an instrument that worked with light and color called the Delaray Lamp. This device had even more resemblance to an art object. It was composed of a brass tube fitted with four pre-adjusted spirals inside it. The spirals were mounted over a blackbody infrared radiator housed in the base, at right angles to the radiation device, and could be exchanged with other similar elements of slightly different design. These spirals were tuners that could be vectored according to a dowsing methodology employed by the operator.

The spirals (as a tuning mechanism) were based on the assumption that radionics energies followed a vortex pattern. A similar, but later, device using light was named the Colorscope. In this design, a light beam passing through optical filters could be reduced in such a way as to accurately define the rates in measurements of light. These measurements were easily repeatable. In later versions, a plate holding a drop of blood (the witness) could be inserted and rotated on the axis of the light beam for carrying out remote diagnoses. The rotational element or Critical Rotational Position (CRP) of every form of matter was now one of the most important features of the de la Warr instrument design.

The Delawarr laboratory also experimented with the therapeutic potential of sound. Radionics author Edward W. Russell states that using sound to carry treatment into the body was part of an attempt by the laboratory to put a "friendlier" face on radionics treatment that wasn't so occult in appearance. In fact, this line of experimentation led to a discovery of great importance for later researchers.

While broadcasting sound into the body, it occurred to de la Warr to see if the same sound was coming out of the body. Pursuing this thought, he discovered that a different waveform emerged from the subject being treated with sound. This waveform would vary with the patient's disease. His discovery led to an invention called an Autoplotter or Psychoplotter that mapped the shape of the emerging waveform. The resulting graph or "Histogram" of this process was a description of the tissue or substance under treatment. The Histogram gave de la Warr the ability to establish a baseline for evaluating the effects his various inventions had on the organism undergoing the treatment. In the case of patients in need of a cure, this baseline could be further correlated with blood tests performed at an outside diagnostic facility.

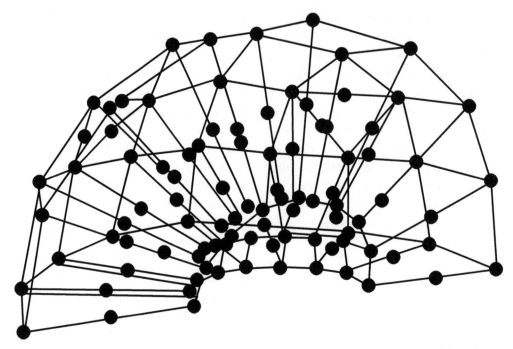

Fig 15-2. Nodal point diagram

In the world of visual art, Duchamp's 1914 photograph, *Air Current Piston*, showing a screen with big black dots in the mesh, is visually similar to de la Warr's large scale Autoplotter experiments that plotted big white dots across a floor to ceiling screen, indicating "nodal spots" detected in the energy field of a subject. No doubt the similarity is purely coincidental, but the persistence of the dot matrix in energetic description and composition has ancient artistic forbearers.

Adding to their therapeutic tools, the lab also developed another purely magnetic device for treatment called the MT/3. This device consisted of a group of small solenoids that permitted magnetic fields to be applied directly to various parts of the body. (The solenoid is a small coil of wire around an air-core carrying one amp of current.) These solenoids broadcast a magnetic field into the body, sometimes pre-recorded, whose effects could then be analyzed via blood tests. When combined with the other therapeutic devices and the histogram, a novel methodology of radionics treatment became available.

It is worth considering for a moment the importance sound was beginning to have within the arts. The power of sound alone now led composers and sonic artists to experiment with it artistically. The electronic music of Cage, Stockhausen, Varese, and others emerged directly from the chaotic envelope of frequencies heard and, more often, felt around us. Many such compositions assigned aesthetic value to radiant soundscapes. This process mimicked the therapeutic value of soundscapes assigned by the radionic devices.

Later, sonic artists fused these experiences with visual art forms and performance. Ambient music became popular as a "lite" version of radionic audio impressions designed to heal or harmonize. Without realizing it and with

    The Secret Art

little or no subsequent credit, the de la Warrs had initiated and explored an important venue for artistic discovery in the late 20th century.

Radionics as art was not confined to sound. In 1919 Thomas Wilfred (1889-1968) produced his first Clavilux, an instrument that allowed light forms to be played by piano type keys, in a performance titled *Lumina*. Wilfred was a dedicated Theosophist and believed that fluid, polymorphous streams of ever changing colored light demonstrated spiritual principles, perhaps suggesting a therapeutic or radionic component. Wilfred performed *Lumina* in front of large audiences, foreshadowing Psychedelic Art, the stroboscopic Dreammachine of artist Biron Gysin and scientist Ian Sommerville, and even the VJ Performance Art of today.

Wilfred also produced a smaller, deco inspired console version called the Clavilux Jr., whereby the operator controlled a kinetic light display housed in the console by means of a wire-connected keyboard. This art device had many thematic and visual similarities to subsequent light-based radionics devices, notably those of de la Warr's Colorscope and Dinsha P. Ghadiali's (1873-1966) Spectro-Chrome light therapy.

More than just structural similarity exists between the artworks of Duchamp and the radionics inventions of de la Warr, Rae, Butcher, and others. The radionics inventors all had one element in common, and that was the utilization of applied intent to overcome the boundaries defined by a mechanistic and deterministic science. Marcel Duchamp was an artist who effectively changed the way we perceive art. He also shared with de la Warr and others in radionics a tendency for overturning well-entrenched ideas about their profession.

If the radionics inventors had been artists

Fig 15-3. Thomas Wilfred playing the Clavilux

instead of healers, they probably would have been seen as contributing to the avant-garde, particularly Surrealism. More specifically, the designs of their apparatuses and their fascination with resonance and energy would have placed them in the deep but narrow confines of Radio Art. Loosely speaking, radio art defines the relationship of sound and radio to the arts. In this case, the name "radionics" implying a fusion of radio and sonics would have instantly insinuated that it was radio art, regardless of what anyone thought radionics actually was.

Craig Adcock, in a chapter for *Wireless Imagination*, a book about radio art, discusses the impact of Duchamp's work upon the world: "The key to Duchamp's seemingly disproportionate success lies in the fact that he was largely responsible for proving that art can be whatever the artist decides it is. In sculpture it can be the unnoticed objects of the world – the ordinary things like bicycle wheels and bottle racks – that lie undisclosed in the oblivion of disregard. In music, it can be the noise that lies hidden in the intervals between the notes or the gaps left empty between the sounds."

Adcock's thesis is that Duchamp wanted to place art once again "at the service of the mind." Later, in the notes, he adds a quote from Duchamp to this end from a television interview in 1956: "I considered painting as a means of expression, not an end in itself. One means of expression among others, and not a complete end for life at all; in the same way I consider color is only a means of expression in painting and not an end. In other words, painting should not be exclusively retinal or visual; it should have to do with the grey matter, with our urge for understanding."

In 1946 Duchamp had said something similar in an article in *The Bulletin of the Museum of Modern Art* (13): "I was interested in ideas – not merely visual products. I wanted to put painting once again at the service of the mind. And my painting was, of course, at once regarded as 'intellectual,' 'literary' painting. It was true I was endeavoring to establish myself as far as possible from 'pleasing' and 'attractive' physical paintings. That extreme was seen as literary."

Duchamp's statements imply that he was making a form of art that continually questioned the nature of what art was. During roughly the same time period, the de la Warrs were initiating experiments of a scientific nature, one that incorporated their own consciousness into the results. Their intent was also to question the assumptions that science was making about the healing process.

The delirious pace of development in the Delawarr Laboratories after the war proceeded unabated. Though expanding quickly,

they remained financially independent, due in large part to de la Warr's engineering position with the town of Oxford. As fast as de la Warr and his team designed and built new devices, Marjorie would perfect their use and treat patients with them. They obtained excellent results.

They were also carrying out their operation with very high professional standards, especially as to who could buy and be trained to use their technology. Aside from the animosity aroused on the scientific issues (or lack thereof), for all appearances the de la Warrs were in the midst of an extraordinary surge of discovery. These discoveries were similar to radionics in the United States after Abrams; only the "instruments" in the visual sense of the word and their ability to function successfully remained subject to the operator's psychic ability. The main difference between the instrument and pure psychic ability was that anyone with the prerequisite skill could learn to calibrate and tune the instrument to a specific goal.

What is not generally known, but what we have tried to expand upon here, is how much radionic technology imitated the arts. We have previously asserted that Ruth Drown should be considered the first radionics inventor of an art form known as Radionic Photography. Later, Delawarr Laboratories, without intending to, took the radionics/art overlay much further. With each refinement of their light boxes, diagnostic tools, radionic cameras, and abstract renderings of the human energy, the Delawarr technology grew closer to art.

In retrospect, their research seemed the convergence of European occult traditions with Dada and Surrealism. Avant-garde thinking permeated all new fringe ideas and drew from them for inspiration. The de la Warr's discoveries could hardly have escaped this scrutiny. Artists fed up with war, materialism, and bourgeois culture could easily have taken joy and inspiration from the odd (and beautifully crafted) therapeutic devices produced by de la Warr and others, which appeared to function through magic.

The fact that the radionic connection to art in Britain remains obscure can be attributed to several factors. The de la Warrs were ultimately hoping to obtain funding and the approval of the medical community. For this reason, their research efforts were structured in a quasi-scientific manner. In order to sustain credibility as a healing technology, radionics under the de la Warrs needed to project a clean, untarnished public image as void of cultural controversy as possible.

All semblances to voodoo or the occult were a liability in this regard. Even the comparison of their instruments to avant-garde art could potentially relegate their technology to mere metaphor. Even without scientific approval, clients were reporting cures and increasingly more people including physicians were beginning to give radionics the benefit of the doubt. Nevertheless, British Radionics was walking a tightrope.

The precarious balance sustained by the de la Warrs was soon to meet a serious challenge. The tension between the self-referential methodologies employed in their research and the "burden of proof" required in meeting scientific standards met headlong in a tempestuous fury when it came to the subject of radionic photography. As the debate over the authenticity of these radionics photographic techniques has recently been resurrected, de la Warr's original radionics photographic efforts are worth re-examining.

Fig 15-4. Mark I De la Warr Camera

On January 18, 1955, the Delawarr Laboratories received a French Patent, No. 1,084,318 titled "Improvements in Research into Fundamental Radiation" for what was being called "the de la Warr radionic camera." In practice, it worked much the same way as the Drown instrument, though it had no design similarities. Like the Drown camera, it could not produce photographs by itself without adding a stimulus from the operator or someone in the room with psychic abilities. This did not prevent the de la Warr Mark I camera from taking more than 12,000 photographs in the eight years following its invention.

A technical analysis, published in the 1999/2000 issue of the *Journal of Theoretics*, describes the way the Mark I camera operated: "The Camera consists of 4 major 'boxes' mounted on a plinth which contains a vibrator driven by a 220 volt supply. The vibrator is turned on during the time the Cassette is inserted into the Light Tight Box, which is mounted superior to the other three specimen and tuning boxes. The Cassette contains the unexposed film or photographic plate (as in the original silver emulsion plates). The film is 'exposed' in total darkness. There are focusing devices inside the top box that 'direct' the information/energy towards the plate or film. The three other boxes are mounted beneath the top box and two of them contain specimen plates, magnetic tuning devices and radionic dials (to specify the information 'codes'). The boxes also contain various types of focusing devices. The technique requires that the photographic medium (film or plate) be 'sensitized' briefly in the dark room (no half-light is permitted at this stage) before being placed in the light tight cassette. When this is done the cassette is inserted through a slot in the bottom of the top box where it is 'exposed' to the information being sought by the operator. After the cassette is withdrawn it is taken to the darkroom and development of the film or plate proceeds normally. Before the cassette is loaded the operator(s) place an appropriate specimen on the plate(s) of one of the 2 tuning boxes beneath the Light Tight Box. The box dials are then 'tuned' directly to the information being sought – e.g. Myocardial Infarction or Tuberculosis etc, etc. The individual doing the plate sensitization is not necessarily the same person operating the camera. The camera will not produce an image if the condition, etc. is not specified precisely. A good example of this occurred years ago when a patient was suspected of having carcinoma in his jaw. The camera would not produce any image until the code was reset for Osteomyelitis at which point the image was produced."

Edward Russell also wrote extensively about the operational peculiarities of the camera. After over 12,000 radionics pictures had been taken, many were images of ailments for which a drop of blood provided the only connection to the camera. With only the blood as a witness, pictures were obtained of growing embryos in pregnant women and animals and all types of other internal conditions, much like a MRI or x-ray. One incident had the laboratory investigating a cow with colic from a piece of hair. The radionic diagnosis detected foreign bodies in the cow's complicated stomach, and ultimately a picture of a piece of stone and a piece of metal were photographed. Stupefied, the vet refused to operate. Another vet had to be found, and when he operated, the objects in question were found.

For a time, the Mark I Camera was loaned to an unidentified doctor and hospital where roughly 400 photos were taken of patients under treatment, allowing for an independent verification of medical benefit.

Edward W. Russell in *Report on Radionics* described meeting this mysterious doctor (later identified by Langston Day as Dr. Foster Cooper of Bart's Hospital). The doctor reported to Russell that the only time high quality photos emerged was when an operator from the Delawarr lab was present at the time the pictures were taken. However, in spite of this drawback, the doctor did not believe the pictures were fakes. Russell, after asking bluntly about their authenticity, quoted the doctor as saying: "No, even if they had wanted to do so – and I have no reason to whatever to think they might, the people at the laboratories simply do not have the anatomical knowledge to produce some of the pictures that came out of the Camera."

The doctor told Russell of an incident where he obtained a cross sectional photograph of the brain of a patient from a drop of blood that revealed a large tumor. An autopsy following her death revealed a tumor in the exact position and of the identical shape and size of the tumor in the photograph.

In spite of the many clear-cut cases of

correct medical imaging and substantial evidence that the camera could become a valuable medical tool, the doctor was forbidden to continue his investigation as soon as word leaked out to higher authorities regarding his success with the camera.

Recently, with the publishing of Arthur M. Young's posthumous autobiography, *Nested Time*, other details have emerged about the helicon years of British radionic photography. Young's invention of the Bell helicopter and his industrial accomplishments, along with an engineering background, make him a potent commentator on the subject of radionics, particularly the camera. He knew both Ruth Drown and the de la Warrs personally, and had set up a foundation later for the specific purpose of funding alternative studies of various kinds.

According to Young, the Delawarr Labo-

ratories had not only borrowed the Drown Radionic camera technology but for a time had built instruments for her. By the time Young met de la Warr, their technologies differed, as Marjorie de la Warr was careful to point out to Young. Like Russell's mysterious doctor, Young confirmed that the camera would only work when its builder, Leonard Corte, loaded the plates.

Corte was more than happy to discuss his work. He carried none of the pretensions of being "psychic" and was only remorseful that scientists viewed his photos with little interest. Young found the camera seemed "to have no limits." He mentions witnessing Corte holding the thought in his mind of a pen knife, then seeing the image appear on the camera plate, with only a drop of blood as a witness in the camera connecting Corte to the photo.

"It seemed extraordinary," wrote Young,

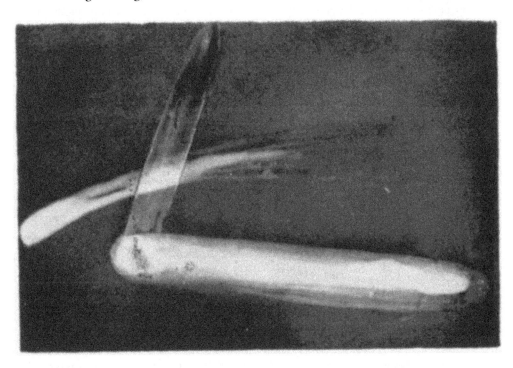

Fig 15-5. Thought photograph of Pen Knife with Mark I Camera

"to think of this important work going on in Oxford; right under the noses of scholars talking about Plato's world of Ideas, the noumenal and the phenomenal, who didn't dream this work existed---nor would they have come to look at it if they knew."

Later on, with the publication of *Matter in the Making* by Langston Day, it became known that indeed other individuals could operate the camera, but there were only four, including the controversial Dr. Cooper. What was subsequently discovered was that the distances between the camera-head, the specimen, and the magnet were critical for each person operating a camera, and each camera needed to be custommade for the individual. It was widely reported that the camera itself had its devilish idiosyncrasies as well.

Day reported that Anthony Broad, of the Cavendish Laboratory in Cambridge, required a custom-built camera with design modifications that resulted in the lower corners of the device being removed to better get at the controls. The revised camera would not work, not for Broad or even for Corte, until it had been restored to its original shape. Even then, the resonance cavity would only respond to Corte

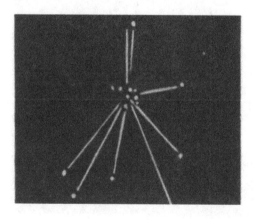

Fig 15-6. Photograph of Nodal Point in Space of Copper Sulfate Crystal

and Broad was forced to use him to load the plates.

From a strictly artistic point of view, there were other discoveries that were made in the Delawarr Laboratories with the camera that are of great interest. First of all, there is the camera itself. If thought photography could work merely by psychic concentration, then why bother with a large, cumbersome instrument the size of a refrigerator? The answer was that while it was possible to produce an adequate photograph by psychic means alone, the camera was needed to produce repeatable identical ones.

Further tests were made to solve the question of how the photos were being made, particularly to determine if Corte was cheating in any way. Broad devised an experiment where Corte was locked in an upstairs home darkroom with no camera while five witnesses sat in front of the camera in another room below. The camera was set to photograph the force fields of a copper sulfate crystal as the others looked on. At the end of the process, one person took the plates to Corte and he successfully developed them, the image being repeatable. Whatever psychic component Corte brought to the photographic process, it either took place remotely from his access to the camera or directly upon the emulsions.

One might surmise that the instrument be recognized as a new type of camera in need of an operator with a unique skill. If radionic cameras function, in part, like ordinary cameras, then any photographer seeking to extend the boundaries of his medium would undoubtedly find the radionic camera design of interest to extend the range of artistic potential.

After radionic photography in the 1950s and 1960s came remote viewing in the 1970s and 1980s. Remote viewing was the psychic

The Secret Art

capacity of an individual to view a remote location without travelling there in person, retrieving details and intelligence in the process. Remote viewing was invented by an artist, Ingo Swann, in conjunction with Hal Puthoff and Russell Targ of the Stanford Research Institute (SRI) in California.

In the 1990s, the Project Stargate was declassified and many details of the 20 million dollar project were made public. Of interest to this discussion is the fact that the way remote viewing worked was that an internally generated (eidetic) mental image of a place could be retrieved from a representation of that location, even if only a set of coordinates. The process was eerily similar to radionic photography, and one wonders with such outstanding psychics in their employ, if the SRI team didn't seek to duplicate the Drown and de la Warr results and obtain actual images.

Such an experiment would have been made even easier by another de la Warr camera named the "Mark V Prospecting Camera" precisely because it was designed to detect inanimate objects under the surface of the ground. At one point a prominent oil company took an interest in this invention. Initial experiments were made that confirmed the camera's potential. For fifteen months, the paid research continued, until the company asked for one last test. From fragments of an aerial survey, de la Warr was asked to discover where the green sand on the east coast of England was located. Without the operator being able to relate his thoughts to any specific points in space or place names, the camera could not deliver better than 50 percent accuracy, and the work was halted. This operational peculiarity was not even suspected by the de la Warrs until this test.

Another subjective facet of radionic photography soon emerged from the outside verification process. People not familiar or dead set against accepting radionic photography could jam the output onto the negative with hostile thoughts. Occasionally, this problem could be circumvented if the operator "pre-conditioned" the negative for positive results. In the end, the case for the scientific analysis of radionic photography became too vulnerable to skepticism.

By contrast, clues to the artistic potential of the camera lay in de la Warr's early experiments. In these, photos of rudimentary elements and simple salts showed the existence of arrow-like shafts of light he believed were the "fundamental rays" of each material. When these materials were combined, so were their rays. These shafts of light had different angles for different elements.

What appears significant about these early radionic photographs is that a baseline for approaching the phenomenon of "rays" or "radiations" could be visually established by experimentation. Once the results were repeatable, variations from the norm could be introduced and catalogued, providing a visual library of overlaying input.

During this same period of time at Yale, modernist painter Joseph Albers was demonstrating the relativity of color. Through his famous series of paintings that demonstrated his Color Theory, every color was subtly changed and shifted in tone and hue by the presence of the color next to it. Within the de la Warr photographs, perhaps an even deeper abstract layer of light had been discovered and photographed, one shifted by thought and intent.

De la Warr also discovered that in order for an operator to capture a photograph, the operator had to stand beside the camera and be aware of what the camera was trying to detect. When developed, the pictures appeared to reinforce the discovery of the measurable "Life" or "L" field discovered by Dr. Harold Saxton Burr and his associates at Yale University, again, at roughly the same time.

There is another interesting aspect of the role subtle light played in de la Warr research. Rotation of the substance caused a single, narrow shaft of light to appear from the element the instant it hit its "critical position." De la Warr photographed (radionically) this light emitting aspect of matter as it hit the "critical position" many times.

The discovery of a fundamental ray within materials has a much earlier precedent in the Hermetic idea of "the prime material." In "The Geometry of the Naked Singularity," researchers Henry Hallmon and Carl Hollingsworth state: "In the centers of form/ The prime material hides/ Informing the host/ That it secretly guides." In presenting a theory that attempts to explain how geometry and dark energy interact in physics, genetics, and neuroscience, Hallmon and Hollingsworth explain Hermetic science this way: "For thousands of years…Hermetic scientists concluded that prime material was a subtle spirit substance, hiding within the myriad forms of the universe by occupying a strictly ordered geometry of locations. Great importance was placed on the golden ratio and the Fibonacci series, both evident in the golden rectangle.

"The golden rectangle is a gnomon which regresses to a potential prime location in a gnomic regression. Gnomon is defined as 'any figure, which suffered no change, save for magnitude.'

"Since everything physical generates from central prime material in a gnomic growth pattern, the material world is considered a network of gnomons without independent existence of their own."

Any tangible connection between visible subtle energy and the gnomon would provide a window into how sacred proportions, and therefore much about aesthetics itself, can be understood energetically. (Malcolm Rae was fascinated with these ideas.)

In the introduction to *Sacred Geometry* by Robert Lawlor, there is a quote by Professor Amstutz of the Mineralogical Institute at the University of Heidelberg who sates: "Matter's latticed waves are spaced at intervals corresponding to the frets on a harp or guitar with analogous sequences of overtones arising from each fundamental. The science of musical harmony is in these terms practically identical with the science of symmetry in crystals."

De la Warr was convinced that his element and crystal radionic photographs supported a connection to geometry. If one assumes that radionic instruments change this geometry through treatment, crystals in a drop of blood would have an energetic signature, both before and after treatment, which could be supported photographically.

Recently, astonishing photographs of water by Masaru Emoto of the I.H.M. General Research Institute in Japan have revealed similar phenomena. Hundreds of pictures taken in his lab suggest that when thoughts, words (written or spoken), pictures, and sounds are directed at samples of water, crystals produced when the water is frozen will be beautiful or ugly depending upon the intent directed upon them. Emoto's critics have been quick to challenge his methods as being less than rigorous and biased toward his beliefs. As usual, lack of scientific duplication has resulted in these wondrous photographs being consigned to the world of pseudoscience and his claims ignored by all but believers.

This situation is most unfortunate. If the healing nature of intent in crystallized water also produces definable changes in the blood or tissue of a patient, an empirical basis for examining radionics effects could conceivably be established. In addition, understanding the process could shed light on how shamans and native healers apply aesthetics in curative ceremonies. A bridge between art and healing long ignored or dismissed could take on new significance.

In their writings and discussions, radionic inventors often return to the idea that it is the basic patterns of geometry at the core of all form that are being changed by radionic treatment. In illness, these geometries have been thrown into distorted relationships with one another. They are out of harmony. It is the job of the radionics practitioner to identify where that has occurred. Once diagnosed, the practitioner transmits an intention or signal through the instrument directly to the afflicted patterns instructing them to return to their proper harmony.

The process of refining a task over and over again until harmony is established is essentially organizing an aesthetic into form. There is no need for the artist to "prove" that this process advances him to his goal. Likewise, someone treated successfully by a radionic instrument finds it unnecessary to "prove" that he was healed.

The Delawarr Laboratories went on to produce numerous variations of their camera. Some were designed to detect inanimate objects in the ground, while others were used to detect lost people and things. Different experiments were designed to use the photographs to impress radionic energies on inert substances and vegetation, in the manner of Curtis Upton.

Best of all, experiments were carried out to see if photographs could be obtained of past events. De la Warr was convinced that a radionic photo he took in 1950, while holding the intention in his mind of "My wedding day 1929" and using blood spots from himself and his wife, produced an image of that day. Edward Russell however, described the picture as "two dark patterns with a very faint resemblance to human beings."

Going beyond the concept of the camera, de la Warr created a device that could be described as a subtle energy communications technology. His Nodal Point Detector was based upon identifying a latticework of points in three dimensions in the space around a magnet, plotted radionically using the stick plate. De la Warr discovered that these points could extend far beyond any possible magnetic field, even miles away.

Apparently, a noise near one magnet could be detected at all the other the nodal points. De la Warr was determined to design equipment that could impress the magnet with recorded frequencies and another that could detect those frequencies at a distance. The reported results were generally favorable in tests that were performed at distances from a few hundred feet (with intervening walls) to thirty miles away. He concluded from the experiments that he was dealing with a hitherto unknown attribute of space. Whether that was true or whether his results were an early form of psychic remote viewing (and hearing) will never be known for certain.

Sadly, after a period of so much brilliant work, the de la Warrs were faced with a legal challenge nine years before his death in 1969. A woman who had bought a radionics instrument from them in the late 1950s claimed, through court proceedings, that de la

Warr had acted fraudulently and was himself unconvinced that the radionics box worked as stated. She claimed that in trying to learn how to use it properly, she had been driven from "a healthy optimist to a frustrated neurotic."

Ultimately, the de la Warrs' honesty and integrity were upheld and the case was thrown out of court. Though not jailed like Ruth Drown and Wilhelm Reich, the de la Warrs were nearly bankrupted in the process. Their savings and vitality were severely depleted, a harsh payback for helping so many people for decades.

What remains fascinating about the de la Warr approach to radionics is the fact that they engineered technology to work with subjective criteria that became comprehensible through the universally familiar experience of resonance. Today, thanks to digital media, we are comfortable in the knowledge that a musical phrase can be heard as sonic energy released by an instrument or pure information described by midi notation. Likewise, any resonant construction can become pure infor-

Fig 15-7. George de la Warr

mation and sent invisibly through the air and be reconstructed as sound or light, music or film on our computer or TV screen.

De la Warr began with the same belief most radionics practitioners have held since the beginning: that some type of energy traveled between the operator and the patient. But, due to experiments with the camera, he was forced to conclude that changes taking place inside the patient were evoked inside the patient's body/mind and were not being sent to him or her by the instrument through space.

It must have seemed preposterous in the 1940s and 1950s to suggest that a set of healing resonances could be decoded from the body/mind of a patient and applied as resonant reinforcement to strengthen that patient's ability to fight off some disease. Yet in a similar sense we know that a set of notes combine to make a melody that in turn can produce a cascade of feeling and catharsis, which many would argue connotes a therapeutic process. This process goes back to ancient Greece, where theater was first used to provoke mass catharsis, a purging of emotion in the audience that was considered healthy for society.

One extraordinary feature of the work of the de la Warrs is the precision with which they were able to translate their intuitive skills into practical diagnostic and treatment protocols. In the appendix of *Matter in the Making*, Langston Day refers to case studies touched upon in his earlier book with de la Warr, *New Worlds Beyond the Atom*, where patients suffering from untreatable conditions found relief through his radionic method.

In one case, a 56-year-old woman suffered from a spasm that caused recurrent head movement and came to Marjorie de la Warr for help. Standard medical treatment had only worsened the condition, and injections of atropine had nearly paralyzed her. Radionic diagnosis showed the torticolis condition to be influenced by three main factors: the sheath of the trapezius muscle, the posterior cervical plexus and sub-trapezial plexus of the nervous system, and the vertebrae of the skeletal system.

Digging deeper, Marjorie de la Warr found that the sheath of the trapezius muscle was injured and showed the presence of Mycobacterium tuberculosis; the posterior cervical plexus and the sub-trapezial plexus had vitamin and mineral deficiencies and imbalances; the presence of Mycobacterium tuberculosis and Clostridium tetani bacterium contributed to the muscle spasm; and finally, that one of the cervical vertebrae was fractured. The situation indicated that the Clostridium tetani was causing the muscle spasm by irritating the nerve. The patient then recalled a suitcase falling against her head while traveling by train some years before.

Radionic treatments for each condition were applied, and at intervals the severity of each condition was measured and found to be diminishing. Within several months the conditions lessened and in time the patient completely recovered.

People like this patient, who had all but given up hope, were being treated by these methods with great success. Not just people, but animals and plants also demonstrated a response to radionics treatment. Skill, training, and an open mind were required, but the de la Warrs had demonstrated an alternative healing methodology that would work on a variety of ills. The manner by which it worked, however, was of such a startling nature that many who were not receiving any direct benefit remained understandably skeptical.

Significant to the discussion of the relationship of radionics to art was the contribution the de la Warrs made to the understanding of how radionics actually functions, specifically "resonance." Consider the various dictionary meanings of the word:

"The quality in a sound of being deep, full, and reverberating…

• Figurative: The ability to evoke or suggest images, memories, and emotions…

• Physics: 1. The reinforcement or prolongation of sound by reflection from a surface or by the synchronous vibration of a neighboring object.

2. The condition in which an electric circuit or device produces the largest possible response to an applied oscillating signal, esp. when its inductive and its capacitate reactance's are balanced.

3. A short-lived subatomic particle that is an excited state of a more stable particle.

• Mechanical: The condition in which an object or system is subjected to an oscillating force having a frequency close to its own natural frequency.

• Astronomy: The occurrence of a simple ratio between the periods of revolution of two bodies about a single primary.

• Chemistry: The state attributed to certain molecules of having a structure that cannot adequately be represented by a single structural formula but is a composite of two or more structures of higher energy."

The de la Warr's use of resonance in his radionics design seems to make use of a number of the overlapping definitions. The figurative sense is clearly one, because Marjorie de la Warr described the importance of holding the image of the patient in one's mind prior to engaging the device. The physics definition of "the synchronous vibration of a neighboring object" captures something of the relationship the detector cavity has to the object of study.

Already de la Warr had stretched the definition beyond a physical vibration into a type of vibration that is a priori to matter. Whether this use of the word bears a relationship to the excited sub-atomic particle part of the definition bears closer examination but will not be reconciled here; ditto the astronomical interpretation. The chemistry interpretation no doubt factors in to how the healing process proceeds from the radionics signal. Perhaps the molecular changes that proceed while a disease is being cured are the result of some form of chemical induction triggered by the radionics signal; it is impossible at this time to know precisely how de la Warr viewed the actual progression of events he termed "resonance."

What we do know from his biographers is that sonic resonance was often a carrier wave for a deeper, virtual resonant phenomenon. Edward Russell illustrated this in a story he told about de la Warr giving sonic therapy to his mother-in-law for her sore shoulder. In the process, he discovered that the sonic waveform that came out of the shoulder was entirely different on the oscilloscope than the waveform going in. In time he discovered that the emerging waveforms varied with the disease of the patient. Not being able to afford a recording oscillograph, he invented a system of plotting the emerging wave forms on a Psychoplotter or Autoplotter, which produced a graph of the state of the tissue being treated called a "Histogram."

With this tool he was able to create a frame of reference for understanding the influence of music, art, light, sound, or any other factor on the human organism. Russell wrote that he believed this discovery to be "one of the most important discoveries of the Delawarr Laboratories." Russell did not elaborate

on why he felt this discovery was so important beyond saying that histograms were taken of subjects treated by solenoids (a device he called the MT/3) placed near points of the body, exposing them to a weak magnetic field. In the course of this study an independent lab analyzed the subject's blood. The results showed a reduction of white blood cell counts and cholesterol. Strictly speaking, these experiments were less radionic than scientific. But before they could publish or obtain additional confirmation of their results, a Russian team of scientists published a similar finding. This event effectively derailed the public relations benefit of the Delawarr Laboratory discovery, as now the radionic findings would be perceived as trying to once again co-opt scientific research to justify questionable radionic methodologies.

At issue was the potential to confirm by scientific means the beneficial impact of a radionic treatment. Had the Russian study been properly employed to confirm the Delawarr study rather than seen as obscuring it, the Delawarr lab may have begun to obtain the scientific credibility it so desired.

By the end of his career, de la Warr had come to believe that the radionics cure was the result of the patient's own organism overcoming the disease, not because the radionics box sent a signal to do so. Rather, the cure proceeded because the operator's mind had linked to the patient on a pre-material level and was able to establish the nature of the disease. Once a numerical rate on the instrument could be identified signifying this connection, the disease could be turned off or overcome.

The de la Warr process was not like a radio transmitter sending a tune across the airwaves and a receiver tuning into audible sound waves. Sound waves could perhaps boost the primary signal, but the actual transaction occurred instantaneously once the mind of the operator obtained "resonance" with the subject and began engaging the healing process. This progression of events was entirely nonphysical until changes in the organism could be detected either radionically or by standard medical procedures.

It is worth noting that the resonance phenomenon that de la Warr believed was responsible for the success of his technology was in fact explored by the avant-garde some decades before. In particular, the experience of synesthesia, where neurologically one sense involuntarily intertwines with another, such as letters or numbers appearing as colors, or sounds are seen as colors (or variations thereof), became of great interest to early modernists. It is fair to say that synesthesia also appears to function according to some unknown form of neurological resonance between the senses and consciousness and can produce measurable behavioral consequences.

Synesthetes of the period, often under the influence of excessive amounts of psychotropic drugs and liqueurs, probed the experience for artistic inspiration. Post-Symbolist and early Futurist groups, especially in early 20th century Russia explored "colored music" and other forms of "anarchistic" sonic composition. The mystic, George Ivanovich Gurdjieff (1872-1949), who had a significant influence at this time, had reported seeing monks in a Christian monastery fully germinate a seed to maturity in 30 minutes chanting "ancient Hebrew music."

In 1910, Aleksandr Scriabin (1872-1915), an ardent Theosophist, completed his fourth symphony, *Prometheus: A Poem of Fire*, a "synesthesic fusion of the senses," wrote Mel Gordon in his article "Songs from the Museum of the Future," noting that it was written to be accompanied by a "light key-board" that projected color images. A color organ designed for the *Prometheus* symphony, which translated Scriabin's Music-Color Symbology from note to color, was later realized (and patented) by Aleksandr Mozer. Scriabin grandiosely began Prometheus with an even more powerful resonant effect, his "Mystic Chord" of superposed fourths that was purported to "dissolve any normative time sense."

Adding to his thesis on Russian Futurists, Gordon also wrote about the work of Mikhail Matyushin (1861-1934), a significant artistic figure in the imperial court who turned to Futurism later in life. Beyond his many other accomplishments, Matyushin also conducted scientific experiments on the relationship of color to form: "Drawing on the theories of French Cubism as well as Ouspensky's Gurdjieffian speculations, Matyushin wedded cogent scholarship with intuitive leaps of the imagination…Matyushin's final discoveries were brought to Germany by Malevich in 1927 and later published in *The Natural Law of Changeability in Color Combinations* (Moscow-Petrograd, 1932), were the result of nine years of precise laboratory work. According to Matyushin, noise levels and the intensity of different colors influence one another. When either a monochord or pure color dominates, the other will appear weaker than it would normally to human receptors. If both are equally strong, then the noise will cause the color to be more visually 'active.' High, sharp sounds lead to a lightening – that is to a 'cooling, or bluing' – of the color. Conversely, low, rough notes have a tendency to 'redden,' darken, and condense the color in the eye of the spectator."

Clearly, early Russian Modernist composers and artists were fascinated by the capacity of sound and color to achieve significant impact, both psychologically and spiritually. Best known in this respect today is the pioneering abstract painter Wassily Kandinsky (1866-1944). Kandinsky believed that the function of art was to reveal inner beauty and spiritual necessity. Through stimulating the inner resonances of the soul, the artist, by virtue of the same mysterious process described by de la Warr that takes place in radionics healing, expressed a communion between artist and viewer, image and sound to intellect, as in any synesthesic combination.

In Kandinsky's work, *Concerning the Spiritual in Art*, published in 1911, the artist discusses a phenomenon that would be familiar to radionics practitioners. The colors of the painting first make a purely sensorial impression on the viewer, as the taste of delicious food would on the tongue. However, the effect can go much deeper, causing emotion and even resonance at a deep soul level. This process, according to Kandinsky, occurs through a foundation of form and harmony which is passed on to the viewer from the artwork in a manner reminiscent of de la Warr's theory of resonance, being not so much energetic as virtual, a transference of inner content through inner necessity. Kandinsky saw this transaction as being a matter of color mixture and movement, implying various combinations and geometries, perhaps analogous to radionic rates.

We can deduce that the aesthetic content of the artwork is analogous to the resonant component of the radionic signal. Something qualitative, not quantitative, is triggered in the subject. In the same manner, the subjective component of the artwork, the part that affects us, follows criteria similar to the de la Warr description of radionic signals. A powerful artistic experience leaves us with a perma-

nent resonant relationship to the art form, one that can be triggered by any representation of it, a picture in a book, music in an elevator, a slogan on a billboard, etc.

Synesthesic events can trigger eidetic memory, flooding the mind with images, as Marcel Proust (1871-1922) found when certain smells produced an avalanche of forgotten memories. Techniques like hypnosis can insert false memories in peoples' minds. Hypnotic commands can also produce involuntary behavior, even long after the subject has resumed normal life. Both experiences point to the enormous unknown power of resonance in triggering the mind and behavior.

The conclusions formed by Kandinsky, de la Warr, and others about the power of resonance has very interesting implications for the artist or media specialist, but also goes far beyond them. We do not readily accept the proposition that a tuned form of thought, color, smell, or sound can manipulate our behavior and even our body chemistry, but that is clearly what many artists and radionic inventors imply. This conclusion reveals privacy issues and a host of other more sinister possibilities, which we shall revisit in the forthcoming chapters on T. Galen Hieronymus.

What is truly beneficial about resonance, as it is thought of by de la Warr and others, is the degree to which the individual can become empowered by simply controlling one's mind, giving it a positive focus in tune with the higher forces of Nature and the Universe. In a sense, the resonance discovery of de la Warr suggests that we are a tunable transceiver; we become whatever signals we tune in. The upside to this discovery is that we can tune to the deepest wellsprings of meaning in the universe, if we so desire, and that this will shape our very being.

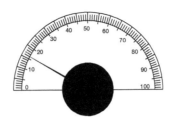

CHAPTER 16
T. GALEN HIERONYMUS

Thomas Galen Hieronymus' career spanned the era between the beginning of commercial radio and the modern era of radionics. In many ways, his work is a synthesis of the two sides of radionics, the speculative, occult side and the empirical, scientific one. He spoke knowledgeably about applied subtle energy, using the term "eloptic," meaning energy + light emanations he detected coming from physical materials. He also coined the term "nionic-nerve influencing energy" for emanations from live organisms.

These unusual descriptions of radionic emanations did not prevent him from obtaining the first U.S. Patent for a radionics detector [#2,482,773] in 1949. Nor did he ever run afoul of the authorities or academia; in fact he was made a fellow of both the Institute of Electrical and Electronic Engineers and the American Institute of Electrical Engineers.

The high comfort level with authority rested upon his solid credentials. He served in the Rainbow Division, A.E.F. in WWI and

later graduated from officer's candidate school. For 30 years, he was a professional engineer working for the Kansas City Power and Light Co. He is credited with designing the phase locking system that connects power stations across the country. He was also a licensed radio operator, later becoming a Senior Member in the Institute of Radio Engineers. Generally speaking, such highly influential positions were reserved exclusively for the brightest and best in his profession.

His work in electronics coupled with a lifelong interest in metaphysics led him to the forefront of what came to be called "psionic devices" or "psychotronic technology" in his later years; these appliances were dependent upon the psychic (PK) energy of the mind to operate.

One other reason Hieronymus was held in such high professional esteem and remained un-censured for his radionics work was because he used his skill in radionics to assist regulatory authorities like the FDA and to solve complicated problems for Big Business. This was especially true when it came to the analysis of substances – in the era before the electron microscope. An example of this assistance comes from my personal conversations with a colleague, Bob Beautlich, regarding work Hieronymus performed for the 3M Company.

At that time 3M was in product development for the now famous product "Sticky Tape." While the glue adhered properly to the tape in laboratory trials, when produced in mass quantities the glue was coming off the celluloid. Hieronymus was asked to use his patented radionics device to analyze the problem. He discovered that a trace element of a solvent previously carried in the container trucks transporting the chemicals was contaminating the adhesive. It had not been detected by normal methods because the trace amounts causing the problem were below what any other methodology could detect. When the containers were changed, the glue stayed on the tape.

Fig 16-1. T. Galen Hieronymus

Because he was savvy in understanding of the dangers of radionics research, he was able to keep close contact with the authorities on the legal parameters of his research. Even his Patent, titled "Detection of Emanations from Materials and Measurements of the Volumes Thereof" was couched in language designed to be acceptable to mechanistic models and reviewers. Yet his actual research couldn't have been more anachronistic to the mechanist credo.

Hieronymus began working in radio in 1913. After he received his license, he began working with KDKA in Pittsburgh, Pa., where he took part in the first-ever public radio broadcast. As a radio operator and electrical engineer with the Rainbow Division in France during World War I, he worked to develop a wireless telephone. It was there that he observed certain metals and minerals had unusual properties or emanations, a discovery that led him to radionics.

By 1930, Hieronymus was working with radionics inventor J. W. Wigelsworth to improve the Pathoclast, the successor to Abrams' Oscilloclast. The Pathoclast was considered to be "the most advanced condenser-tuned radionic instrument ever made," incorporating vacuum tubes for amplification and other electronic features. It is also important to realize that by the time Hieronymus began designing his own version of the Pathoclast for Wigelsworth, mainstream doctors had adopted radionic-type therapies for clinical diagnosis and treatment throughout the country. In retrospect, one can sense a fusion occurring of homeopathic medical principles with electronic gear. For that period in the 1920s and 1930s, there seemed every reason to believe that radionic medical devices were evolving into a modern form of medical instrumentation. It was this favorable climate that clearly made the issuing of the Hieronymus patent possible.

In addition, the grassroots success of the Pathoclast/Radionics technology must also be considered when it comes to comprehending what Hieronymus faced later on in his career when his patent was popularized in a famous 1950s science fiction magazine. By then, Hieronymus had already witnessed thirty years of medical successes using these technologies across America. A great deal of technical evolution in radionics had occurred in the interim, with a large number of highly respected electrical engineers and instrument designers providing expertise and experimental insights. The world of radionics that Hieronymus entered in the late 1920s and early 1930s was an exciting place, as this fast developing, non-invasive, revolutionary medical technology had universal appeal. He was in the vanguard and was well positioned professionally to advance a technology being created as quickly as the healing successes were being reported. Before him lay a business venture that was successfully providing quick and inexpensive health care to ordinary people.

Aside from the history, it is informative to look at the nature of radionics in this period from the vantage point of art. Art movements often begin with a renegade group of artists following a course of action in conflict with the status quo. They self-organize and collectively begin to project their ideas upon the world. Individual artists with little else in common discover a common theme; soon they begin to articulate and develop ideas from one another, cross-pollinating their efforts. The radical nature of their ideas is often the key to their success. But both medicine and science, unlike art, have much more efficient means of policing their turf and squashing dissent.

Fig 16-2. Pathoclast

Another parallel of radionic technique to artistic technique lies in examining how intent becomes focused and realized through instrumentation. In the 1920s and 1930s, the radionic inventors seemed relatively comfortable with the notion that their technology functioned much as an artist's brush does for the artist. A certain amount of intent is required, which is then tuned through the instruments influencing a medium to produce a desired outcome. By the 1940s and 1950s, when Abstract Expressionism was overturning representational art, substituting impulse for carefully crafted imagery, radionics was developing a more intuitive and energetic approach to healing, where the curative process seemed to proceed far more from releasing and balancing natural forces than from any set of mechanical medical skills. At that time, medicine linking the intuitive guidance and skill of the doctor to a device inexpensively resonating with the curative forces of nature seemed highly desirable.

By the early 1950s, Hieronymus was also collaborating with Brigadier-General

Henry M. Gross (Ret.) in Pennsylvania and the Homeotronic Foundation (of U.K.A.C.O. fame) on the development of agricultural radionics. It is at this point that radionics, and Hieronymus in particular, had their famous brush with popular culture. Coincidentally, the notoriety given the success of radionics in destroying predatory insects in controlled agricultural experiments briefly brought radionic theory and technology to the attention of big business and science. The fascinating details of these circumstances will be examined shortly.

It is important to realize something about what the Hieronymus patent represented at this time. As the power of the American Medical Association grew and the allopathic medical model became dominant, radionics pioneers and other alternative health and agricultural innovators were systematically persecuted for introducing and practicing what was considered pseudo-scientific bunk. But the better the radionic techniques, the higher their rate of cures, which exponentially increased professional animosity from the establishment. In the midst of this struggle, Hieronymus and his colleagues were trying to establish a scientific basis for the way these instruments worked, even accepting the fact they employed the skill of the operator's mind. Even the most dedicated and pragmatic of instrument designers believed that it was only a matter of time before science confirmed their suspicions that a new form of energy was being engineered.

While many radionics inventors were being persecuted, a host of other bright scientific minds were clamoring for a better scientific understanding of life energy and consciousness. J.B. Rhine of Duke University was busy making a statistical case for the existence of parapsychology and psychic ability in general. Carl Jung in Switzerland was exploring the landscape of the unconscious and linking alchemical knowledge to dream psychology and art. Harold Saxton Burr of Yale and Leonard J. Ravitz Jr. were measuring the life or "L" field of all living things with sensitive voltmeters. Robert Rosenthal of Harvard was demonstrating that bias, or the thoughts of an experimenter, could influence the behavior of laboratory rats. And, as mentioned before, S.W. Tromp, a geologist from the Netherlands, published the first scientific review of dowsing and radiesthesia entitled, *Psychical Physics*, in 1949.

In prior decades, German scientists Gurwitsch, Stempell, Rahn and others were publishing papers about their discovery that living matter produces volatile components and radiation that could pass through selective membranes and act on colloidal substances, even without direct contact. In 1944, Soviet scientist V. S. Grischenko raised the possibility of a fifth state of matter termed "bioplasm" existing in living organisms. Much later, in 1962, physiologist L. L. Vasiliev at the University of Leningrad published a comparable study, his 178-page monograph *Experiments in Mental Suggestion*. The Russian work was taken up later at Columbia University by three scientists, I. I. Rabi, P. Kusch, and S. Millman, who developed an apparatus that "conclusively proved that some kind of ray or vibrations pass between one molecule and another."

Joseph F. Goodavage's article, "The Incredible Hieronymus Machine" in John White and Stanley Krippner's book *Future Science* elaborated on their discoveries: "They showed that each molecule, living or inert, is a small radio transmitter (and receiver) that broadcasts continuously. These waves range over the entire electromagnetic spectrum--often beyond! The sheer volume of these vibrations is apparently limitless. A single molecule can give

The Secret Art

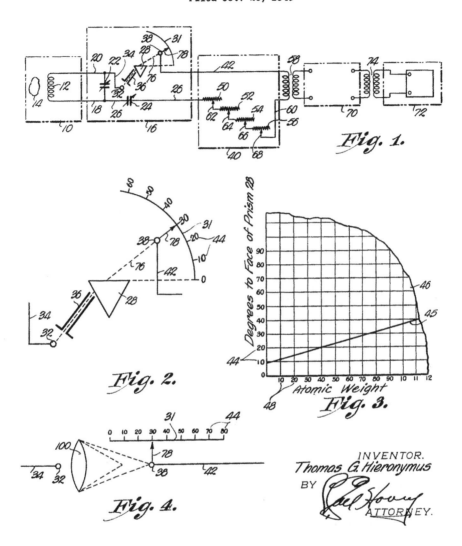

Fig 16-3. US Patent #2,482,773

off rays of a million different wavelengths, but only on one frequency at a time."

Popular sentiment, supported by universal experience, was at long last pressuring scientists into exploring venues outside the mechanistic/reductionism credo advanced in most academic quarters. At the same time, other researchers, actually helping people with these ideas, were facing ruined careers or even prison.

The possibility of a non-material, biologically active force present in space was generally taken for granted, if not officially condoned, by the early 1950s in many quarters. It was through this medium that consciousness and paranormal phenomena were thought to operate. Hieronymus cleverly put a simple description of this force in his patent: "radiations from each of the known elements of matter produce some form of energy, probably electrons." He went further by including a prism in the design through which "the radiations may be refracted, focused, diffracted, or otherwise manipulated in the same manner as the radiations of the visible spectrum."

This patent clearly gave language to a force that was not strictly electronic, opening a door once again to the scientific investigation of radionics as an instrument utilizing subtle energy.

Hieronymus' references to light in his patent have a direct relationship to some of his agricultural radionics investigations. In particular, he had experimented with growing plants in complete darkness with only a copper wire to the outdoors to conduct energy from the sun. A full account of this experiment in Hieronymus' own words appears in numerous online sites dedicated to his research. In a nutshell, Hieronymus became convinced that he was measuring a solar influence other than light. This force was received by living organisms and could be transmitted over certain types of conductors and insulated by others, much like electricity. The developing radionic current analogy to light achieved greater significance through the evidence of radionic photography.

Unlike its mechanistic counterparts, eloptic energy could be influenced by consciousness and required human sensitivity to be detected. Hieronymus, to his credit, never skirted this issue. His patent clearly states that his apparatus "preferably relies upon the element of touch and, therefore, the skill of the operator."

Contemporary writers on Hieronymus,

such as engineer William D. Jensen provide additional insight into exactly what allowed the Hieronymus device to obtain a U.S. Patent: "Dr. Thomas Galen Hieronymus has the unique distinction of having the only US patent of a psychically operating machine. At first glance, what he invented was a machine to detect the type and quantity of any material matter under scrutiny, by analyzing the previously unknown 'eloptic' radiation that seemed to emanate from all materials. No one had ever thought of such a machine, and mainstream science is perplexed that his patented device does indeed work. His secret ingredient was that the experimenter became a part of his own machine, bridging the real and psychic worlds."

W.D. Jensen, in an article posted on the internet entitled "Preliminary Report on the Patented Hieronymus Machine" continues: "Patent number 2,482,773 was awarded in 1949, after three years of very careful consideration by the United States Patent Office. There are strict criteria that must be satisfied before a patent is awarded. A 'utility patent' for a machine must be something new, unusual, and unobvious. These points are easy to satisfy. In addition, the invention had to be useful for at least one believable thing that could not be done before. He did not need to explain 'How' it worked, only to prove 'That' it worked, sufficiently enough to have undeniable merit. Under extraordinary cases, where an invention seems to defy the basic precepts of science, extra proof is requested by the Patent Office. Hieronymus backed up his claims with live plant experiments, and made working models of his invention.

"Traditionally, psychic machines fall under the Para-psychological field of Psychotronics. Radionics is a specialized field within Psychotronics where the machines

The Secret Art

have electronic components that operate in the region of radio waves. There are two basic types of radionic instruments: Receivers and Transmitters. The patented Hieronymus machine is a Receiver instrument, also known as a Detector. It amplifies and detects the presence of Eloptic rays which occur at different vibrational frequencies coming naturally out of elements, like channel signals on a radio. Hieronymus also made Transmitters of Eloptic radiation, sometimes called Eloptic Beam Projectors, or Eloptic Radiators. They projected specific frequencies of Eloptic radiation into materials, and living things. These transmitters could be made to store the radiation in alcohol or other materials.

"What we have from the Patent is a working model of a psychically operating machine. From tests by Hieronymus and other independent researchers, the machine will work for 80% of the population. The percentage is even higher if you have the will and desire to be successful with the machine. This is a phenomenal rate of success in a psychic experiment.

"But the story doesn't end there. It has been found that each of the subsystems in the machine can be unbelievably generic, replaced by symbolic representations, or eliminated altogether. What this might mean is that as the machine is built to contain fewer parts in the material world, psychic parts within the experimenters themselves replace them, as they gain proficiency. But few individuals are immediately able to operate it with proficiency. Thus, the device is an objective incremental teaching tool that can provide a fundamental starting point for the psychic studies in Radiesthesia, dowsing, clairvoyance, remote-viewing, interdimensional communication, healing, etc."

Other writers on psychotronics, like Col. Thomas Bearden, have tried to illuminate the

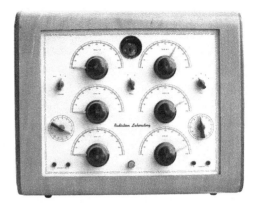

Fig 16-4. Three Bank Hieronymus Radionics device

issue of exactly what a Hieronymus device is detecting by using the language of modern physics. Ever so slowly, we see emerging a linguistic attempt to bridge the divide between energy perceived as "in the mind" versus energy "in nature." Bearden, in a section entitled "Typical Hieronymus Detector" from his book *Excalibur Briefing*, states:

"The Hieronymus device, patented by Thomas G. Hieronymus in 1949, is one such device. It has an optical front end, a prism that passes waves and does not admit particles. So a wave entering the front end will go through the prism and be refracted at an angle that depends on the frequency of the wave. Inside the surrounding box, which acts as a light shield, is a small tuner, a little copper rod attached to a rotating wheel so that the rod may be moved through the various refractive angles from the prism. The prism is mounted on the box with a thin slit in the wall, so that only a small and narrow field of view exists external to the box. The tuner rod is wired to the input of a three-stage RF amplifier where each stage is separately shielded against light, which is very interesting, because of a similar requirement in the two-slit experimental apparatus if the electron was to act as a wave. The output of the RF amplifier comes out of the box and ends in a flat coil of wire between two parallel plastic plates.

"Coming into the box through the slit in the prism, there can be single-state entities and dual-state entities or quitons. The physicist does not have a good name for a dual-state entity. They used to be called wavicles; today we talk about wave packets. But what after all is a wave packet? It is a three-dimensional bunch of two-dimensional waves! So that is where the physicists have hidden the idea of the dual-state wavicle today.

"Only single-state waves and dual-state entities or quitons can pass through the prism and be refracted at an angle dependent upon the frequency. If we then tune the rod into the correct angle of refraction, the refracted quitons hit it, as do the single-state waves if their frequency should happen to coincide with the frequency of the quitons. Now the single-state wave dies when it hits the copper rod; it may chip a single electron or two off a copper crystalline grain, but that is lost in the thermal noise anyway, below the detection threshold of the RF amplifier. The quitons, however, simply say 'Oh! Now you want us to act like a corpuscular electron, and go through those wires and conduction paths. That's all right, that is just our right hand side.' So the quitons will go through and be amplified, just exactly like ordinary electrons would do. But now it is not electron energy, it is a dual-state analog of energy – let us call it anenergy, for analog of energy. (Hieronymus called it eloptic energy, since it could act as electron flow or as optical waves, but was neither exclusively.) The amplified anenergy will come out in the coil of wire and it will generate field and it is not a magnetic field, and so it cannot be measured on normal laboratory instruments. The simplest way to detect the anenergy fields is to use the human sensory system, because the human body knew about RF energy, frequency modulation, and anenergy long before we had modern electrical and magnetic instruments. (The use of anenergy is illustrated by acupuncture, a very ancient medical system dealing with the fact that a peculiar type of energy-like stuff flows in the body, and in certain points and structures of the body, it can interact with other energies and fields.)

"Now if we believe we cannot sense the an-energy fields, then we cannot. We can turn the entire an energy detection system in the body off with the unconscious mind. The negative psi effect is a well-documented effect in parapsychology. There are goats as well as sheep. Some persons do worse on psi tests than chance would possibly allow. They are the goats. They exhibit the negative psi effect, for unconsciously they want to show you that psi does not work, so they use psi effects to do worse than is possible by chance.

"At any rate, the human sensory system can get a tingle from the anenergy field generated by the flat coil of wire in the Hieronymus machine's output. What type of tingle one gets depends upon one's own type of body sensory tuning. It may feel as if the fingers on the plastic plate are in thick syrup, or as if the plastic plate were vibrating. Or it may feel greasy in a peculiar way. And the negative person does not get a tingle at all.

"The Hieronymus machine has been built by many persons, and it works for those who are not negative. It processes entities that exist in the dual-state, or that obey the fourth law of logic. And we can do some almost magical things with these dual-state nothings, these nothings, if we set our minds to it. This is what psychotronics is all about."

Even before contemporary thinkers like

Col. Bearden grappled with how radionic transactions work, other well-known scientists had struggled with the same dilemma. One such figure, Arthur M. Young, the helicopter inventor and friend of Ruth Drown, quoted earlier, had been one. Young made a point of meeting many radionics practitioners. He visited the Delawarr laboratories in Oxford. He met Hieronymus and even funded his research. He did not take issue with the fact that certain individuals were able to direct their devices to heal or augment agriculture. But he was frustrated by its theoretical underpinnings: "Initially, my goal was to encourage other people to develop a general theory of consciousness, with different minds contributing. I envisioned it to be an overall theory, not too complex, which would permit the adoption of new tenets towards a science of what I then called the nonphysical, but now term the projective realms of Nature.

"There seemed at first to be two possible methods: we could work from the higher realities down to the realm of the accepted, or from the accepted towards the paranormal or projective levels. By 1952, my experiences had shown that the former method could not succeed because individuals who are able to function in the paranormal sphere (such as Dr. Brunler, de la Warr, and Dr. Drown) feel no pressure to make scientifically acceptable explanations for their achievements. The latter approach has difficulties because most scientists are so intrigued by their own procedures that they care little for what lies beyond. It began to look like a shotgun wedding with neither bride nor groom a willing participant."

Arthur Young encountered the true paradox of the radionics inventor, that the mind of the operator seemed to play a predominant role in the operation of the device, while the

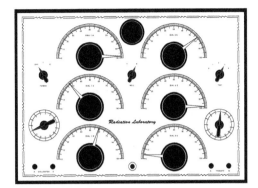

Fig 16-5. Three Bank Hieronymus Radionics device

instrument itself was more like a facilitator for some and completely unnecessary for others. In the course of his investigations, Young founded and became President of the Foundation for the Study of Consciousness.

He was also a friend of John W. Campbell, who was a trained scientist and editor of *Astounding Science Fiction Magazine* (later known as *Analog*). Campbell was already a famous science-baiter and counted many professional scientists among his readers. Seeing the potential for a scientific breakthrough in Hieronymus' work, Campbell constructed a device from the patent and found that it worked. As a result, he published a favorable report in his magazine in the early 1950s that caused a run on the patent office with people eager to build the device.

Young told Campbell that he thought the instrument was only an aide to concentrating the mind, and the focal point of the radionic transaction was the operator's own organs, or physiology. Young's deduction meant that the instrument's functionality proceeded from the body/mind of the operator, and was not dependent upon the electronics in the device at all. With this thought in mind, Campbell unplugged the instrument from its power source and discovered that it worked just as well.

Going further, Campbell designed a Hieronymus device consisting exclusively of a circuit diagram with only symbols of the components shown on paper. In other words, it was a purely an illustration of the device, a ready-made artwork consisting of a paper drawing, India ink, wire, thread and a dial. And he found this drawing worked just as well as the electronic version, provided none of the lines of the schematic were broken.

John Campbell wrote Hieronymus on June 4, 1956, concerning his unusual discovery: "When I began working with the machine, I learned that it didn't need a power supply. Then I learned that it wouldn't work if a tube were missing or defective. I saw some of the other psionic machines and saw that they worked, despite the fact that their wiring system made absolutely no logical sense. From that, I derived a new concept, a theory, and made a crucial experiment.

"I have a model of your analytical machine, simplified and streamlined to the ultimate. It consists solely of the circuit diagram; I have a symbol of a prism, not a real prism, mounted on a National Velvet Vernier dial; that, and a small copper loop, alone appear on the front surface of the panel. Back of the panel, the circuit diagram is drawn in India ink on standard drafting paper; the prism-symbol rotates in its appropriate place in the circuit diagram. The spiral coil is drawn in India ink on paper glued to the back of the panel; it is connected with the symbolized vacuum tube plate through a condenser-symbol by means of a nylon thread; the other end of the coil-drawing is connected to the symbolized vacuum tube cathode by a second nylon thread from my wife's sewing kit.

"The machine works beautifully; the consistency of performance is excellent...

We're working with magic – and magic doesn't depend on matter, but on 'form' – on 'pattern' rather than substance.

"Your electronic circuit represents a pattern of relationships; that is important. The electrical characteristics are utterly unimportant, and can be dropped out completely. The machine fails when a tube burns out because that alters the pattern. It works when there is no power, because the relationship of patterns is intact. My symbolic diagram works because the pattern is present."

The question that no one seemed to ask at this point was: If the Hieronymus device assists the mind in expanding the boundaries set by science for how the world works, essentially allowing the improbable to occur, does this possibility also open up an ability for the artist to radionically reverse engineer artistic tools to more effectively influence culture and events?

Given the fact that popular culture was having a hard enough time absorbing non-representational art in the 1950s, it is not surprising that a theoretical reach of this magnitude was put on hold. What did occur was actually fairly close to a contemporary art event. People went out and built radionics devices, demonstrating to themselves and others that even the drawings of the circuit would work.

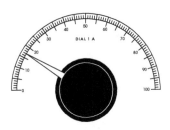

CHAPTER 17
RADIONICS MEETS POPULAR CULTURE

Anything as hopeful as radionics likely casts a shadow, and the shadow in this case is the lethal potential of the technology. There is a famous story about how Ed Hermann, an engineer at McGraw-Hill, Inc. publishing company in New York, upon learning of radionics, asked Hieronymus to treat a caterpillar-infested tree on his lawn. He never expected that from 300 miles away Hieronymus, using a photograph (and negative), would be able to exterminate in a few days the insects that had resisted every other treatment!

For safety's sake and national security, Hieronymus later claimed to have deliberately removed some critical factors from the patent. Whether this is true or not remains unresolved. Today, some manufacturers claim that they have installed components in their radionics devices that prevent them from being used for harm.

In retrospect, Hieronymus was anything but pleased by the notoriety his invention was accorded, especially the focus on its potential for pest control. In this regard, it's worth mentioning the correspondence between Hieronymus and *Astounding* editor John Campbell, as it serves to illustrate and illuminate many aspects of radionics that remain mysterious and unresolved to this day. It also helps the reader understand the technical and cultural difficulties about why that should still be the case.

The following excerpts are drawn from *The Story Of Eloptic Energy, The Autobiography Of An Advanced Scientist Dr. T. Galen Hieronymus*, which was authored by his wife Dr. Sarah Williams Hieronymus and published in 1988 by the Institute of Advanced Sciences. In Chapter V, Hieronymus writes that he chose these letters because "they represent, on the part of Mr. Campbell, a viewpoint of a man who seemed wedded to an opinion common to many people, that of regarding the study of Eloptic Energy as something magical or supernatural. He ignored the long years of research and application of the power of Eloptic Energy for healing the human body, and dwelt on the conducting powers of India ink to create a replica of the schematic of my Eloptic Energy Biometer (Analyzer).

"I appreciated Mr. Campbell's interest in my work, but over the years since then, I have concluded he set back the acceptance of my work at least a hundred years by his continual emphasis on what he termed the supernatural or 'magic' aspects of a mind-control device he built by drawing the schematic of my patented instrument with India ink. The energy flowed over the lines of this drawing, because India ink is conducting, but it wasn't worth a tinker's damn for serious research or actual treating."

Hieronymus is referring, of course, to Campbell's ability to make a symbolic drawing of the device function as well as the electronic one. This development, while boding poorly for the study of eloptic energy, has just the opposite potential for applying subtle energy through art. Clearly, the operating assumption is that an India ink drawing can conduct eloptic energy, and if the artwork is so designed, it can also become an instrument conducting this energy. The Campbell model goes a long way towards encouraging artists interested in experimentation to validate for themselves the potential of radionics. In a similar fashion, it casts light upon the function of art works of various designs in indigenous healing ceremonies.

Cultural Implications of Death By Radionics

On June 4, 1956, Campbell, writing to Hieronymus, maintained that there are two aspects to the problem of publicizing eloptic energy that must be considered: a reliable demonstration of effect to win public approval and an acceptable type of demonstration.

Campbell wrote: "Evidence of many, many years of trying strongly indicates that no demonstration which operates at the level of living forces is or can be made acceptable.

"It is also apparent that no demonstration that negates the privacy-protection concepts will be tolerable. It makes no difference how valid it is, or how clearly demonstrated it is — the very idea is psychologically anathema. Unbearable. Rejected because it true, not despite it is truth."

Campbell's point was if you can kill pests with nothing more than a photograph, especially at a distance of thousands of miles, it implies that you can kill him with such a machine, despite all he might do to hide, with no chance of protecting himself. By making a person know that such forces exist, the more insecure and insignificant you make them feel.

Campbell wrote: "True, you're attacking only insects; you're helping human beings. But the inherent implications are there, and cannot be denied. You cannot tell me how to defend myself against such an attack; if I acknowledge the reality of those forces, I acknowledge that I am helpless, and know of no defense."

Ironically, Campbell explained that he originally selected the Hieronymus machine because it was patented specifically as a mineral-analyzer, thereby allowing life-affecting characteristics to be ignored. Appearance played a role as well; it looked like an electronic-physical machine and almost made sense at the physical-science level.

Campbell continued: "A man can learn only at the boundary of the known; your machine appears to be right on the boundary between pure-electronics and psionics. Therefore it appears as though this were a learnable-understandable device that can, with a little study, be comprehended with just a little extension of already-understood concepts."

If Campbell was hoping the life force as-

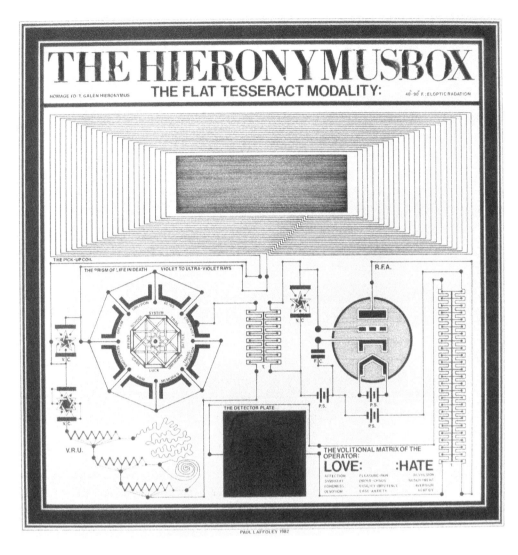

Fig 17-1. THE HIERONYMUSBOX - Paul Laffoley 1982

pects to the design could be totally ignored – allowing physical scientists to ponder the problem of operation without stirring deep, and extremely powerful fears – in point of fact, his letters to Hieronymus portray the opposite:

Campbell wrote: "That machine of yours is almost pure Magic. In the old, real, and potent sense; it casts spells, imposes death-magic, and can be used for life-magic. It operates on the anciently known laws of Sympa-thetic Magic; it, like Voodoo dolls, applies the law that 'The Symbol is the Object, and that which is done to the Symbol occurs also to the Object.'

"Magic is dangerous; it's a bred-in-the-bone fear that lies in every human being, be-cause there have been generations, hundreds of generations, who lived with the threat of Magic hanging over them. Mankind finally combed the damned stuff out of the picture;

now you and the other psionics investigators are bringing it hack. But this time you're bringing it back with a new, and enormously more powerful technique; the scientific method of stabilizing and reinforcing ideas will be backing it, and making it so powerful that we'll never again be able to drive it out of our lives.

"You're scaring the hell out of the people who understand what you've got. You may be using it well – but release it, and what limits it? If a magician can destroy a man tracelessly – who is safe from threat, from ransom demand, from the vengeful hate of an unjust enemy? You can name no limits to this powerful technique!

"When I began working with the machine, I learned that it didn't need a power supply. Then I learned that it wouldn't work if a tube were missing or defective. I saw some of the other psionic machines, and saw that they worked, despite the fact that their wiring system made absolutely no logical sense. From that, I derived a new concept, a theory, and made a crucial experiment."

A Radionics Device As Symbolic Representation Only

In pondering how the device worked, Campbell asked Hieronymus to consider the impact of 10,000 years of history and the millions of experiments humans have conducted during that time. He pointed out that "Magicians weren't the silly fools our culture says they were; they had something, but something inexpressible in terms of logic." The result, he maintained, is that our logic-oriented language can't handle those ideas; they can't possibly understand them today.

"The Magicians placed immense value on symbols, and on Charms – which, if you recall, were frequently symbols inscribed on something."

Campbell then wrote to Hieronymus about the major shortcoming of the psionics researchers: "they get turned down cold by scientists, every time." He guaranteed that Hieronymus would be turned down as long as he tried to make scientists believe that his device was scientific.

Campbell wrote: "No physical-science method can produce the results you produce. Therefore, claiming that you have a scientific device which does it, simply tells the scientist that you're a liar, a nut, or haven't the foggiest notion of what science is. He'll decide you're a mixture of all three.

"My claims were: (1) That it was not a scientific device. (2) That the eloptic radiation theory was inadequate, mistaken, or seriously incomplete, and (3) The machine did something. Having denied all explanation, and denied that I knew of any explanation--- the reader was completely unable to argue with me. He was forced to argue with the machine itself---which, of course, can't be done.

"The Scientist is then caught in a trap; he insists that science can explain any real phenomenon. If you demonstrate a real phenomenon---an action-level objective effect – and deny that it is scientific, he is now forced to prove you're a liar, to prove that it is so scientific! (He can't, of course, because it isn't – but he'll be forced to study the dratted thing, much to his own annoyance.)"

Campbell's letter didn't offer any ideas at all about the machine's operation and denied that any idea available was valid. He simply offered the fact that it did something, somehow. He denied his own ideas, Hieronymus' ideas, and Science's ideas. Campbell's cautious approach should be considered when presenting subtle energy devices as art works.

Several hundred readers scattered around

the world began building their own devices as a result of the publicity Campbell provided by writing about the Hieronymous device in *Astounding*. Campbell wrote: "They'll prove that they're smarter than we are; they can explain it. My business for a quarter century has been trying to make people consider ideas that they were sure were impossible. Gradually, I've learned some of the things you can and cannot do. First of all, you must convince them that you haven't got anything really new; that puts it on the border of the known, and you can get them to consider it. Then you expand it a little bit at a time, till, before they quite know how it happened, they've gone so far out into the pure unknown that they can't very well back out."

Campbell told Hieronymus that to fulfill some interesting requirements from the cultural perspective and to make his invention acceptable to the general public, he would need the following:

"1. It must be immediately useful in a way they want to use it.

"2. It must not appear to be really new – not importantly different, and must not appear to imply any great changes

"3. It must be so simple that making it can be a routine moron-operated action. No intellectual consideration required, no engineering talent needed.

"4. It must be something a business man – who doesn't give a damn about why's so long as how can make money – can apply directly, personally, and without the help of a technician.

"5. It must achieve something that is badly needed and can't be achieved scientifically, or can't be achieved economically.

"6. It must not require any research whatever before it can he used commercially.

"7. It must not hint at the violation of privacy-concepts or life-force problems so that it will not call up the old, deep fears."

Campbell pointed out that Hieronymus' plant-treating techniques fulfilled all but number 7, the violation of privacy concept. He suggested that the answer to the privacy problem was to introduce the device as a communications unit, surmising that psionics evidently do not involve energy but rather work with information. This interpretation of psionic functioning would mitigate the life force complications, leaving only the problem of producing the sonics of a vibrating loudspeaker cone, etc.

"The unsolved problem," wrote Campbell, "is how psionic forces can be made to modulate physical-action energies without the intervention of a living organism? I can't proceed from where I am without a damn sight more data on psionic machines. I don't know the exact set-up of your diagnostic machine. I don't know the set-up of the plant-treatment machines. I don't know the experiments you've made. I know damn well that the object isn't important – the India ink machine shows that. But I do need to know the order of effects, the things that did and didn't work, etc. And the things that did NOT work are just as important as the things that DID in revealing the pattern; light short-circuits the effects in your machines because it establishes an all-over, every-which way relationship by multiple reflection. It makes everything inside the machine related to everything else. I need to understand the pattern of developments. The pattern of the various machines."

On June 14, 1956, Hieronymus replied to Campbell saying that when the patent specifications were written, his patent attorney thought it would be a good idea to include an explanation that would be accepted by the uninitiated (i.e., those unfamiliar with psionics). Hieronymus also pointed out that he had learned a lot since the days the patent was written and not to hold him to the original explanations.

Hieronymus wrote: "Let's face one fact right now. I don't like to even put this in writing, but you have already done so in part and I might as well finish the job. We can kill insects at a great distance. We have done it repeatedly. Some have been worms the size of your finger and several inches long. We have made mistakes in technique of operation or in handling situations or have had apparatus work backwards from what we expected with the result that we have been really scared by the results obtained. There is terrific power in Eloptic Energy. It can be generated, it can be directed to a pinpointed objective halfway around the globe. What we can do, others can do.

"If we allow ourselves to be shoved aside because some so called scientist says he doesn't believe it, and we do not do all we can to learn all we can about the behavior, what can be done, what can be done to prevent it etc., then we may some day awaken to find that another power on the globe where they are not tied down by so called scientific tradition, where scientists do what they are told to do whether they like it or not, another power may direct such unscientific forces against us and our scientists who said, 'It can't be done,' will be helpless to protect us or themselves.

"I have tried to get our government to try the idea out but I got the same old run around. I have a letter from the Department of Defense signed by Donald Quarrels that you will appreciate. Will show it to you some day."

Hieronymus went on to say he did not care whether anyone had the answer to how or why it works. He made it clear that he did not need scientific approval "to get this to the American people." He was just looking for the right person to take his knowledge forward.

Hieronymus wrote: "It is all right for you to say that the world is afraid of Magic. I do not agree with your entire premise. People are afraid of the unknown or what they do not understand. The cave man was afraid of lightning. We have harnessed it and put it to work. The rank and file still know about as much about electricity as the cave man. What do we know about it? We know a lot about controlling it and using it. That is enough for most people.

"Explorers took movies into the jungles and had their entire audience run like mad into the dark woods to get away from the devil magic of the white man. Cousins, only a few times removed from those natives, are quite respected citizens of the community here, today. They go to the movies. Why don't they run away like their native cousins? Education and familiarity; that is the answer."

Hieronymus argued that everything man has devised for warfare purposes has eventually been enhanced in peacetime. He pointed out that radar, invented by two Americans, was turned down by some VIP in Washington as an impractical dream but was utilized by England. The end result was that we had to go to England to learn how to use it during the war, but it had far broader applications in peacetime.

Hieronymus believed that within metaphysics lay the real answer to how eloptic energy works and is controlled. He believed the reason the general public couldn't accept the possibilities of eloptic energy was due to our spiritual advisors inability to accept the truth.

Hieronymus wrote: "A Chinese person can take an Abacus and do some very intricate mathematical problems with it. There, both the man and the device are necessary. There are a few people who have the ability to do very complicated problems mentally, without any device to assist them. In this case, it is wholly the personal equation that counts. The same analogy holds good when it comes to doing things with apparatus for the diagnosis or treatment of disease."

At this point in the correspondence, Hieronymus addressed the question of how a radionic device actually functions. He attributed the capacity for most alternative healing techniques to three possibilities: (1) The super-conscious mind; (2) Discarnate entities guiding the healer; (3) Those without clairvoyant ability opting to use a psionic device. (Learning through trial and error, tuning into the emanations of diseased tissue, etc.)

Hieronymus wrote: "These three categories are so mixed up in various people that they seldom know when they are using one and when using another. The important point is to be able to know that all three do exist and not confuse them."

In reading Hieronymus closely, it becomes apparent that he may also have been confused at times by how these categories apply to the functioning of his technology. This confusion surrounding the operating methodology becomes a source of increased importance in the ensuing correspondence.

Hieronymus continued: "We can set the dials of one of our instruments to a specific frequency rate, put the leaf from a tree in the instrument (to form the connection with the specific tree) and even though the tree is hundreds of miles away and has no 'ideas' on the subject, we can produce definite results in the tree. Anyone can do this. Not just me, or my wife; anyone who will take the time to learn the motions of operation of the device.

"When you made the paper drawing of the circuit of that instrument of yours, you gave it a terrific shot of power to do what you wanted it to do. Someone else might or not get the same results. When a man has an ability very well developed, it is difficult to convince him that he is the exception."

Here Hieronymus states that the operator actually injects energy into the device. He attributes personal ability, not the mechanical function of the device, as the direct source of the art of making a psionics device operate successfully. This statement in many ways contradicts Hieronymus' own insistence that construction details of the device are as important, if not more important, to its functioning ability. If the device truly functions as a product of directed intent cultivated over years of practice, combined with innate ability, then it seems likely that his technology is far more artistic than mechanistic.

Radionics Devices as Transceivers

Perhaps sensing this dilemma, Hieronymus began describing his experiments on how a radionics device could function in communications: "You have undoubtedly heard about Nelson's attempt to get RCA interested. In anticipation of his being sent here to see the idea at work for communication, I built a transmitter and a receiver for the sending of dots, spaces and dashes. Until we get a mechanical detector, we must necessarily depend upon what we have for getting reactions.

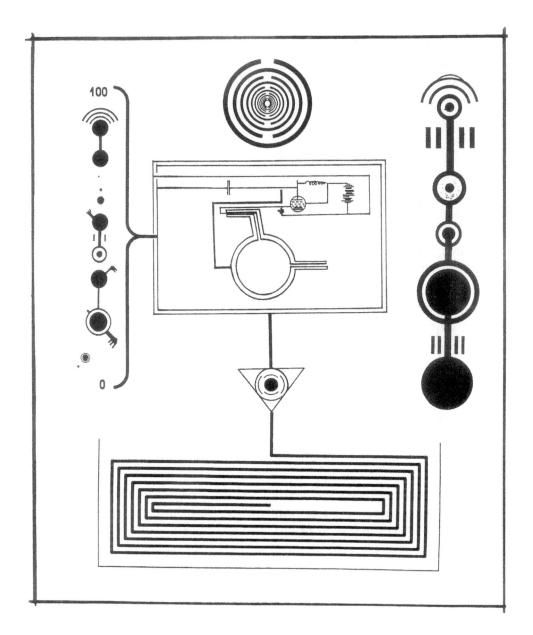

Fig 17-2. Radionic T-Shirt design — D. Laurie

"Since I have already written up the idea and had it notarized for future patent coverage, I don't mind telling you about the details, however, I would rather you held all this as between us for the time.

"I took a piece of gold that had been a filling from a tooth as the carrier frequency source. This had some very specific characteristics that would hardly be found elsewhere. I tried several pure form elements such as silver, antimony, selenium etc., and found those that had very distinct frequency patterns differ-

The Secret Art

ent from each other. The carrier was caused to radiate from the transmitter, continuously. In order to send a dash, I caused the energy from the dash element (e.g. selenium) to be superimposed on the carrier (gold) and thus so modulated. To send a dot, the same procedure, only the modulating frequency was from another element.

"The receiver consisted of three complete prism units in the same case with separate quantity measuring devices for each, with a switch that would cut in first one then another of the preset prism units, each being tuned to a different frequency, one for the dot (antimony e.g.), one for the dash (selenium), and another for the space to be sent between characters to separate them.

"Before putting the gold filling in the receiver, I photographed it. The photograph was placed in the receiver so it would respond only to the energy from the one source, the transmitter. The device does a very good job. If I were going to do this for an important demonstration, I would want to search very carefully to get some good elements for the dot, dash and space. I find that some elements work one way and some another."

Source of the Radionic Function

Hieronymus believed God endowed us with the ability to create, and therefore make use of eloptic energy, which can alter physical patterns: "He made us in His image and likeness. I believe this means that He gave us those of His abilities (likenesses) that would enable us to create most anything we chose to create."

As far as radionics was concerned, he added, "with our imaging, with our cold reason and mental picture, we form the pattern. With our emotional energy, we fill the form or pattern or mold and thus create. The mental form must be made of something. The emotional energy must come from somewhere. It comes from this sea of all pervading something. When something has been formed, it must be kept in form by some binding energy or it will revert to the original state. There is a constant interchange of some kind in which there is a constant disintegration, reverting back to the original state, and a constant replenishment, to hold the form created. It is this 'disintegration' part in which we are interested when we tune in to the energy emanating from a substance and find out what frequencies are emanating from it."

Hieronymus also believed that he could measure emotions and thoughts through radionic detectors. The rationale was that by measuring the effect of a thought or emotion directed at some unsuspecting person, a rate could be obtained with the same device used in the detection of the emanations from solid substance.

Hieronymus wrote: "When we can find the resonant frequency of a pest like a corn earworm and subject it to that frequency and the worm just goes from a lively worm to a moist spot in 24 hours, what have we done? Have we not probably offset the 'binding' energy or what have you, and allowed the component elements to revert to their original state?"

In a postscript to the letter of June 14, 1956, to John Campbell, Hieronymus wrote: "You mentioned the fact you could do without any electrical power to actuate the original copy of my device. This is true for diagnostic work that is, just getting your reactions. When it comes to treating or producing such results as changing a disease condition in a person or in killing a pest, there is need for more power."

Campbell Confronts Hieronymus on Terminology and Approach to Radionics

On June 17, 1956, Campbell, writing to Hieronymus, stated that his education was in theoretical physics, in the period of 1926 through 1935, "when nuclear physics was the grandest mess of theories that had ever come down the pike. They had a dozen different theories, all of which were good for explaining some aspects of the observed data, but none of which would explain all."

Campbell told Hieronymus that he has spotted the basic flaw in modern science, so far as his work is concerned. The problem was using electronic terminology, words like "frequency" and "vibration," in ways no professional scientist could tolerate. He asked Hieronymus to develop new terms.

Campbell wrote: "Physics has their territory too well mapped to allow the existence of any major features such as we've been working with. Insist that they have to fit it into their territory, and they'll know for a fact — and be perfectly correct – that you're a crackpot. IT IS NOT SCIENCE AND CANNOT BE EXPLAINED WITHIN SCIENCE. The problem, then, is two-fold; explain that it is not science, and explain what it is."

Campbell recommended that instead of saying that science's present maps of the Universe must necessarily be deficient, one should point out that perhaps the method of observation is inadequate: "Physical science has no map whatever of the forces of purposive influences, no description whatever of want, or desire. But purpose is direction; a purposive organism can – unlike Einstein's One Eyed Logician! – tell Past from Future; any living organism has a sense of purpose, of direction-in-time. O.K.; now let's consider what that psionic machine that controls insects, etc., is

doing. Suppose for a moment that it somehow influences purposive force; it can influence want-energy.

"Let's imagine a young, healthy vigorous aphid resting on a nice, tender young rose shoot. It is in a perfect position to be able to eat; in that situation it can eat. If it were a purely inanimate system, then, it would eat. But it isn't inanimate; suppose what the machine does is to block the want-to-eat. The aphid sits there, not wanting to eat, and starves to death.

"I have a hunch that the psionic machines, so far, have largely served as means of concentrating or focusing human attention on a specific target; the purpose-energy of a human being is stupendously greater than the purposive energy of any ordinary animal. The purposive energies a human being exerts in such ordinary jobs as driving in traffic must represent a purposive-power sufficient to blast out of existence hundreds of thousands of caterpillars or beetles!

"Any method by which the enormous purposive energies of a human being could be focused against such fragile purposive structures as Jap beetles, for instance, should make it possible to kill tens of thousands without much noticeable effort on the part of the human being. But...don't try it on another human being! There you'll be running into a purposive dynamo of your own magnitude! If, moreover, you tie into a violent neurosis in the patient's structure, he'll swing more and more of his total life-energies into defending it against the attack of the therapist, and you might find yourself darned near knocked out yourself.

"The other side of the matter is Meaning. Efficiency could be defined as 'maximizing the ratio of P/A' – maximizing of purposive result to action expended. Your diagnostic-analytical machine is an effort to maximize a different ratio – the ratio of M/D. The maximum of Meaning obtained from Data used.

"Meaning, I suspect, is the intellectual side of Purpose, while Logic is the intellectual side of Action. Just as many actions can yield the same purpose, so many logical structures can yield the same meaning. There are a dozen different logical proofs of the Pythagorean Theorem, for example, each equally valid – but only one Meaning.

"How much data is enough? The answer to this question, in Logic, is absolutely definite; 'All the data, and only all, is enough.' That's why Logic, real, formal logic, works only in mathematics, where the Universe of Discourse can be fully defined.

"Meaning is different; you do not need all the data to determine meaning. Simple example: A newspaper half-tone print visibly does not present all the picture; the half-tone dots visibly interrupt the pattern. But the meaning is complete! The most successful method of attacking the problem of the Universe has been that of physical science; it yielded more Meanings per man-year than any other technique philosophers ever tried."

Campbell then challenged Hieronymus at the functional level of the apparatus: "The trouble we're going to run into in this field is that Will, Purpose, is effective in this area! You say glass doesn't hold a charge. O.K. – that's fine. Then your glass won't – because your purposive energies prevent it. But if I say it does, then my glass will!

"You say light conducts the force; I say it doesn't. In my machine, as a consequence, it doesn't!

"I built that symbolic machine, and installed a 6.3-volt transformer, power line, and switch, with a little pilot bulb. Reason: plugging it in, and turning on the pilot light helped convince people that 'something' inside this box is now ready to function.

"The light from the pilot bulb, however, bathes the entire circuit diagram. The machine works just as well with the light on as with the light off. So, in my machine, light does not conduct the force." (Note: Hieronymus had always alleged that light interferes with the operation of his device.)

Campbell stated that what was missing in the technology was an actual, genuine barrier to purposive energy: "The damndest part of this research is just exactly that problem; purposive energies can saturate matter, as a magnetic field can saturate steel, and magnetize it. I very studiedly saturated my symbolic drawing with a conviction that this would work, by reason of the laws of symbolic magic. I agree that that was important. I know I have very special talents along that line; hell, man for 30 years I've been specializing in developing my talents in the line of presenting imaginative concepts with conviction that produces a sensation of reality! That's what a science-fiction writer-editor does for a living…and in that field, by God, I'm good."

Campbell saw that the experimenter's own powerful purpose can impose the quality of excellence on material that may be inherently poor, and deny effects in material that may inherently be excellent. He wanted Hieronymus to design a mechanical detector of purposive energies. The very best experimenters would be the ones with greatest purpose and understanding who can impose magnificent results on an experiment that others find impossible to recreate. Campbell was looking at the role consciousness plays in dictating the outcome of a psionic experiment. When life force is being studied or applied, he argued, then the nature of the person doing the evaluation will impact the result.

"Sure, you're a Grade A magician," he told Hieronymus. "You can plant a Charm on a bone, some mud dug from a graveyard at midnight, and a three-stage broad-band impedance coupled amplifier, after which the darned thing will work for ordinary people. But ordinary people can't; therefore, for them, the things are no good, and your theory obviously is nonsense.

"Ed Herman's no doubt told you about the trouble the de la Warr people have with their photographic machine? It works just fine, for anybody…provided Mr. Corte loads the plates! Unless Corte puts the Charm on the plates – saturates them with purposive energy, so to speak---the plates can't be used!

"Until we can get instrumentation of a mechanical order…we're stuck."

Campbell and Hieronymus Define the Working Relationship

On June 19, 1956, Campbell wanted to talk about the business of protecting the symbolic device. The patent system at the present time did not offer them any protection whatsoever, as it was not set up to handle the type of problem they had. The purely symbolic machine obviously was not what Hieronymus patented. Furthermore, Campbell believed he could use a different set of symbols and get results that were just as good, as the symbols had their characteristics arbitrarily assigned to them. He realized that getting effective patent protection on a psionic device was completely out of the question. He had also discovered why doing business in psionics was not looking profitable to corporate investors.

"You can't patent a law of nature," Campbell wrote. "What we're doing, however, is discovering laws of Nature. No patent pro-

tection possible."

Campbell wanted to go back to the Trade Secret system. Since no technique of scientific analysis could find out why psionic devices work, then why worry about patent protection? Campbell believed that as a team they could create a viable product. Here again, a growing disparity between the two men becomes apparent. Campbell wanted a psionic product that will financially justify the trouble it took to convince people to use it and a device that avoided the stigma of magic. Hieronymus did not need a product beyond his existing device, which made money through serving the needs of its buyers. He only wanted some scientific approval of its function.

Wrote Campbell: "A theory is no damn good, unless it can lead you to a piece of hardware that works."

Hieronymus: On the Manipulation of Eloptic Energy

On June 20, 1956, Hieronymus replied to Campbell. Hieronymus preferred to discuss eloptic energy and how it worked. Today, decades later, it may seem odd to be concerned with these deliberations. Yet throughout the world numerous devices of similar design claim to work using similar principles. It is a huge business. Suffice it to say, businesses cannot survive selling products that never work. One senses Campbell is very attuned to this reality, but wants to promote one that has at least a veneer of scientific validity. For today's skeptical researcher, the debate over the function of psionic devices continues, very much as it did fifty years ago. Is it energy or is it mind (i.e. information) that makes the device work?

Hieronymus wrote, "It seems to be necessary to keep pounding away at the idea of trying to get over the important fact that we

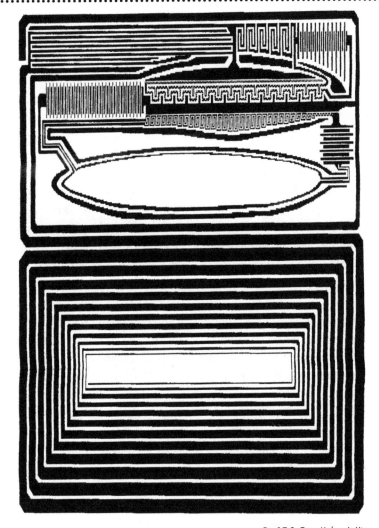

Fig 17-3. Tony Malone's Hieronymus Circuit

Notes on the Hieronymus Circuit

Here are the facts:

1) a wire dangling in the air is an antenna.

2) a wire in a loop is coil and/or an inductor.

3) a wire next to another wire and not touching is a capacitor.

4) a wire of two different metals (or colors) is a battery.

5) an inductor and a capacitor together is a resonant circuit and will vibrate.

Deduction:

If you colorized this circuit – it would work.

— *Tony Malone - retired Electromechanical Spacecraft Engineer, JPL* are dealing with a force or energy that is as different from electricity and radio as electricity differs from heat. In fact, there is more difference since we are in a different medium than that involved in the electro-magnetic.

"Electricity flowing through a wire will produce heat. This does not mean that electricity is heat, any more than saying that since a flow of electrons, up and down an antenna will produce something that radiates out away from the antenna; the two phenomena are one and the same.

"Might just as well take off on the subject of why a burned out or missing tube works as it does. I have been able to make a device without any kind of electricity involved that generated much more energy than the best radio amplifier. It was all mechanical, no chemicals or batteries. Form or configuration was most important. We are using the amplifier tubes for other than their typical radio characteristics."

Hieronymus made even more exaggerated statements about eloptic energy and what can be done with it. Here he claimed that he had made a mechanical device that generates "much more energy than the best radio amplifier." The two men had diverged in purpose. Campbell wanted a working device that people can use, that can make money, while Hieronymus wanted a scientific investigation of eloptic energy and approval of his discovery. The problem is that eloptic energy involves the use of consciousness. In the end, neither individual would get what they wanted.

Hieronymus was still insisting there was a physical basis for eloptic energy. He wrote that some of his most time consuming and heart-breaking experiences resulted from not knowing enough about conductors and insulators of eloptic energy. He explained that

after building many devices over a period of time and finding they would not work, he discarded them and went on to other experiments, usually because some material used was not an insulator, but a conductor. He did not accept Campbell's claim that none of the design parameters made any difference; that it was all in the mind of the operator.

Hieronymus debated endlessly about how eloptic energy travels, its relationship to ether, its similarity to high frequency current, and how at times it didn't work with an electrical device. Then he talked about how electricity can be converted to eloptic energy and the role of magnetic fields. He wrote about the infusion of life energy into chemicals, animating matter. Finally, he described, using the third person, an experiment he had obviously made that he thought would make a good science fiction story:

"Take a similar combination eating away on said ear of corn. Find by use of an Eloptic analyzer, some substance (we call it a reagent) that will reduce his vitality value to near zero. Take a bit of the shuck from the ear of corn, place this and the reagent in an Eloptic transmitter, removed many feet (e.g. 20) from said ear and worm and start the transmitter going. Then leave town. House vacant. The only one who knows what is going on is 250 or more miles away, having a good time with a lot of people and not thinking at all about the worm. Two and a half days later, the knowing ones return to find three out of four of the worms are just spots of moisture. The fourth worm when tested shows one-twentieth the vitality he did three days before. Keep him on the ear of corn while the treatment continues over night and next day, he too is a moist spot. What happened there? He did not dry up and become dust. The components were disassociated. The binder was removed or nullified. Instead of a worm, intact, he became carbon, oxygen, nitrogen etc., again. That would make a swell Astounding Science Fiction Story. It is astounding but not fiction."

Hieronymus told Campbell that he was manipulating the so-called, binding energy that holds the electrons together in a molecule. He said that the amount of energy required was so little compared with that required when atomic energy was used; there is no comparison. The reason is easy to explain. Hieronymus wrote: "The brute force method used in atomic fission is very inefficient. When you find the resonant frequency of a molecular combination and feed this frequency into it, the amount of energy necessary to neutralize the binding effect is relatively small." This is a fascinating possibility. It is hard to imagine accomplishing such a task on mental functioning alone.

Hieronymus kept referring to the worms. He pointed out that many other instruments require an operator in the room with the instrument while it is operating, to furnish the necessary energy. With his own device, they could treat the corn earworms 250 or more miles away and they completely dissolved; they did not need to fulfill the requirement of having to supply energy to make the instrument work. Hieronymus seemed to think that this device was the product, in spite of Campbell's admonitions against it. They were not connecting, but some useful information for the radionic artist/inventor is forthcoming, namely that emotion and thought shape eloptic energy as much as any material.

Hieronymus wrote: "There is a lot of difference in the way different instruments operate. We are quite sure we are dealing with a form of energy that is not a flow of electrons (electricity), or a wave motion in the ether (radio like propagation), or magnetic, or heat, or light. We know that there is a great similarity between Eloptic energy and the energy involved in thoughts and emotions, and in the nerve impulses (not the electrical part set up by the chemical action). We know that Eloptic energy exhibits several different states. We can store it like a static charge; we can generate it in a manner similar to the generation of electricity; we can manipulate it by thoughts and emotions. It can be transmitted over great distances without attenuation. It can be made to disassociate the atoms in a molecule. It can and does manifest something akin to frequency, as we use the term in connection with audio or radio etc., whether pulsing or alternating."

Hieronymus referred Campbell back to a letter where he divided operators and their instruments into a least three general groups. For those working in radionics, these were important potential distinctions to consider. There were individuals who are able to function psychically and only use a stick plate to get yes or no answers to mental questions. Their questions are either consciously or unconsciously asked. This group would include those who experience the dowsing reflex instantaneously, such as skilled artists, cooks, survivalists, psychics, etc.

Next, Hieronymus said that there are those who have a smaller measure of psychic ability but are very sensitive operators. This group required some type of instrument that would tune to different frequencies. The last group had little developed psychic ability and would deny having it if they did. These individuals required a good instrument to do almost all of their work, arriving at their skill through practice and perseverance.

Furthermore, said Hieronymus, the first group usually never knew whether it was the instrument or themselves that did the work. This group's work and findings were most often unrepeatable by others. The second type of operator was generally the most reliable, when and if he had a good instrument to work with. They knew they must guard against too much interference. The last group of operators was completely lost without a well-built and well-calibrated instrument.

Campbell's letter from the previous October had dwelled at length on the cost and elaborateness of some of the instruments on the market. Some were much larger than others and very complicated to operate. Of those, he observed, some were made to sell at a very high price for the sole purpose of making a lot of money for the builder. Many were built on contract for $5,000 (in 1950s money) and the builders later went bust. In radionics as with so many other appliances, price was no guarantee of quality.

"As a case in point," Hieronymus wrote, "I have two instruments of the prism type. One refracts the entire spectrum of 90 odd elements in a pick up arc of about 30 degrees. The various isotopes are so crowded that you can only pick up one energy peak, get a reaction, at one place on the dial for each element. The other instrument is so constructed that the same band of elements is spread out over 60 degrees and we can pick up each isotope of an element without trouble."

What Hieronymus was trying to tell Campbell was not to put all instruments in one bin and classify them as Psionic Devices; each individual design could impact its functionality. This observation went counter to Campbell's deepest convictions regarding psionic function and remains a matter of dispute today.

Campbell Describes People Using the Hieronymus Device and What It Implies

On July 11, 1956, Campbell wrote to Hieronymus: "I've had a lot of people test the devices here at my house. I've gotten a lot of interest among highly trained technical people, because of my magazine. And I've observed the results. Also, I've had friends of my daughters' try it. The results work out this way:

"1. The blasted thing won't work for me except on a highly erratic, unpredictable basis. I can predict, however, that the frustrating contraption will not work any time I am trying to make a test of something new!

"2. Every one of the dozen or more professional scientists I've had out here has scored a flat zero. Not one of them has succeeded! This includes men from Bell Labs, Esso Research, Sperry Electronics, and several other outfits. They are real, Grade A research men too, and have approached the problem with genuine good faith and open mindedness.

"3. Kids of high school age and under have about 99% success.

"4. Housewives, lawyers, doctors, insurance agents, business executives – score about 85% success.

"5. It won't work for my wife, except erratically and uncertainly.

"6. It works for both of my younger daughters, but best for my 11-year-old.

"The remarkable fact that stands out is that it won't work for scientists: I've heard from a number of the gang that tried building it from the magazine. All of them complained it didn't work. Not one success reported to date!"

Campbell then pondered about what scientific training does to a man, or possibly, what kind of a man becomes a scientist, and why it is that a scientist can't do what most people can. Or, put another way, what type of problem so matches the search-pattern of the scientific method that the scientific method is inherently incapable of solving it?

"The answer, I think," said Campbell, "lies in this: A scientist is rigorously trained – and trains himself to a strong self-discipline – to avoid injecting his own wishes, hopes, desires, or feelings into his experiment. He must determine what is there, and must not seek to 'prove his point.' He must conduct his experiments with absolute objectivity; if the experiment is going to disprove the theory he spent half a life-time building – why, he must conduct it with the same honest, detached, and purely-factual attitude he would if, instead, it were proving his life work.

"It was the introduction of, and development of that completely objective, honest approach that made Science what it is. It's the foundation of scientific ethics, and every scientist worth his salt accepts it deeply, and with a degree of self-discipline that few laymen appreciate."

What would happen, Campbell wondered, if such a sincerely dedicated and honest scientist tried to use something that worked only if he entered into it and drove it with his own desires and wants?

Nothing.

If, as Campbell suspected, psionic devices are dependent on the application of human purposive energies, then the scientific method gives 100% absolute assurance that it won't work.

"The scientist must not inject his own purpose," wrote Campbell. "He must be purely objective. Which means he won't do a thing to help it! He has trained himself to a state of completely withdrawn, perfectly neutral observation-without-participation. Which is precisely what will not work in a psionic experiment!"

Campbell had the training and could not make the device work when he wanted it to work. It worked only when he accepted without question that it did work and was asking about something else.

Wrote Campbell: "These are tools, but not yet machines. A tool is a device by which a man can do something, or do something more easily, that would normally be impossible or very difficult without the tool. The tool is, however, essentially a passive device, like paper and pencil, or a typewriter that works only when I push on it.

"A machine, on the other hand, is a dynamic device; it can work itself. An oil burner is a machine. A power shovel is a machine, where a shovel is a tool.

"The scientists are looking for psionic machines; devices that do-it-to-them, rather than psionic tools, with which they-do-it. The scientist makes 'objective' and 'passive' mean the same thing."

The crux of the matter lies in these observations made by Campbell in 1956. Artists rather than scientists should be building and developing radionic technology. The devices work because the operators direct a subtle intent through the tool, something to do with consciousness that's not yet understood. Artists understand better than others; especially the artist that allows inspiration to flow through their being into the artwork.

Campbell drew the analogy to a skeptical person reporting on the first bicycle. He will try to ride the thing, but the inventor's claims are "clearly preposterous." The device is inherently unstable; how can it stand upright with a load on it? Where is the power source? If it travels faster than a man can walk, then it will violate the law of conservation of energy.

Then, true to form, the man takes the test and the bicycle doesn't move; it falls over. Only later, with practice, does the genius of the bicycle become apparent. Campbell pointed out that had the inventor of the bicycle not entered the experiment and demonstrated to himself the means of riding, thereby violating a cardinal rule of scientific detachment, the invention could have been written off as a hoax.

"Unfortunately," wrote Campbell, "the professional scientist is in precisely such a position with respect to psionic devices. The best, most dedicated and ethical, honest scientists are precisely the ones that, you can guarantee, will not get results!"

Influence of the Mind; Scientists Working Psionic Devices

On July 24, 1956, Campbell wrote to Hieronymus: "Now see if you can check this point: Call it psionic, call it eloptic, or call it frahmstahl-moisenbur – names make no never mind. But there definitely is attenuation over intervals. Many of the scientists have blown their stacks over the idea that distance has no effect. Believe me, an increasing interval does have effect – only the proper measure of interval is not distance. The parameter for measurement is relevance. Relationship-separation, not space-separation."

Is this observation not precisely the nature of art? Take a great painting; no power supply, no moving parts; nor does distance from the painting limit its power and influence; the energy broadcast by the work is con-

sistently strong. Even a reproduction conveys part of the power and meaning of the artwork. One can recall it in his mind to the same effect. The artwork is dependent upon "attenuation over intervals," because the farther we distance ourselves from it emotionally, the less relevance it has for our lives.

Wrote Campbell: "You found, I understand, that if you were working with a photo print, and the negative was destroyed, the print didn't work any more.

"Betcha: It does respond, still! BUT…it responds far more weakly. Reason: There is no longer as close a relationship between print and object as there was."

Campbell went on to argue that he could attenuate the effect of this mystery force by introducing irrelevancy. He could, in effect, reduce the power and importance of the signal by dumbing it down, by "spinning" it into absurdity. With this observation, we see the heart of radionics in media today. No devices are necessary; the medium is the message. No wonder we aren't supposed to study radionics. Invert the equation and we can "charge" objects with relevance as well – witness the onslaught and merging of powerful electronic advertising media with consumer culture from the 1950s onward.

Campbell told Hieronymus he was looking for "a psionic-to-electronic transducer."

"I think we have to work with patterns, not with quantities," said Campbell. "You see, the total number of electrons arriving at the screen need not be changed at all; no energy change is required. We simply shift the place of arrival, and get a clearly visible difference. We shift the relationship, without shifting the objects.

"Item: You'd be surprised how many psionic devices have started coming out from

Fig 17-4. 13th Century Geomantic Device - front

behind the weeds. Friend of mine at White Sands Proving Grounds has suddenly started discovering that dozens of the boys there have psionic devices they've been working on privately – and secretly, so they wouldn't be jeered at. Now that ASF has revealed there is such work going on, and that there are patents…the boys have started talking to each other.

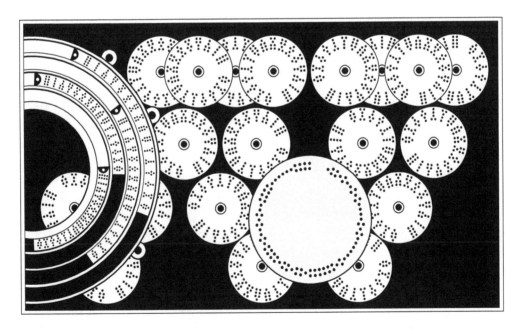

Fig 17-5. 13th Century Geomantic Device - reverse

"One of the best is an Ouija board. The rocketeers have, for years, been trying to predict the point where the rocket will land when it falls back. Their best aerodynamic, physical, and whatnot theories, worked over on huge electronic computers, scored about a 10% correlation. One of the boys, as a gag, brought in an Ouija board. From the start, they scored 80% correlations – including an accurate prediction of the failure of their nice, new $50,000 Aerobee."

Treating People with Eloptic Energy Instruments

On October 6th 1956, Hieronymus wrote to Campbell: "My daughter called from Kansas City, about 2000 miles away. She has one of our treating instruments but had not used it for quite a while. We wanted to check it to see whether she could use it as the granddaughter was sick. We took a specimen (several years old) of the daughter and tested for certain things. While still talking on the phone, we had her start treating herself on her instrument and a recheck here, showed changing conditions, indicating that the treating instrument 2000 miles away was functioning correctly. What happened?

"If I subject the daughter's specimen to a magnetic field, there is no longer any value to the specimen. It acts as if it were never a specimen. Why?

"All this adds up to the drawing of some conclusions. When a person makes a specimen, by writing on a piece of paper, by being photographed, by putting a little saliva or blood or perspiration on a piece of sterile paper etc., he has taken a little bit of himself and separated it away from himself so far as appearances but actually, it acts as if there were a telephone line running between him and his specimen. If we

take a photograph of a person, then make a print from the film, we find that either will act as a good specimen. If we put the film in a metal box, then the print loses its contact with the person and is not a useful specimen of that person. When we remove the film from the metal box, instantly, the contact is restored and the print is a representative specimen of the person again.

"Now about the use of power. I built dozens of instruments without any power of any kind and they work well. The reactions are harder to get. I used chemical amplifiers. They help a lot. The Drown instrument uses no power. I built instruments for sale to doctors for several years. I had too many doctors who had spent $2000.00 for Drown equipment, put it aside and spend a like amount for my equipment because they could demonstrate that they could get in fifteen minutes treatment with my equipment, what it took eight hours to do with the Drown equipment.

"I didn't kid anyone. I required a week of schooling at my laboratory for doctors who wanted to buy one of my analyzer-treating units. They paid $1945.00 for the instrument and never questioned the price. They knew what they could do with it. I did no advertising. A doctor would get one of my instruments and go to work on his patients. His doctor friends would note the results and he then wanted one. They were not kidding themselves. They wanted results. They got it."

Relationship of Psionics to Art

On October 16, 1956, Campbell wrote to Hieronymus, pointing out to him that his work is art, even a "black art." Campbell offered some advice: "The reason people don't like Arts these days is quite understandable; throughout history it has been held that the Artist works for the love of his Art, and shouldn't be paid for it. This stems from the fact that no one who doesn't have a built-in, practically inescapable compulsion toward doing the darned job would undertake such tough, unrewarding work. Since such a man is going to do it anyway, by reason of his built-in compulsion, why…why pay him? You can get him to do it for nothing, because the poor slob has to do it anyway.

"You're quite right that you're not in the business to make money; believe me, you won't…so long as it's an art. My own field of Art, writing, took centuries to get into the class of Business. I'm an Artist; like you, I've spent years learning by experiment. It's a psionics field in itself, you know; the Art of making someone want to understand something he hasn't the slightest desire to understand. My specialty is making people interested in something they 'know' is 'imaginative nonsense.' You think I haven't had years of practice at that? Hah! We were working out the problems of nuclear energy in 1935; the problems of space flight in the '30s and '40s to such an extent that's all old hat stuff for the magazine now.

"The problem is of a totally different order from the area of problem you're working on; you're working on 'How to make it work,' and doing nicely. The problem I'm making my principle effort on is 'How to make people believe it works.'"

In one respect, Campbell deserves a lot of credit for even trying to make people believe that psionic devices work. He did his best, as the following letters will show. The problem was that radionic technology was already understood and being developed at a level of sophistication far beyond that of psionic healing devices.

Recent investigations such as Adam Curtis' 2002 BBC documentary, *The Century of the Self*, illustrate exactly how well media can be adapted to insert directed intent into human motivation, "using Freud's theories to try and control the dangerous crowd in the age of mass democracy," as Curtis put it.

To render this process visible to the masses was not entirely in the best interests of those who understood its true potential. By introducing psionic devices into a public mainstream discussion, even couched in the literature of science fiction, Campbell and Hieronymus were inadvertently risking the exposure of a potent new means of mass manipulation. God forbid the poor consumers, upon realizing their vulnerability, suddenly discovered they had the means to "render those manipulations irrelevant" by employing their own homemade psionic devices for protection, or worse, retaliation.

Getting Respect for Psionics: Claude Shannon and the Hieronymus Device

Campbell advised Hieronymus that the fundamental problem with getting psionics recognized was that it was almost impossible to reach the top men in any field of study. This problem was compounded by the fact that it was very difficult to find out exactly who the top men were; they tended to remain as invisible as possible, hiding from public notoriety.

Campbell said, "Col. Gross Flopperoo with Dr. Vannevar Bush is an example; Bush is one of the most finely stuffed shirts in science. The way such a man stays in business is to be very careful to watch what the back-room gang who do the real thinking are doing, and not making any original statements of his own.

"The admittedly second-line men in any field don't make original statements; that's why they're second-liners, of course, but it's their uncanny ability to quote the right authority at the right time that got 'em up from third-line. Neither the Front Man, nor the second-liners, are going to do psionics any appreciable good; we need the real, genuine, backroom-front-line men, who don't attend the banquets, but tell the Front men what the score is."

Campbell told Hieronymus that an example of a front-line scientist of the highest caliber was Claude Shannon of MIT, who is often credited today with the invention of Information Theory. He informed Hieronymus that the fundamental theoretical work on which 90% of all modern automation, cybernetics, computer design, and communication equipment design is based upon Shannon's formulation of information theory. Shannon was, however, "a backroom boy who avoids the banquets like crazy."

Campbell then told Hieronymus that Shannon had taken an interest in psionics, and coincidentally had been an *Astounding* reader for years. He wanted to see a demonstration of a repeatable effect. He wanted experimental data; he wanted to see things work.

Said Campbell: "His gang won't give you the 'pish-tush' treatment; they're the ones who everybody else watches to see which way science is going to jump next – and they don't have to watch what anybody else thinks of what they're doing. Therefore they're completely free to evaluate, without fear of being considered out of line. Hell, they make the line!

"When, and only when, you reach people at that level will your communication be unhampered. Let the news get out that Claude Shannon and his group are interested in the Hieronymus machine, and every major technical school in the country, plus half the major scientific research industrial labs will

start looking frantically into the subject."

By comparison, Campbell continued, "Nelson of RCA has the required free-investigating mind…but he has orthodox bosses who report to David Sarnoff."

On the other hand, "Shannon doesn't have bosses."

Other scientist friends of Campbell's were growing interested as well. Said Campbll: "Randy Garrett, one of the authors, and a professional chemist, was the first professionally trained scientist to get good, solid results. Tom Scortia, another professional chemist, and another of the writers, also tried the machine, but got no results. Tom and Randy have been friends for some years; Randy suggested trying it together. So Randy tuned, and stroked the Plate, with Tom's fingers interlaced with his. This time Tom felt the tacky effect with his own fingers!

"Apparently, when a successful operator interlocks fingers with an unsuccessful one, the non-operator can feel the effect too.

"Thereafter, Tom could tune the machine quite accurately…but in a completely cockeyed manner! Still no tacky feeling – but he could tune to 45 on the nose, tuning entirely blindfolded, and did so five times running – by tuning to the point at which he felt absolutely sure the whole thing was impossible nonsense, that simply couldn't happen: The intensity of his doubt-feeling reached a sharp peak at precisely the correct setting!"

Resistance to Psionic Phenomena

Campbell pointed out in his correspondence that intuition is a natural, instinctive ability, the ability to abstract a general law from a collection of data. Logical thinking, however, was not an instinctive ability. It was something the individual had to learn and it imposes se-

  The Secret Art

vere limitations on intuitive thinking.

Wrote Campbell: "Once, Europe bred for a team type of human being; recently Europe has been breeding for a logical type human being – and that required the rigid suppression of psi-type thinking."

Campbell argued that logic, by its very nature, is communicable. We learn logically; we can't intuit for another, or show someone how to intuit. Differences between intuitive processes tend to break up teams. Logical communication allows them to stick together and work together.

"For the good of the race," wrote Campbell, "psi powers had to be suppressed until they could be made communicable. So long as psi is a purely individual thing, psi is an anarchic force, a culture-destroyer. When science was secret-science, it led to wars of conquest."

Campbell argued that the long history of the anti-psi mentality was founded on a longer history of psi forces being used to break up cultures. "Suppose you have a death-magic machine and you use it to murder a man in New York," he wrote. "Who can prove it? How can you be punished?" He asked Hieronymus how an organized group could exist, when there are individuals who cannot be organized and controlled by the group?

Campbell felt that if a person was immune to all external punishment he was absolutely free to do anything he wants, and naturally he would. If he has no power to punish some other individual, then he must also be deathly afraid of that individual.

One can begin to understand why aggressive legal action was being taken against people advocating studying and working with life energy. Dr. Wilhelm Reich, perhaps the leading exponent of subtle energy research and its importance to health, died in prison

after his books were publicly burned and his devices smashed.

Ruth Drowns' career and health were destroyed using similar tactics. The de la Warrs in England suffered a long, expensive litigation to defend their work. Many other researchers and practitioners have been branded quacks and their efforts crushed, as the history of alternative science readily demonstrates.

Wrote Campbell: "Psi is safe for the race only when psi powers are strongly coupled with ethical restraints. History indicates that they weren't – particularly during the Dark Ages. You don't get a tough, hard, driving race of people like the European tribes of the Dark Ages that scared, for that long, without something most bodaciously potent to be scared of. There were magicians, and they were unethical, and they raised as fine a demonstration of Hell on Earth as you could ask for.

"In the primitive tribes, the magician is controlled by Ritual and Taboo – which apply as strongly to him as to any other. But in the non-tribal culture, ritual and taboo are banished; then the magician is free to do anything he can."

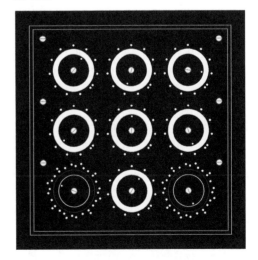

Fig 17-6. Butcher Upright Diagnostic Instrument

No doubt the emerging revelations in the 1950s of the occult origins of the Third Reich, illustrated with pictures of emaciated Jews hugging barbed wire fences in concentration camps, solidified this fear in the eyes of many.

Wrote Campbell: "My mother always knew she was a sweet, kind generous, gentle woman, who was constantly resisted by selfish and mean-tempered people. My mother was a brass-tailed hellion on wheels, as a matter of fact. I have the greatest suspicion of rosy-minded mystics who know that only good can come of it; my mother would have agreed so warmly, and so happily swung to the task of making her ideas go over via psionics. She was the type who wouldn't think of killing someone who she considered un-nice to her; she'd afflict him with assorted plagues until he admitted she had been right in the first place, and thanked her for making him see the error of his ways.

"The race has every reason to suspect that psionics is dangerous. It is. Torquemada tortured people only for the best of reasons; to save their souls for them.

"One reason Claude Shannon is so important: his Information Theory represents the first time in human history that a completely structured, logical demonstration of the existence of a non-physical reality has been achieved. Information is not physical, and Claude achieved a full, mathematically exact definition of it!"

On November 6, 1956, Hieronymus replied to Campbell: "I am quite interested in your friend Claude Shannon. He sounds like the type of physicist I have been looking for all the time I have been trying to find someone with guts enough to stand back of his convictions if shown something not in the book. I can see now that I have contacted only stuffed shirts."

The Military-Industrial Complex Takes Notice

On February 4, 1957, Campbell wrote to Hieronymus: "I've been very slow in replying on your article, because of some long, deep, and serious thinking about the problem of optimum presentation.

"Look at the results so far:

"1. Claude Shannon of M. I. T. is interested; that's a real load in.

"2. I got a call from a captain at the Sandia Base; that's the Special Weapons research base. (The home base for atomic bombers) The captain was calling to check with me whether the Army should set up a Psionics Research project at this time. He felt that it wasn't quite time – but that the Army should keep a very close eye on what the amateurs wore doing.

"3. The Rand Corporation – one of the top pure-research outfits in the country – sent a man to see me, and get what information I could give him on psionics. They want in.

"4. I was visited by the Director of Research for Bell Aircraft; he wanted to find out more about psionics. They want to keep track of it.

"5. *The American Weekly*, the Hearst papers' Sunday magazine, sent a couple of men around; they were planning an 'Out of This World' issue, with some clean fun spoofing the psionics business. Their science editor and a reporter came around to see me. Their science editor got his ears pinned back, because I could show him wide-open holes in science that he had never noticed – and then Ed Hermann swamped the pair of 'em with sheer data and facts. Their attitude was mighty different when they left. The fact that Sandia, Rand Corp., and Bell Aircraft were interested was not without effect.

"6. There are various modified versions of that mineral detector of yours being tested all over the world now. And there are positive reports coming in slowly. A man over in England, Eric Jones, built one working from the Astounding diagram and a copy of your patent. It worked fine.

"7. A group of top executives of the Esso Research Labs was out at the house; three of them were research department heads. All three of them got 100% solid results on the symbolic machine. And, being professional researchers, they really gave it the works.

"PS. I've been asked out to the Texaco Research Labs, in Beacon, New York, to give a talk and demonstration out there next month.

"In other words, this thing is, right now, growing like a snowball rolling down hill.

"That's never happened before – not at the level of professional, corporation-and-university scientists. Every earlier effort to put it over, from Sir William Crooks and D. D. Home, through Edgar Cayce, and Dr. Abrams, was soon smashed, with severe damage to the men who tried to put it over."

Ask for Advice; Don't Tell Them How It Works

Campbell then warned Hieronymus about an article he was writing. "Whatever you do," he warned, "don't give the reader facts. Cayce had facts. Abrams had facts. Sir William Crooks had facts. Galileo had facts, and for all that, he was damn near destroyed. Our success, so far, seems to me to be due to

our insisting that we don't have facts!"

"Rather we should present ourselves," Campbell suggested, "as bewildered, confused, uncertain, with no understanding of the thing whatever. Say we don't know what it is, and can't figure it out. The trouble with this article, is that you're telling them answers; why it works, and what the theory is; they want them to be their answers!"

Rejection by Big Medicine, but Claude Shannon Shows Interest

On May 15, 1957, Campbell wrote to Hieronymus: "First, Mr. Fowler has asked me to tell you what happened on the effort to interest the doctors at Memorial Hospital. As you expected, the answer is very decidedly no. I had expected that, of course; I've told you before this that I have a strong conviction that the opposition to psionic devices affecting life energies will, at this stage in the development of our civilization, meet the most vigorous, active opposition. It is not simply ignored; it's positively and actively suppressed.

"Let's put it this way: if all the very great power of the Catholic Church has not, in many decades of trying, and with hundreds of solidly documented case histories, attested to by highly qualified physicians, been able to induce the medical profession to acknowledge that miracle cures do happen at Lourdes…it seems sort of foolish for us to try to do what the Catholic Church can't accomplish!"

Three weeks before, Campbell was in Cambridge, Massachusetts, talking with Claude Shannon and Wayne Batteau, a close friend of Shannon's, and several other people about psionics. He had brought along the symbolic version of Hieronymus' mineral analyzer. None of the group then present was able to get repeatable results, but he presented a letter from Harry Stine, of the White Sands Proving Grounds research staff who had built the symbolic mineral analyzer from the published description. Stine had gotten very solid, repeatable, and useful results, as had Clyde Tombaugh, the astronomer best known for his discovery of the planet Pluto.

"Dr. Shannon is very decidedly interested in exploring these phenomena," wrote Campbell. "I've known Claude for some ten years, off and on. He's been an *Astounding* reader for many years. He's a man whose reputation is, in his field, as great as Einstein's was in his own field. Claude is not a formal-orthodox type of scientist; he's more of a Natural Philosopher. He's too big a man, and too competent, to be ruled by orthodoxy; orthodoxy is, instead, powerfully swayed by him. He is acutely interested in communication – any and all means of perceiving and conveying information.

"He genuinely wants a demonstration of your mineral analyzer. His statement was that if the real workability of the device can be demonstrated on a repeatable experiment basis, under sound test conditions, it represents an extremely important discovery, one which must be developed vigorously. He meant that, and means it in full honesty.

"Convince him that there in a real phenomenon present, and he will turn his very great talents to the task of making that phenomenon understandable in terms of modern science. Once science has been shown how to understand the phenomena of psionics – medicine will, as usual, tag along behind, proclaiming their wise leadership."

Campbell asked Hieronymus to make the trip up to Boston to work with Shannon at M.I.T. in demonstrating the mineral analyzer. He wanted *Astounding* magazine to publish a detailed report, describing the test conditions and test results, naming all the people who set up and carried out the test.

Thoughts and Emotions Use Eloptic Energy

Hieronymus continued to write about his tests and techniques, making it clear to Campbell that he was setting aside important, revenue producing business, not to say time and expenses, to throw himself at the mercy of the minds at MIT.

On May 19, 1957, Hieronymus wrote Campbell: "I just finished writing a letter to Eliot Pratt of New Milford, Conn., who is interested in the application of Eloptic energy to destroy insect pests. I have a commitment to finish some research started for Mr. Pratt. I expect to receive his O.K. to set it aside and take the trip to Boston.

"As you probably know, we have put on demonstrations several times with the same results. Even with complete 100% perfect results of the operation of the equipment, we have been pushed aside with the comment similar to that of the farmer who visited the city zoo and saw a giraffe for the first time. 'There ain't no such animal,' says the farmer."

In addition, Hieronymus also did not want tests run in public, with a number of people looking on who were "just skeptical" and not actually involved or necessary to the work to be performed.

On June 29, 1957, Hieronymus wrote Campbell: "It has been six weeks since I wrote you and I am at a loss to figure out what gives."

Finally on July 10, 1957, Campbell replied to Hieronymus: "The reason you haven't heard from me is that I haven't heard from Claude Shannon.

"It might also be that the question I raised, 'Define what is meant by "an adequate

138   *The Secret Art*

demonstration of a new principle'" has caused him to do some thinking and discussing that leaves him uncertain as to how to proceed. There's not much point in doing something unless you have some idea as to what you're doing, why you're doing it, and the meaning of what happens as a result of doing it."

On August 26, 1957, Campbell wrote Hieronymus: "I finally heard from Claude Shannon – and learned why there has been such a delay. He's been transferred from M.I.T. to the Institute for Advanced Study of Behavioral Problems, at Stanford, California, for a year. That's a major Ford Foundation set-up which has been inviting the top creative thinkers – not the highly publicized men – of science to help attack the major problem Man faces right now. The problems of psychology and sociology.

"For another year at least, Shannon is unavailable. It is suggested that a friend of Shannon's, Dr. Wayne Batteau of Harvard, might conduct the tests instead."

Campbell then added another detail to the difficulties he was encountering: "We're being stopped by the ancient 'Galileo Problem'; Constituted Authority 'knows' the idea is impossible, and 'knows' there is no point in dignifying such nonsense by 'looking through the telescope.' No amount of scientific data helps on that problem; the only force that will combat Constituted Authority is, of course, Authority. Wayne is a brilliant man, he's perhaps as competent as Claude…but at the moment, Claude is an Authority, while Wayne is simply wise and competent. (One doesn't need to be wise and competent, actually, to be an Authority. One needs only reputation, not wisdom.)"

Campbell promised to investigate remedies for the situation. He explained: "Claude is marvelously unaware of the fact that he is an Authority, and that his Authority is a real, important, and critical factor in the problem. So far as he sees it, he's just another one of the gang working on problems. He's quite sincere in holding that Wayne is fully as competent to do the job as he himself."

Meanwhile, another angle on the problem had also emerged: the American Medical Association (AMA). Much of the important data on psionics lies in the psycho-medical area. "The AMA has been solidly, powerfully, and effectively clamping down on it," wrote Campbell, "with all the very great and real weight of their Authority. As you well know."

Hieronymus: "We Found Life Energy on Venus and Saturn."

Just at this most critical juncture in Campbell's negotiations with scientists, Hieronymus dropped a bombshell.

At an unspecified date in 1957, Hieronymus wrote Campbell: "A long time ago, I discovered that one of the laws of behavior of Eloptic energy was that the energy would flow on light rays. The next stop was to photograph an object and find the energy from the object on the film. Several other experiments verified the fact that the energy could be picked up from light rays after having traveled quite some distance.

"We borrowed the films taken of some of the planets and found that we could analyze them. We did find that there was a showing of life energy on both Venus and Saturn but not on Jupiter. Back to Venus, it would seem that Venus has plant life in plenty and of an order very similar to that we have on this planet. I cannot believe that Venus has animals or human beings of the warm-blooded type as we have. There is no reason why there might not be men of a higher order than we have here.

Definitely, we are of the order just slightly above the lower animal.

"We tested the Venus rays for several of the common violent diseases found on earth. We found no cancer but did find tuberculosis; no gonorrhea or syphilis but did find one of the flu's and one of the undulant fever rates. Then we tested the plants and found that they also show several of the same diseases.

"This is just one analysis chart on Venus. Others made over a period of time might show different results. We are positive of the results obtained in each test. We have done too many over many years so we know when they are to be trusted and when there are other forces working that effect our results. Several individual tests were duplicated to be sure of the results."

So now, after all this time, Campbell had to risk watching Hieronymus completely discredit himself in front of the Boston scientific community by talking about discovering life on Saturn and Venus, using the very equipment he hoped them to scientifically validate.

On top of that, Hieronymus was balking about making the trip, now that Shannon was unavailable: "I do not want to spend time and money (either my own or someone else's) going to Boston or New York to run tests for someone to disregard. Naturally, I am quite disappointed in not having an opportunity to work with Dr. Shannon. However, if he recommends Dr. Wayne Batteau, I am sure that Dr. Batteau would be as interested as most anyone else and I believe that Dr. Shannon would believe anything that Dr. Batteau told him resulted from our tests. That would mean that Dr. Shannon would probably use his 'authority' in the matter later."

Ironically, Hieronymus appeared to have no clue about how his revelations about life on Venus must have seemed to Campbell. He even surmised that they would provide good material for his readers: "I can see where the planet analysis could fit into an [*Astounding* magazine] story and result in many future stories based on the results found. It would also knock a lot of former science fiction stories about the other planets and stars, into a cocked hat."

Frustrations were mounting in both men. On February 4, 1957, Campbell's letter mentioned that Hieronymus was no longer participating with General Gross in the UKACO research. No explanation was given. We sense Hieronymus was growing increasingly isolated. Campbell would not let go of the Eloptic Energy = Magic rhetoric. Claude Shannon, the real rainmaker for Hieronymus, departed for the West Coast without warning. Business prospects, killing insects for farmers, were being put on hold while testing by Harvard's Wayne Batteau was being negotiated.

Just as the thin thread connecting Hieronymus to Big Science was getting deeply frayed, Hieronymus announced that his patented technology had determined that life exists on Venus and Saturn from an analysis of recent NASA photographs. If that claim wasn't the kiss of death for radionics in the 1950s scientific community, what was?

The long and complex correspondence that took place between Campbell and Hieronymus is quite instructive. While Hieronymus was both a respected electrical engineer and radionics pioneer, his heart was more invested in folk medicine, helping the small farmer and in the study of esoteric teachings. From his perspective, trying to convince the AMA or Big Science that radionics was a viable technology must have seemed a long shot, yet, to his credit, he felt obligated to try.

When Campbell brought national attention to his patent, it was a rush of fresh air that would eventually turn into an ill wind. For a time, Hieronymus must have felt his work and life were finally vindicated. Campbell was more circumspect, constantly trying to caution Hieronymus as to the subtleties of the PR game he must play and all the cultural pitfalls. From Hieronymus' perspective, his reticence may have seemed a bit condescending. He had been in the trenches since his late teens, watching people getting healed by these "unscientific" devices. He was the one who first placed radionics on a viable commercial platform by obtaining a U.S. Patent. The ideological tension between the two men, in spite of the immense good will on both sides, must have grown extreme. There is something to learn from all this, especially for the artist interested in working with radionic tools today.

In a sense, Hieronymus was like a visionary artist, not exactly a primitive, but in a different spirit than the purely professional individual who knows the business of art and the right career moves. Hieronymus navigated a world split between the rigors of scientific materialism and the intercession of higher forces upon daily life. In the end, it was the artist in Hieronymus seeking freedom from theoretical and political constraint who won out, wanting only to practice and develop his technology and see it prevail over the need for approval from institutional authority. At least, that is what is indicated from their correspondence.

Hieronymus appears somewhat naive to the whirlwind of cultural and political forces unleashed by Campbell's publicity. It is certainly a tragic component to the story. Even more so considering the fact that many distinguished scientists had actually obtained results using his device and could have possibly been persuaded to investigate the technology further, had someone of Claude Shannon's caliber spearheaded the campaign. Without him, and with Hieronymus claiming his experiments had demonstrated that life forms exist on inhospitable planets, radionics became a professional embarrassment.

In retrospect, the derailment of promising subtle energy research seems tragic. It appears that in this era before the internet could instantaneously link research efforts, scientists from around the world were making serious efforts to tackle similar issues.

In 1977, John White and Stanley Krippner published a collection of brilliant essays that illustrated the scientific efforts being made to understand life energy entitled, *Future Science: Life Energies and the Physics of Paranormal Phenomena*. Perhaps it was not the first book to do so, but it did reflect growing worldwide interest in making parapsychology a serious part of scientific discussion during the late part of Hieronymus' life.

In many ways, the articles in *Future Science* collaborate the difficulty encountered by Campbell and Hieronymus in understanding phenomena that act like measurable quanta on one hand and purely aspects of consciousness on the other.

On May 19, 1957, Hieronymus told Campbell: "You will agree with me that a thought and an emotion are not the same thing. I have found that they are activities that employ the same energy but in a different way, just as a beam of visible light is not the same as a radio wave to the average observer, even though a physicist might classify them both as 'the same thing.' Where you and I differ on one thing is that you lump all as 'Psionic,' regardless, and I separate into groups, depending upon the special characteristics displayed.

"The Eloptic energy that radiates from a pure element, such as silver, is not to be effected as easily as the Eloptic energy involved in the nervous reactions of a human being, even though they are both related. You can direct a 'beam' of Eloptic energy to a human being and cause a change in their actions or reactions. With many people, this effect can be felt immediately, while with others, it is not felt at all.

"We have been able to direct the Eloptic energy from a drug into a human being and produce the same results as if we had administered the drug. You cannot direct such a radiation to a pure metal and cause a change in the structure of that metal.

"There are many things we have discovered about the behavior of Eloptic energy. We are firmly convinced that thoughts and emotions are using Eloptic energy. We know that every element that makes up our material world radiates Eloptic energy. What binds two elements in a chemical compound? We have untied the binding in many cases by manipulation of Eloptic energy. Might they be similar?"

Campbell replied: "I can give you an exact term for your status; nobody can be a true 'professional' in a field that's still as indefinite as psionics now is; neither is it proper to make no distinction between a man who has just started diddling in the field, and someone who's spent many years working at it. There's a perfectly good term, however, and it applies; you're neither a professional, nor an amateur – you're an artist. An artist is a professional, highly skilled worker in a field that has not yet been reduced to a formulateable, definable system. Such work is known as an Art."

If Hieronymus was making art, then maybe artists should be exploring and using radionics.

CHAPTER 18
AGRICULTURAL RADIONICS TODAY

Fortunately, agricultural radionics still exists in our world in many guises and forms, especially simple ones, like having a green thumb. A number of technical approaches remain available as well, one of which will be examined here. But first, an impartial review of what is meant by "agricultural radionics" appeared in 1997 in an article posted on the internet entitled "Radionics In Agriculture" by Steve Diver and George Kuepper. The article was written as a Current Topics publication for the ATTRA (Appropriate Technology Transfer for Rural Areas) Project. ATTRA, funded by the USDA, disseminates information on sustainable agriculture.

The authors begin by stating that radionics usage for plant and animal diagnosis and treatment is receiving some attention in alternative agriculture circles, but little information about it is available through conventional channels, such as the Extension Service or land grant colleges. They believe that this is due in part to the fact that, in America, ra-

dionics is primarily what they term a "practitioner-based technology," meaning that it is under the regulatory radar, whereas in Great Britain and parts of Europe, it is a licensed medical discipline.

The objective of their analysis is "neither to persuade nor dissuade the reader regarding the validity of radionics. The purpose, rather, is to shed light on a poorly understood practice that is being adopted by a growing number of people within sustainable agriculture."

The authors then set forth the basic facts of Radionic Agriculture today: "Radionics is controversial because it is a metaphysical science. It is not recognized by mainstream agricultural science; thus, useful information is available only from select sources. Even within the alternative (sustainable, organic) agricultural communities, there is disagreement regarding its utility and validity. Yet, there are many reports of success among those who have given radionics a serious look; and the number of practitioners— farmers, gardeners, crop consultants, veterinarians— appears to be growing."

The authors then summarize their interpretation of the basic assumptions of radionics: (1) Subtle energy fields exist at a sub-atomic level. (2) They can be accessed by communication with cellular DNA and can be detected by the human nervous system via the dowsing reflex or stick and through a galvanometer attached to the skin. (3) Radionic instruments essentially help in facilitating and discriminating among the energy fields used in diagnosis and treatment. (4) Quantum physics research, while not a proof of radionics functioning, supports its theory and application to some extent. That said, Diver and Kuepper break down agricultural radionics into three parts: analysis, evaluation of materials, and vitalization.

Analysis: As with human radionics, the initial effort is made to identify imbalances in the subtle fields around the subject. By successfully employing such an analysis, the farmer may identify a potential problem before it physically manifests. This approach can save money and time as well as have favorable environmental consequences. Sprays or nutrients can be applied selectively, or replaced with radionic treatment; veterinarian bills can be reduced and farm resources conserved.

Diver and Kuepper offer two examples: (1) "An orchardist monitors her trees radionically to find evidence of fungal diseases. Because she does not detect any disease problems until midway through the season, early sprays are not applied. This saves money and reduces impact on the environment." (2) "A horse breeder has a valuable animal with health problems, and the usual spectrum of testing reveals nothing. Radionic analysis suggests that the problem is a relatively rare amoebic

infection. A specific conventional test confirms this and the proper treatment is given."

Evaluation of Materials: This category of agricultural radionics applies to the consequences of having a reliable means of testing feed, soil, fertilizer, or nutrient and other aspects of farming. To farmers sensitive to subtle energy fields, testing for the suitability of various products for their farm can be important. The subsequent impact of the materials can be measured by establishing a baseline and then radionically measuring the impact of the materials on what is being treated. Inappropriate usage and amounts can be identified early and appropriate remedies taken. Similar methodologies can be devised for insects, weeds, and pests, of which there are numerous theories and applications.

Vitalization: Older methods of vitalizing fields and crops focused on the elimination of pests. Technology borrowed from radio broadcasting technology were said to transmit reagents to the soil or crop to destroy pests or eliminate parasites. Newer approaches to agricultural radionics do not focus as much on getting rid of pests as on building up the strength of the seeds, soil, and plants. The methods emphasize constructive balancing and nurturing, which strengthen the crops against predators and disease.

The introduction of pollution and chemicals from the atmosphere and water has stressed the environment and can be hard to rectify using ordinary means. Radionic treatment today is employed systematically to balance all aspects of the farm's ecology. To this end, potentized preparations made with radionics equipment can be sprayed, drenched, or injected into the feed, soil, crop, or animal to address specific needs.

Diver and Kuepper offer two examples:

(1) "A farmer with a sandy-loam soil determines, through radionics analysis, that an expensive humic acid product would help to build soil humus levels, as would the Biodynamic preparation #500. To encourage natural humus, specimens of humic acid and BD 500 are inserted into a Hieronymus tower that has been installed on the farm. (2) A race horse, suffering from lung bleeding, will be disqualified from competing if treated with the appropriate drug. A veterinarian, skilled in radionics, prepares a water-based potency of the drug, and effectively treats the horse without generating side-effects, or incurring disqualification."

The authors discuss various methods for implementing radionic agriculture, many of which are discussed elsewhere in this text. Printed guides are available from some manufacturers for those unable to attend workshops. Crossing inventions and their methodologies are not recommended.

"Radionics can be learned successfully by most individuals," say Diver and Kuepper. "Instructors and researchers estimate that better than 90% of the population possesses the intuitive ability required. Those suffering nervous system disorders or injury; on some forms of medication; or those having drug and/or alcohol problems, may be unable to do radionic work, however. Furthermore, due to the subtle nature of the fields being evaluated, the highly skeptical or hostile individual will also have difficulty getting things to work properly."

Costs can vary widely for the instruments as can the competence of the instructors, consultants, and sponsoring organizations. There are no objective guidelines to help an individual with such a selection. Most radionic practitioners do favor the sustainable approach to farming. Various organizations such as The United States Psychotronic Association (USPA) and the Radionic Association of the UK can offer valuable information and training. It is a testimony to the lasting effects of pioneers like Curtis Upton that these techniques have continued to flourish and expand throughout the world in spite of official condemnation.

We will turn our attention now to the case of Little Farm Research, a Utah homestead that has been successfully using and promoting radionics in all aspects of rural family life. Lutie Larsen of Little Farm Research is a radiant grandmother, radionics pioneer, and one of the best educators in radionics alive today. From her homestead in Utah, Larsen

Fig 18-1. Little Farm Research

approaches radionics in a family-oriented way, treating her garden, her animals, her family, and her spirit with equal dexterity. In each case, radionics has proved to be a creative, efficient way of managing the many challenges of day-to-day life on a homestead. Her simple "down to earth" approach is what makes her methods so attractive and effective in a cultural environment that still remains quite hostile to radionics.

In 1999, Larsen received a diploma from the Keys College of Radionics, Oxford, England in Radionic Agriculture and Horticulture. Many would say that by the time she received her diploma she was already in a class of her own. Since 1974, Larsen has studied and developed radionics in such a way as to make it familiar, comprehensible, and eminently natural, without losing any of its magic and wonder. Finding herself in the position to help others, she began teaching radionic theory and application in 1983.

Today, Larsen and her daughter call their operation in Utah, Little Farm Research. She is also a partner in Wise Woman Ventures, a company that supports and consults with women in business. Recently she disclosed that for many years, she was a consultant with cosmetics giant Estee Lauder. Larsen is the mother of 10 and grandmother of 14 children.

Larsen's model demonstrates how radionics can benefit normal day-to-day life. Using radionics appropriately can free us of many false assumptions, services, and products we have grown accustomed to and dependent upon in our lives. In her system, radionics becomes much more of a philosophy of applied balance, more a technical Taoism, than a type of occult technology. As much as a radionics device utilizes the mind of the operator to work, so does the reverse become true.

Through radionics, the mind of the operator is brought to bear on the critical details of daily life, addressing each with love and patience and care. In Larsen's hands, radionics becomes more a metaphysical approach to life than a tool or technique.

As a result, one learns that attention is not to be wasted. We can constantly reinforce meaning in our lives through directed attention, instead of dissipating it. Radionics may not be a cure for every problem, but in the world of Little Farm Research, it goes a long way.

The radionic device of choice for her work is the computerized SE-5, which is described later on in this book. More important is how she approaches the use of the instrument. Insights into that process can be found in a January 2001 interview with Lutie Larsen by Marie Allizon, entitled "Lutie Tests MZ Alchemist Oils," from which an excerpt follows.

When asked to define subtle energy, Larson replied: "We all have a sense of the meaning of subtle - in the background, less obvious, more yin-like - but I think we misunderstand the meaning of energy in this context. Most of us think of energy as force like the motor of a car starting and moving, or the energy activated by turning a switch. I would like to define subtle energy in a different way. I feel that subtle energy is more information than force, or perhaps it could be called intelligent energy/force. The subtle energy fields were called Formative Force Fields by Rudolf Steiner and George de la Warr spoke of the 'Formative Rays' coming from the 'Counterpart body.'

"The great physicist David Bohm once gave an illustration of Quantum Potential by describing a huge airplane flying on autopilot and having a computer on the earth radio a correction in course to the airplane's computer. That radio wave carried information that changed the course of the airplane. It did demonstrate force but from information not physical force.

"Subtle energy is like that and the subtle energy we use in healing and strengthening the physical form, I believe is more information than force. Coherent subtle energy activates manifestation. It is truly a formative or creative force in a subtle way. Every physical form has a subtle field -a complex informational pattern. And the physical form and the subtle pattern are inherently linked.

"This is David Bohm's 'Implicate Order' linked with the tangible, physical 'Explicate Order.' Once we understand that this subtle information is the manifesting pattern or formative force we can begin to understand the importance of supporting health and well-being. Our focus will change from what is wrong and placing all our attention on disease, disharmony to what is right, coherent, harmonious and synergistic. We will start building, supporting instead of trying to fix by tearing down."

Of interest to artists studying radionics are Larsen's Radionic Balancing Cards. These colorful, two inch square, computer generated images describe various color washes with superimposed geometric forms, such as cones, also of the same color and texture floating within the image. In fact, the cards could very well be considered miniature paintings. They not only provide aesthetic pleasure, but also function as radionics rates, much as the Rae cards do.

Later in the interview, which was primarily devoted to Larsen's testing of an "Alchemical Oil" product by using the Radionic Balancing Cards, she provides additional in-

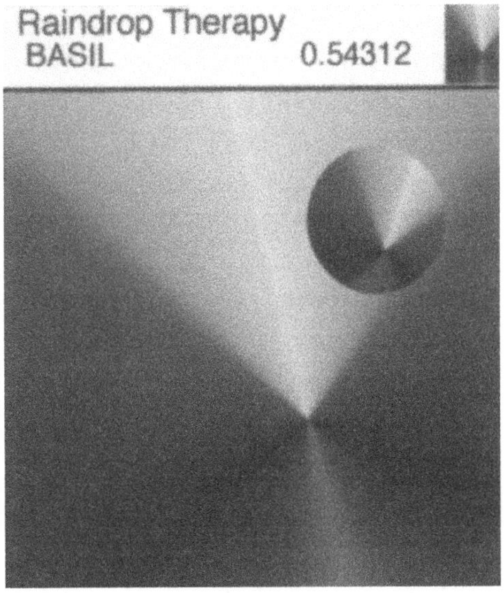

Fig 18-2. Lutie Larsen Meridian Raindrop Therapy

sights into her approach to radionics: "The individual oils are all (no matter who prepares them) identifiable by an inherent archetypal pattern. You know this. Radionic 'identification rates' link with these archetypal patterns. If the setting is right on, the linking perfect, then we can use the information in many ways. We can broadcast the pattern. We can im-print it into water or another structured base. (These bases act as carriers of the subtle pattern.) And interestingly enough the physical form is very responsive to the archetypal energy even at a distance!"

Larsen goes on to explain her methodology and its basis in the work of George and Marjorie de la Warr, and what she teaches people to do with radionics: "In my study of the de la Warr system of radionics and particularly studying their experiments that led to the development and use of the de la Warr Camera, I came to appreciate the difference between establishing a link with the manifesting patterns of a life form, the identifying or recognition Rates, and linking with condition or action of that form in its physical [manifestation]. The de la Warrs used these 'condition rates' to identify many disease conditions. They were able to demonstrate them with 'pictures'. Those pictures got them into a lot of trouble because they could identify a specific condition by linking with the information of that condition and they could do it at a distance. The Camera's exposed 'picture' would confirm (to the affirmative or negate) the presence of that condition pattern...

"At the time I was developing rates in the de la Warr format for horticulture and agriculture. There were a number of links I wanted to create and wasn't sure which type of setting would be most appropriate or useful. One of these I remember was 'tilth.' Now tilth is the structure of the soil, a good blend between sand, clay and silt. So I needed an identification setting, a recognition rate for tilth. But tilth is also the 'health' of the soil, a condition. I needed a linking setting for that subtle pattern. Another thing about radionic patterns is that they can be 'resonated.' In Radionics we call this 'treatment' or 'broadcasting the rate.' It is the way we use these settings (aside from using them to monitor). It is a lot like tuning. Just like an orchestra takes time to tune itself before a concert."

Some areas of research being conducted a Little Farm Research, include:

"Measurement of positive subtle energy fields associated with living systems and a comparison of them with normal healthy fields.

"Measurements of negative or pathogen-toxin subtle energy associated with unhealthy or otherwise distorted living systems.

"Experiments to balance and utilize subtle energy fields.

"Experiments using potentized vibrational or homeopathic-type preparations.

"Experiments to measure and compare the energy compatibility between a substance and a life form.

"Experiments to develop consciousness."

In regards to consciousness, Larsen has this to say: "Much knowledge from the golden era of the past is being restored. The ability to tap into natural law and to understand the principles that govern the physical world is taught through working with the subtle body fields. For us this is the greatest gift of radionics, that unique, utterly amazing view of our whole being and the 'beings' we interact with daily on this marvelous earth plane."

    The Secret Art

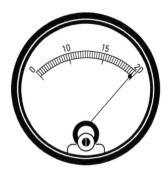

CHAPTER 19
RADIONIC PHOTOGRAPHY TODAY

In an interesting twist, just as radionics was becoming comfortable with itself as a true occult technology, new scientific information concerning the de la Warr radionic photographs became available.

For all intents and purposes, this change begins with a paper by a Ph.D. and RN named M. Sue Benford, entitled "Empirical Evidence Supporting Macro-Scale Quantum Holography in Non-Local Effects" and published in a 1999/2000 issue of the *Journal of Theoretics, Inc.* In this paper, Benford describes her discovery of "a spatially-encoded three-dimensional (3D) effect similar to those possible via Magnetic Resonance Imaging," on the surface of the original de la Warr glass plate radionics images.

Benford then suggests that this holographic component of the photos is an indication of a macro (i.e. in our world) quantum effect. (Quantum effects are presumed only to occur at infinitesimally small, "quantum" levels and not at our level of reality.) This life sized quantum effect of the de la Warr camera also presupposes a quantum "action at a distance" (non-local) effect that is reminiscent of psi and pk events. Furthermore, Benford believes that the ability of a radionic "witness" (such as a drop of blood) to represent the organism in producing a photograph or a treatment can be explained holographically.

A holograph is essentially a three-dimensional light picture. One intriguing feature of a holograph is the property called "distributedness." Benford believes this property helps explain the "witness" phenomena. "Distributedness" means that any fraction of a hologram contains enough information about the whole hologram to reconstruct it in its entire three-dimensional form, albeit with less detail, according to the size of the fragment. By analogy, a hair or blood sample could therefore contain a holograph of the biophysical radiation of the host.

Benford cites research at the Russian Academy of Sciences supporting the existence of this mysterious biophysical radiation. She points out in the Russian papers that this radiation is linked to physical DNA. In her words, the radiation "may support the hypothesis of an intact energy field containing relevant organism information that is capable of being coupled to an optical imaging device," and by implication, other electromagnetic fields.

To support her thesis, Benford quotes the 1999 paper, "Nature's Mind: The Quantum Hologram," by noted astronaut and astrophysicist Edgar Mitchell: "The percipient and the source of information are in a resonant relationship for the information to be accurately perceived...[The] discovery of the non-local quantum hologram created by the absorption/remission phenomenon and characteristic of all physical objects provides the first quantum physical mechanism compatible with macro-scale three dimensional world as we see it...Non-locality and the non-local quantum hologram provide the only testable mechanism discovered to date which offer a possible solution to the host of enigmatic observations and data associated with consciousness and such consciousness phenomena. Schempp (1992) has successfully validated the concept of recovery and utilization of non-local quantum information in the case of functional Magnetic Resonance Imaging (MRI) using quantum holography. Marcer (1995) has made compelling arguments that a number of other chemical and electromagnetic processes in common uses have a deeper quantum explanation that is not revealed by the classical interpretation of these processes. Hammeroff (1994) and Penrose (1991) have presented experimental data on microtubules in the brain supporting quantum processes."

The keystone of Benford's thesis, which combines DNA, holograms, and non-local quantum connectedness at macro levels (read that as psi), is her discovery of the 3D nature of the de la Warr images. Using the VP-8 Analyzer (analog) and the Bryce4 Software (digital) she is able to convert the image density of the original plates into a vertical relief. This does not occur when using it on a normal photograph or even on an X-ray.

The de la Warr images by contrast yield "very accurate and well-formed three dimensional reliefs...Full rotation around the organ and/or object is possible with the digital computer software, thus permitting significantly enhanced medical assessments." Upon closer comparison with the original images, Benford was surprised to discover that the 3-D representation contained information that wasn't even on the original pictures.

De la Warr and his associates believed that their images contained a holographic element. However, the VP-8 technology needed to decode spatial information in 2-D images wasn't developed until 1976; twenty years after de la Warr published his first pictures. Another twenty-three years would go by before Benford used her tools to demonstrate it.

What remained to be addressed in her evolving theory was the issue of operation. How did this quantum photography work?

Benford's theory gets into the knotty issues of how a holographic pattern is frozen in space-time, particularly the relationship between the two optical waves that combine to make the image appear, called the "interference pattern." These two waves are called the "optical" wave and the "reference" wave. How they affect each other, the relation between intensity and phase-shifts that occurs when they cross, is what freezes the holograph in space and time in the air. Normal photographs record only the intensity changes in the optical wave. It is the phase shifts of the optical wave in relation to the reference wave that produces the added dimensionality to the image.

It will be remembered that its inventors have described radionics as "pattern manipulation" at very basic levels, often involving light-like "eloptic" energy. In Benford's theory, the reference wave originates from the "directed intention," the now familiar radionics mode of action. The camera operator puts that directed intention "in circuit" with the object wave (i.e. the object being photographed). This transaction completes the necessary requirements of creating a radionic holographic image on a 2-D surface (the photographic emulsion, which is otherwise completely normal).

To substantiate her theory, Benford references papers on quantum non-locality first proposed by Einstein, Podolsky, and Rosen in the 1930s, which hearken back to the very roots of quantum mechanical "entanglement," as well as the 1993 proposal by IBM physicist Charles H. Bennett and others on quantum teleportation.

According to Benford, quantum teleportation means that the "Photon quantum informational characteristics can be transmitted instantaneously between two laboratories independent of space-time." In 1997, according to her paper, two independent groups successfully demonstrated quantum teleportation. This experiment is creatively used to support her theory that recognizes a quantum hologram as "a macro-scale, non-local information structure (that) extends quantum mechanics to all physical objects including DNA molecules, organic cells, organs, brains, and bodies…"

Benford's work calls for a paradigm shift in thinking. She also enhances our knowledge of radionic functioning by stating: "The intention required by the operator of the de la Warr system to extract usable information from a quantum hologram forces us to conclude that evolved consciousness is antecedent in producing measurable non-local causal events."

The rigor of Bedford's thesis will not be debated here. It is enough that we compliment her for the courage to approach the rancorous topic of radionic photography from an open-minded and novel direction. In so doing, she stimulated a resurgence of scientific interest in radionic phenomena. Shortly following the release of this paper, Benford joined forces with Edgar Mitchell (of the Institute of Noetic Science [IONS]), Peter Marcer (of the British Computer Society Cybernetic Machine Specialist Group), and Peter Moscow (President of the United States Psychotronic Association). They produced a paper for the Fifth International Conference on Computing Anticipatory Systems, Liege, Belgium, 2001, entitled "QuantaGraphy: Images From the Quantum Hologram."

The expanded thesis took a much harder look at the de la Warr photographs and their implications for quantum theory and holography. Initially, the decision was taken to carefully examine the original de la Warr plates to determine their chemistry and composition. The Ohio State University Microscopic and Chemical Analysis Research Center (MARC Lab) undertook this work in April 2000. This investigation sought to determine whether pigment had been added to the glass plate and concluded that it had not, refuting earlier charges of tampering.

The analysis also included using a scanning electron microscope (SEM) to determine the chemical composition of the glass plate itself. The same SEM was then used to examine the image chemicals on the plate,

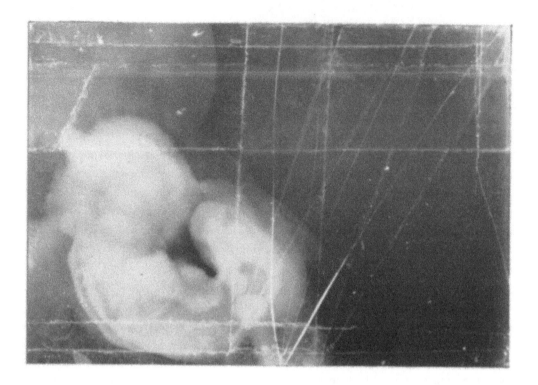

Fig 19-1. 3 months' pregnancy photograph taken with de la Warr Mark I Camera

which were the standard silver-based photo emulsions that de la Warr had described using. In short, there was nothing irregular regarding the actual glass plates themselves. The MARC Lab concluded that the 3-D images present on the plates were probably the result of a "high energy radiation" that eluded their analysis.

Additional analysis by the group of the 3-D component resulted in a return to an earlier hypothesis. This hypothesis concluded that the image was in fact similar to the layering of single slices of the image accomplished by Magnetic Resonance Imaging (MRI) techniques. In June of 2000, MRI expert, Philip Morse, a professor of chemistry at Illinois State University, undertook a blinded evaluation of the original de la Warr images.

The report states: "In attempting to ex-

plain the de la Warr images in terms of the principles of MRI, Morse used the cow's stomach image. He commented, 'The object is one dimension (wire), so bends will be reflected in the intensity differences depending on the amount of other material surrounding it. The 2-D image actually encodes the spatial distribution of the object because it is only one-dimensional in the first place, so position (location in the stomach) could be encoded by intensity…I'd need to see your (computer) code to figure out what you are doing. I don't see any need at the moment to postulate anything other than graphical manipulation (in the most positive sense) to generate the images you produced. However, if you are using some other method to obtain the image, then…THAT is interesting!'"

Morse believed that he was evaluating

152   *The Secret Art*

computer-generated MRI-related renderings. He was very impressed with the 3-D nature of the images, considering them even superior to ordinary MRIs, which rely on multiple images from different angles and a complex reconstruction algorithm to achieve similar dimensionality.

In their summary of the functioning of the camera system, Mitchell, Marcer, and Moscow stated: "The camera system consists of a trained operator, a receptacle for the test object, a control panel to adjust and 'tune' the system, and a light tight compartment for the photographic plate…The need is, however, is to explain the most remarkable aspects of QuantaGraphs® experimentally demonstrated by DelaWarr [i.e. de la Warr] in his creation of unique reproducible images for simple minerals, tissue, organs and organisms as already described above. The evidence presented above strongly suggests, in our view, clear parallels with the quantum holographic operation of MRI, which concerns the nonlocal quantum coherent holographic properties of matter [Binz, Schempp 2000a; 2000b] not formalized in quantum theory until the present period. DelaWarr's work would then presage and support the later discovery:

"(a) that there exists in nature a nonlocal quantum holographic representation of macro-scale objects.

"(b) that each substance possesses its own unique and distinguishable characteristics,.

"(c) that spatially encoded holographic information can be 'recorded' as in the case of the QuantaGraphs®, on a photographic emulsion, or indeed, as evidenced from the medical work of Abrams, on physical or biological objects, and

"(d) that, as with MRI, the precondition for production of a 2-D brain/body slice im-

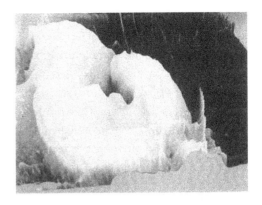

Fig 19-2. de la Warr 3 month's pregnancy photograph enhanced with Bryce 3D software

age, or as in Magnetic resonance microscopy a 3-D one, is one of phase-conjugate-adaptive-resonance [Schempp1992]. That is, to say, both in the Radionics of Abrams, and of DelaWarr, the brain/mind (of the physician or respectively that of the camera operator) is able 'recognize' the point of resonance, which signifies the desired spectral signature, or image being sought, which corresponds to a quantum gauge condition. That is, the physician's or operator's brain/mind and sensory apparatii act as quantum holographic transducers [Schempp 1992; Marcer, Schempp 1996; Marcer, Mitchell 2000] in order to perform what is, in effect, a quantum holographic measurement. Noting that such quantum holographic measurements may indeed apply to any kind of physical field, electromagnetic, acoustic, etc; such as, in the case of Abrams, the acoustic and tactile percussing of the stomach of his patient."

The authors also revisited the issue of quantum non-locality, teleportation, and entanglement, drawing observations from the work of Bohr, Bohm, Pribram, Aspect, Dubois, Schempp, and Wilson to strengthen their theoretical assumptions. They conclude the de la Warr camera seems to employ both quantum and conventional means in its operation. When information from the object being radionically photographed is transferred to the photographic plate, the authors assert that a quantum potential is evoked that cannot be explained by ordinary means. Therefore, classical, repeatable measurement paradigms fail to account for the quantum processes employed in the camera's operation.

In addition, the puzzling necessity to achieve the proper orientation or rotation of the subject to the Earth's magnetic field described by various radionics inventors emerges in the holographic research. Their hypothesis (which occurs in full accord with Schempp's quantum holographic, mathematical foundations of MRI, describing the production of 2-D and 3D imagery) demonstrates that quantum holograms require a definite orientation, both to be detectable and to be decodable. This fact, they point out, is highly relevant to both the diagnostic percussive observations of Abrams, and to those of de la Warr, regarding the orientation of the subject to a specific magnetic direction.

In conclusion, the authors say that based upon the evidence they have in their possession, the potential benefits to medical science of radionics and radionics photography are significant enough to warrant a full scientific investigation. Without detailing here the complexities of the holographic component of the theory and the means for defining and measuring "intentionality," they conclude: "To posit a full theory of operation of the system, a number of questions must be fully examined: 1) What is the relationship between the test object and the subject? 2) How does the test object carry and transfer the complete information of the subject? 3) How is this information optically obtained by the de

la Warr system? The proposed theory is that the test object is a specimen from the subject that emits a complete quantum hologram, representative of the subject for the condition tested, and that such hologram represents quantum entanglement/coherence with the subject. That the quantum hologram can be caused to affect the optical part of this system through mediation of the operator's focused intention; such mediation creating resonance, entanglement/coherence of the entire system, and, under the right conditions, produce a holographic-like image."

Radionic photography, in its initial analog manifestation, did not appear to be overly technical. Many of the photographs still in existence from Ruth Drown's era did not even require an electrical apparatus to work. De la Warr's work is particularly well documented and his camera(s) are still in storage or being studied.

The biggest obstacle to a recreation of de la Warr's work remains our scientific belief system. Scientists find it impossible to believe that techniques like radionic photography actually work. Scientism has been very successful at suppressing research of this kind, as the history of radionics demonstrates. We hope these discoveries will re-emerge in an artistic platform, in a manner capable of being repeated in other studios. Under those circumstances, unprejudiced researchers might then step forward to scientifically examine the evidence, and radionic photography could then advance to the next level.

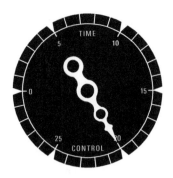

Chapter 20
FROM COMPUTERIZED RADIONICS TO RADIONICS WITHOUT DEVICES

Radionics, both in theory and practice, changed dramatically in the digital age. More than ever before, the computer brought home the notion that Information becomes Energy (I > E) once it enters the brain and nervous system. Within a few decades, the whole civilized world was using computers like radionics devices, electronically moving information around the world, translating it back into energy at any point of action.

A few modern radionics inventors were quick to respond to this irony. They designed radionics devices using computer processors and theory in an attempt to re-cast radionics in a fresh and positive new light. In one brilliant stroke, much of the voodoo and mystery surrounding "Black Box" technology was rendered irrelevant. As people picked up their PCs and Macs and began to work, create, and play in a new virtual reality would radionics become re-interpreted as cybernetics? One thing was certain: it no longer seemed implausible that individuals directing their intent into a box of electronic circuitry could summon magic into their lives.

No one can blame radionics inventors today for distancing themselves from past controversy. Information science encouraged a far broader approach to the integration of neurology, semiotics, data processing, electronics, and many other fields of study than ever before, bringing us what is now known as "cognitive neuroscience." The widespread use of mind-altering drugs by each new generation, the growing public fascination with mystical and shamanistic studies, and the rapid development of the World Wide Web brought a profound open-mindedness to millions if not billions of curious ordinary people. Instinctively, as if in response to these developments, radionics began to morph into a more socially conscious discipline. The new devices addressed ecological concerns. They challenged New Age idealists to demonstrate proofs and employ scientific protocol. They put agricultural radionics back into full view on the home and farm.

An organization called the Leadership Alliance gives us some insight into this process, through an article by its founder, Matthew Cross, and Franz Lutz, at that time director of the Institute of Resonant Therapy. They wrote: "Various European governments and landowners report that forests that were once dying are now being miraculously rejuvenated. Farmers report measurable increases in crop yields and livestock reproduction. People visiting and living on treated land areas experience enhanced wellbeing and a greater sense of community. What is going on here?

"The answer is a remarkable method for conscious restoration and rejuvenation of ecosystems, people and the planet: Resonance Therapy. This new science, which at first sounds like something from a science fiction novel, defies 'modern' scientific paradigms. Yet the results from Europe's Institute for Resonance Therapy (IRT) near Düsseldorf, Germany are attracting increasing international attention from many agriculturists, environmentalists, therapists, scientists and governments.

"IRT has now been using its unique energetic principles to revitalize dying ecosystems for ten years. Recognized by the Gorbachev Foundation and the European Economic Community (EEC) Environmental and Agricultural Department, IRT has been involved in revitalizing reserves in Russia, restoring parkland in Austria, and treating depleted farmland in England. Resonance Therapy has also demonstrated positive results for treating people as well."

The SE-5 Intrinsic Data Field Analyzer

Critical to the success of the IRT projects was the selection of a newly designed computerized radionic device, the SE-5. Physicist, electro-engineer and inventor Willard Frank created the SE-5 in 1986. In 1998 it was updated and called the SE-5 Plus. The SE-5 was not originally labeled a Radionics instrument. It was designed as a spectrometer to analyze the energies emitted by mineral samples. The SE-5's use as an experimental research device increased dramatically with those who accepted the fact that subtle information fields surround living systems. Soon, the SE-5 was used for analyzing and balancing these fields, which the inventor calls Intrinsic Data Fields (IDF).

It was also described as a tool that can expand and amplify the senses, with the purpose of establishing a communication link with subtle energy, termed the bio-field. The idea was to apply the instrument to locate imbalances or obstacles to the flow of energy in the body and change or remove the negative influence. To this end, the SE-5 transmits IDF wave patterns to the subject under treatment. The SE-5 Plus was computerized for rapid processing of information. With its increased memory capability, it was able to detect, quantify, and transmit a full spectrum of IDF signals. Because it did not operate directly on the physical level, the SE-5 Plus was able to restore to normal the waveforms of the bio-field. It functioned, according to the inventor, as a receiver, transmitter, and modulator of information found in the subatomic, magnetic, and gravitational energy fields that precede the manifestation of matter in its elemental atomic and molecular forms.

Today many radionics practitioners have accepted the concept of Intrinsic Data Fields, as a new, informational way of viewing radionics. Perhaps this shift from the language of energy to the language of information helps to circumvent the legal quagmire surround-

The Secret Art

ing classical radionics; it certainly helps justify the $3,000 plus price tag (which includes the IDF32 Windows software). Whatever the reason, the environmentalists at the IRT were attracted to the versatility of the SE-5 Plus.

Environmental Recertification

One source of information on the IRT methodologies is Don Paris, who stated: "Their primary area of experimentation has been in the area of restoring forests in Germany and surrounding countries. They have done many double-blind studies that show the beneficial effect of the SE-5. When they first began, they were using radionics equipment of almost every type and design. In 1987, ProNova Energetiks, a company that is representing the SE-5 Plus in Germany, demonstrated the instrument for them. After a demonstration of the SE-5, someone commented, 'You are driving Cadillacs, and we are driving around in old Model Ts.' They promptly put their radionics instruments into the closet and purchased seven SE-5s. They realized the differences between Radionics, and the superiority of the SE-5. They now use 14 SE-5s in their work."

By increasing the vitality of the forests through deliberate augmentation, the IRT treatments assist the forests to adapt to new circumstances. This process, called "Resonance Therapy," introduces a new "organizing field" into the ecology of a forest, which reinforces the system to accommodate new environmental challenges.

George de la Warr first employed the term "resonance" in describing radionic healing. The implication was that a disease had a pattern or resonance that could be identified by the device and destroyed; in the same fashion a wine glass can be shattered by a specific frequency. In Resonance Therapy, however,

the idea is that, under the guidance of the local forest service, the ecosystem designated for treatment is analyzed instrumentally and the appropriate IDF (Intrinsic Data Field) resonators are used to re-balance the systems. These sessions normally run for two to four hours a day, five days a week, with two people monitoring the results.

Like traditional radionics equipment, the SE-5 Plus uses a "stick plate" as a detector. In place of the usual rubber membrane, a thin piece of circuit board material was placed over geometric designs and "scalar" antennas underneath. These devices were said to fine tune and amplify the scalar informational fields, another term for Intrinsic Data Fields. Knobs no longer were necessary to dial in the "rates." Instead, one could type them into the computer on the instrument. This much simpler diagnostic and treatment method saved time,

Fig 20-1. IRT Laboratory, Germany with SE-5s

Fig 20-2. SE-5 Plus

and the overall procedure complications were greatly reduced. The number of usable rates stored in the device was enormous and accessing them could be virtually automatic.

With the SE-5 Plus, detailed examination can be made of all aspects of foliage growth, soil conditions, and environmental contaminants. Balancing often takes place over months and years before the forests again become self-regulating. This process reveals itself on many levels, from increased species in the forest to more humus on the ground to increased leaf mass and many other factors.

Paris describes other experiments at IRT that show photographs of these forests, before and after treatment, with all the treated trees showing much improvement over the controls. Similar tests are shown with seeds and sprouts, where roots, stems, and leaves are readily measured for comparison. Emphasis in the IRT system is put on building the soil, seeds, and plants, making them healthy and strong, rather than in destroying pests and other plant predators, as was the case earlier on in radionics. However, in the case of pollution and chemical toxins from pesticides and other contaminants, the capacity of a forest to adapt to change becomes compromised from the onslaught of the new compounds. The

adaptive signaling systems within the ecosystem cannot function as designed. Resonance Therapy, as conceived by its founders, reintroduces a new informational and organizational structure to the forest in an attempt to balance the harmed ecosystem on the semiotic level where the damage first appeared.

Little substantiating information concerning the IRT program is readily available in English. What we do learn from a mutual friend and co-worker of the founders, biologist Hans Andeweg, is that German natural healer and radionics practitioner Irene Lutz established the Institute for Resonance Therapy with Countess Marion Hoensbroech in Germany in 1986. Both ladies were interested in developing an energetic response to accelerated ecosystem degradation in Europe. In their collaboration, Ms. Lutz supplied the radionics and Countess Hoensbroech provided the capital. Andeweg was brought into the organization to establish the scientific research concerning the effects of treatment and to guide the projects. Later on, when the organization hired a new director, Rijk Bols, Andeweg continued working with her until 1998. Together they managed projects in the Netherlands, Belgium, Germany, France, Austria, Spain, England, Scotland, Czech Republic, and Russia. Later on, in 2001, IRT closed down permanently.

"At first the forests were 'small', 100 hectares," Andeweg says of his work, "but they soon grew to 20,000 hectares in the UNESCO Biosphere reserve Krivoklat in the Czech Republic. The largest project was 40,000 hectares in the Niznesvirsky Reserve, above St. Petersburg. This was by order of Michael Gorbachov. Results were almost everywhere; personal announcements by people that everything went better and also an abundance of hard, significant, scientific proof of improving vitality.

"So both Rijk and I know full well what you can attain by balancing from a distance. Next to the great possibilities, we also know very well what not to do. As it turned out very soon, the method worked like clockwork but this at the expense of our own health. Apart from that, people at the scene were happy with the result, but at the end of the project nobody knew how to keep the energy at the same level. There was no involvement and no responsibility for the people themselves."

Andeweg wrote about his experiences with resonant therapy in a book called *In Resonance With Nature*, which was published in the Netherlands in 1999. He eventually mastered the problems that previously had left him sick and drained. Today, he continues his work with Bols in their own establishment, The Center for ECOtherapy. Their goal is to develop methods to heal both within nature and culture on a large scale. To this end they have refined Irene Lutz's radionic tools into a therapeutic system that works for humans, agriculture, and institutions.

Unlike the IRT, ECOtherapy employs no actual radionics devices in their methodology. Their approach does appropriate some of the language and techniques of earlier radionic systems, but in place of a device is a specially trained ECOtherapist. The therapist uses a map in place of a device. The map is essentially an energetic scan of the various components of the project being treated. They liken a scan to the therapist making intuitive contact with the "morphic field" or informational content of the entire project parameter, like a blueprint. This scan also provides various energetic values for all underlying conditions, a baseline for future energetic comparison.

Another concept borrowed from Lutz

Fig 20-3. SE-5 1000

is the creation of a holon. A holon in the ECOtherapy system is made by surrounding a topographic map of the project with "an energetic resonance-box." essentially a boundary definition of some kind. The holon is an actual object, a map, but it is also a semiotic representation of the whole project, which "enables the projects own healthy vibration to sound in an optimal way." Once created, the therapist can proceed with the balancing procedure, using the holon as a witness. Ironically, before the balancing begins, the holon is manually turned by the therapist to its "Critical Rotation Point" (CRP), where it can pass on information and energy most efficiently. It will be recalled that CRP has its origin in the earliest radionic experiments.

Balancing is a therapeutic process with numerous steps and objectives, all following a prescribed course of action. Within this process, a number of other energetic "medicines" can be employed, such as colors, music, remedies, symbols, etc. These are brought in contact with the holon, with the view towards transferring information from the medicine to the holon, as prescribed by the therapist. All this effort at balancing is accompanied by affirmations, testing, and regular evaluation.

The objective of the process is to produce results that demonstrate enhanced functioning. Unlike strictly medical or agricultural radionics, ECOtherapy is regularly applied to large systems and institutions such as businesses, farms, cultural institutions, nature preserves, and schools, at this point apparently, mostly in the Netherlands where the company is located.

ECOtherapy is also an educational institution with a vocational training program for therapists with a staff of 12 persons. On its website it publishes the names of its graduates and information about the projects they devised and completed while undergoing their training. There is also statistical data quantifying the results. They claim to be coaching over 200 projects a year in the Netherlands. Overall, the impression one gets is that of a competent group of individuals who have taken radionics into a very contemporary platform. The word radionics doesn't appear once in their literature, yet the methodology at its core seems deeply derivative of radionics. Clearly, the group is teaching a methodology for attaining higher functioning through balancing energy. ECOtherapy is a business that seems ideally suited for many applications, and they aren't afraid to publish their results.

The Quantec Device

Twenty-first century computerized radionics owes a lot to Peter von Buengner, the founder of M-TEC AG, a German company currently manufacturing radionics software and hardware. Mr. von Buengner calls this methodology Quantec, a registered trademark for what is described as "the leading computer-system in instrumental biocommunication." In the brochure, Quantec purports to exploit a new technology of diode and white noise

technology, such being considered a "generator" through which a bio-field can be scanned in a few minutes. With Quantec, Buengner has integrated radionic philosophy into a packaged approach that can be used in numerous applications with an ordinary computer.

The Quantec generator serves as the basis for a therapy plan that is described in the brochure as "a very objective method, [in that] the therapist has no influence on the analysis." Instead, the plan itself provides for all necessary detected remedies to block or rectify the path of the intrusive condition. The database of more than 50,000 remedies stored in the computer is designed to respond not only to physical maladies but spiritual and mental ones as well. The database includes remedies from many comparable disciplines such as homeopathy, acupuncture, Bach flower essences, psycho-kinesiology, and many others. New or personalized entries can be added at any time. At the time of this writing, Quantec's automatic processing capability can function night and day for up to 500 targets, individually adjusted by the therapist for duration and intensity.

However, in a different context, von Buengner describes his technology as a means to concentrate and guide consciousness, in an operator dependent manner, to complete the stated goal. He calls this process "Instrumental Biocommunication." It is not clear exactly where operator consciousness guides this technology and where it is automated. The procedure is further complicated by the assertion that his instrument functions as a symbolic representative of an abstruse physics that only becomes active when it is in use by the operator. I'm not sure exactly what he means by this, but it sounds a lot like Butcher's idea of a "downpouring" of energy that the instrument automatically captures and applies to the patient. However, Von Buengner asserts that when his procedure is combined with computer processing, the best of the old and the new of radionics is integrated into one device.

It is also a complicated way of saying that Quantec is a radionic technology without referencing or using the term radionics very often. Yet he goes on to add the common caveats found in most radionic technology today: restricting practical use to areas outside of human health, excepting where legally permissible, etc, etc.

The actual underlying radionics technology bears a closer look. I have no direct experience with von Buengner's methods, nor any reason to believe they don't function entirely as claimed. I simply wish to make the reader aware of his methodology, especially in relationship to the historical evolution of radionics. In that regard, of great interest is his utilization of a white noise diode as the primary component or "generator" of the technology.

In Von Buengner's application, the white noise diode, essentially a random event generator, becomes slaved to the operator's intent. In his words, "The noise of the QUANTEC diode itself can be compared to a radio that is not tuned into any station…completely at random and with no recognizable pattern." But when this noise is connected with consciousness, it changes. These changes can be processed and interpreted by a computer. QUANTEC claims to optimize this interaction between consciousness and white noise to search its databases for relevant entries (e.g. affirmations, acupuncture, Bach blossoms, homeopathy, colors, etc.).

Von Buengner attributes the success of his Quantec technology to a mysterious quantum-physical property inherent in white noise itself. He states that once linked to a computer, it "is so complicated that QUANTEC is the only device on the world market that can handle this technology." I will leave it to the interested reader to conduct their own analysis of the merits of this approach and its viability. Ample information and analogy is provided on the Quantec website and in von Buengner's book, *Physics and Dreamtime.*

As I understand it, first, the operators' consciousness gets connected to the noise, at which point the Quantec software takes over and automatically responds to the operator's intent, selecting a treatment from the appropriate (symbolic) remedies stored in the computer's data bank. As Von Buengner puts it in his analogy, "Figuratively speaking, white noise is a keyboard that can be used by the unconsciousness for communicating information."

In his radionics design philosophy, von Buengner relied heavily upon research conducted at the now closed Princeton Engineering Anomalies Research (PEAR) laboratory at Princeton University. As mentioned previously, PEAR operated under the guidance of Robert G. Jahn, Brenda J. Dunne, and Roger Nelson. Since the late 1970s, PEAR has accomplished significant work, using scientific and statistical methodologies, on the topic of "mind-machine-interactions."

Beginning in the late 1980s, PEAR began employing diode white noise generators to illustrate whether directed intent could alter the normal statistical distribution of a Gaussian Bell curve of many binary events being randomly generated over time. A binary event takes place when only two reactions are possible, yes or no, 0 or 1, etc. Should the bell curve of the average statistical distribution vary as a result of some mental intent (causing that distribution to shift significantly over a long period of testing), then one would be inclined to interpret such deviations as indicative of an influence of consciousness upon the outcome, and therefore upon the generator itself.

The pattern of deviations from normal collected by the PEAR researchers covered years of statistical research and numerous refinements of procedure. Their first decade of results were published in the late 1980s, ultimately in book form as *Margins of Reality: The Role Of Consciousness in the Physical World*. While this serious and revolutionary study demands careful study by the interested consciousness researcher, we will consider here only the impact on von Buengner's radionics innovations.

First, the PEAR study indicated that *distance* between the test person and the white noise diode (also called the random-event generator) had no significant bearing on whether focused mental intent caused significant deviations from a random distribution. PEAR data reinforced what radionics inventors had been claiming for decades: that distance played no role in diminishing the effective treatment employing applied intent.

While the overall results in the PEAR studies of an individual test subject's influence upon the generators varied significantly throughout the testing (with the majority not achieving statistically relevant deviations), taken as a group, clear deviations were statistically evident through time.

The PEAR research into the human psychokinetic (PK) potential appears to support certain aspects of the empirical results of radionics research. Von Buengner optimized the PEAR data for his own inventions, although that data has been virtually ignored by mainstream scientists. Referencing Jahn and Dunne in his own writing, von Buengner drew his own conclusions from their convic-

tion that human consciousness can interact with physical systems under certain conditions. Von Buenenger employs the PEAR work to suggest a scientific rationale for the radionics transaction, one that considers both the role of consciousness and the role of tools.

One condition von Buengner emphasized that produced success in his testing is loss of body-centeredness and relaxation of analytical thought processes while trying to influence an outcome. This "turning over" of control to the natural flow of the process is consistent with successful creativity as well. In his discussions with Jahn and Dunne, von Beuneger learned that altering the outcome of the random event generators was achieved under similar conditions.

According to some models, the psychokinetic energy necessary to accomplish the shift away from random generation is derived from energy liberated by a neural transaction in the brain, perhaps at the nerve synapse junctions, termed minute Casimir Effect thresholds. The Casimir Effect demonstrates the existence of huge amounts of energy (Zero Point Energy or ZPE) available throughout the vacuum of space. ZPE has become a favorite term for scientists and alternative thinkers alike in describing a universal energy substratum.

Von Buengner's fascination with the radionics potential of the white noise random generator, supported (in theory) by the PEAR findings, led him to design his Quantec technology. While his radionics designs remain proprietary and details on the studies, which substantiate his theories, are not publicly available, nevertheless clues to his design intent are to be found among his published writings.

Basically, if random generators can be influenced by intent, then those test subjects whose intent can most easily be projected into a computer or diode, or in some other fashion influence the outcome with their mind, that person should have an inherent ability to optimize software designed to direct this ability into a desired radionic outcome. This thought gave von Buengner the idea for developing a computer program called Syntec.

The Syntec program controls a visualized Galton Board on the computer screen. A Galton Board is a mechanical device invented by Sir Francis Galton to demonstrate the law of error and normal distribution. The machine consists of a vertical board with interleaved rows of pins. Balls are dropped from the top, and bounce left and right as they hit the pins. Eventually, they are collected into one-ball-wide bins at the bottom. The height of ball columns in the bins approximates a bell-curve.

Theoretically, the Syntec software gave Von Buengner the ability to test "whether the human mind could influence matter in the form of a computer." This development, he adds, was followed by unspecified tests performed in various settings, including the University of Freiburg in Germany. "The initial evaluations of the results," he claims, "have shown that the PC must meet certain technical conditions to allow it to be influenced by the human mind."

He doesn't say specifically what these technical conditions are. As computers are literally filled with noise, with each connection and soldered joint making its own respective contribution, the computer may well have been too diffuse a "target" for such a PK task without significant modification. This may simply mean he had to separate the diode he was using for his treatments from all the noise generated by the computer.

Von Buengner asks us to envision a new type of radionics device emerging from a computer program. In short, it's a very complicated way of saying the dowsing reflex has been replaced by a new system. The Syntec program is designed to carry out high-speed radionics analysis, but it does so by slaving the operator's intent to a diode "target," which in turn automatically selects from the software the proper treatment. How does Von Buenenger explain why this happens?

Like the PEAR generators, the von Buengner generators utilize thousands of binary events to show significant statistical deviation. But von Buengner asked his operators not to target "plus or minus" binary decisions, but to think of nothing at all, neither "plus nor minus." The results demonstrated to von Buengner that over time when a person was asked "not" to influence the random distribution of the test in any way, they generated a pattern that was uniquely their own. The way I interpret this function is that radionically, a reflexive condition was established between the generator and the operator that allowed for automatic diagnosis and treatment. It is confusing, but this unique connective relationship between consciousness and generator is, for von Buengner, a radionics "witness" as good as any DNA: "The generator therefore knew who was connected with it and not thinking about anything!!!"

Von Buengner believes it is possible and practical to establish a purely psychic link between the computer and the mind of the person being treated. According to his design, the computer is slaved to the radionic intent of the operator, like a direct feed, which in turn influences the treatment selection for the patient.

"Would the generator again search out what was characteristic for the person involved?" von Buengner asks. "In the development of my own radionic device, this was the deciding thought: the generator reacts to the presence (physical and/or spiritual) of people, and, as was proved in later series of tests, to animals, plants, and even stones, houses, etc. What now might occur if instead of the white noise diode being asked to choose between only a "+," a "—," or a "0" value, it was asked to choose between thousands of possibilities? And of these thousands of possibilities, could they include all the radionic rates, homeopathic remedies, acupuncture points and every other form of energetic data capable of being entered into a computer?"

Apparently it could, because his Quantec radionics equipment and software are enjoying worldwide success today in a wide variety of applications. He unequivocally states that the proper remedy for the patient's current situation is produced from the relevant databases via the generator. "The reliability with which this happened was stunning and shows that a device has actually been successfully developed which is capable of independently discovering problem areas within a few minutes."

It is fascinating to see how far von Buengner took this hypothesis. On his website, he references the experiments of French researcher, Rene Peoc'h, of the University of Nantes, first published in the *Journal of Scientific Exploration* in 1995. Peoc'h built robots whose movements were controlled by the same type of white noise diode, or random event generator utilized by Quantec. In control experiments, the movement of the robots was haphazard. In his next experiments, chicks hatched in an incubator were imprinted and become attached to the robots; as the first thing they saw moving, they believing it was their mother. Later on, Peoc'h demonstrated almost the reverse impulse. When the chicks, instead of being allowed to follow the robot

around, were held in a cage at the corner of the enclosure where they could still see the robot, they managed to make the robot move toward them. Somehow, the chicks' need for the robot/mother caused the random number generator to guide the robot over to their cage. Chicks that were not previously imprinted by the robot had no such effect upon the robot.

In other experiments, Peoc'h placed rabbits in an enclosure with robots, which at first frightened the rabbits. The robots in turn moved away. After the rabbits became familiar with the robots and were no longer scared of them, they tended to draw the robot towards them. The implication was that fear and desire, expressed through intention, influenced random events from a distance. The intent had to exist and travel outside of the rabbit's brain in order to influence the generator.

Von Buengner interprets Peoc'h's work as though an unconscious, instinct-guided wish of the chicks or rabbits influenced the position of the robot. He suggests that because the chicks believed the robot was their mother, they generated a field that took control of how the white noise generator directed the robot, slaving it to their own needs. Under the same premise, von Buengner has reasoned that human intent focused upon a similar random event generator linked to treatment modalities within a computer database will also elicit the most favorable treatment from among all the possibilities available in the computer's memory.

Von Buengner suggests the Peoc'h's studies in human unconscious control of robot activity support his hypothesis that a selection process can be done instinctively, in an automated fashion by anyone operating his software. In further Peoc'h studies, a robot making an unpleasant sound, but controlled

The Secret Art

by a diode, randomly navigated a room with an empty bed, shutting off after 20 minutes. Then, the motions of the same noisy robot in the same room are tracked as a person sleeps in the bed, but is not awakened by the robot. The robot in this instance is steered into the farthest corner of the room from the sleeping person, indicating that even in an unconscious state, as measured by brain wave data, the sleeper was still able to influence the random event generator to suit their own need for better sleep.

This experiment suggests another. Try inserting the intent of a person wanting a good sleep into the bed, in the form of a Quantec technology programmed for that task, in place of the actual sleeping person. Will the robot respond to the intent only and still hug the opposite corner of the room? Once the door is opened to demonstrating a mechanism or the conditions for the transmission of intent, it can only follow that radionics equipment designed for a similar purpose must also submit to the same tests. It's surprising more such tests haven't been conducted over the long history of radionics.

Von Buengner soon discovered it was not necessary to be anywhere near the Quantec system to derive benefit from it. A digital picture of the patient or whatever is being treated can be scanned into the computer. The Syntec software enables the Quantec operator to quickly derive a diagnosis and treatment schedule, and then print a report. At the required intervals, the computer can automatically call up the picture and treat it with predetermined rates.

However, for certain environmental radionics treatments, von Buengner provides an external component. It is made up of a plate glass triangle with three discs of rose quartz

Fig 20-4. Quantec triangular detector

attached to the points. A golden metallic clip is fixed to a portion of the glass triangle on the top. The Quantec computer system can transmit whatever "frequencies and oscillations" the operator deems necessary to whatever sample is placed upon the golden clip, at any distance. The triangular assembly acts as a surrogate radionic transceiver that can be imbedded in its surroundings.

The triangular detector radionically monitors minute-to-minute diagnostic details of the chemistry and life force characteristics of whatever it is imbedded in. The operator periodically adjusts the treatment protocols from the computer to support the transforming ecosystem. A device of this sort would be ideal to use in experiments where intent is used to control robots.

In contrast to earlier complex and time-consuming radionic procedures, the Quantec system seems like a dream come true for the practitioner of radionics skills. The implication clearly exists that Quantec technology is a self-adjusting system that also bypasses the danger of incorrect diagnosis and treatment by non-medical professionals. If true, this feature alone would be of tremendous merit. In radionics there exists the great danger of the individual able to use the device but being untrained in treating illnesses.

With regards to veterinary medicine, the M-Tec website provides testimonials by horse lovers of successful treatment for their mounts. According to an article by Sabine Heuvelop, "Health Management of Show Horses Using Instrumental Biocommunication," a high-level dressage trainer, Ralph-Michael Rash of Hesselhof in Warendorf, Germany, has integrated the Quantec system into the care and management of the horses under his care.

The form this treatment takes if five fold. First, the fodder is analyzed to insure adequate vitamins, minerals, and trace elements are reaching the horse in its feed, as subsequently provided for by additives or radionic treatment. Second, regular instrumental treatment of the intestines and immune system helps manage the parasite status of each horse, in many cases avoiding worming and the noxious chemicals involved. Third, Quantec treatments help horses exposed to frequent transport and other stresses that occur in equestrian showing to regain balance through treatments, reducing the risk of colic, sleeplessness, and circulation problems. Fourth, geo-pathological disorders associated with barn locations, water, and inoculation complications can also be addressed with the appropriate treatment. Fifth, overall physical fitness can be monitored and advanced with Quantec management, including treatment of tendons, ligaments, and discs.

In agriculture, the M-Tec website also describes successful treatment of varroa mites attacking European bees suffering from weakened immune systems. While standard chemical treatments caused noxious environmental problems and had to be abandoned, all bees treated with Quantec radiation proved successful, according to the literature and published reports on the website. Similarly, other pest treatments for agriculture can be found on the site, including forestry projects in Germany, a vineyard in Vienna, and a flower farm in Africa, several accompanied by testimonials.

One other fascinating case study involved the environmental re-certification of a small pond around Berlin destroyed by pollution, highway run off, and accumulating mud. The project was undertaken in a joint venture with Berlin-based environmental and water purification company Mundus GmbH.

According to Anton Stucki, a Swiss environmental purification specialist working for Mundus, the situation in September 2000 was dire: "The Dreipfuhl pond was in many aspects a hard nut to crack. The pond has a surface of about 1 hectare, has no outlet and is the final destination of a road drainage area measuring several square kilometers, including two main access roads to Berlin.

"For many years heavy metals have piled up in this lake and the continuous lack of oxygen has led to a pollution process creating a mud slick several meters thick at the bottom of the lake. The slick was disturbing living conditions of the flora and especially the varieties of algae that are absolutely essential for the biological balance in a broad stretch of water. Consequently, this pond was choked two or three times a year, especially during heavy rain bringing along dirt from the road. Every time as a result the stench was like an open sewer and the fish suffocated from lack of oxygen, leaving them floating belly-up on the surface."

The city of Berlin then asked Mundus to clean up the mess, as other methods under consideration proved to be too costly. Water samples were taken. The Mundus approach called for installing three remote devices directly in the pond called Primary Energy Generators, or PRIGE towers, developed by a researcher named Elmar Wolf. The dual purpose of the generators was to supply the pond with life energy and restore balance.

For some time, according to Stucki, the company had been looking for a technology that would allow them to direct the energetic balancing process in a more precise way. By employing the Quantec system, Mundus was able to achieve this objective. They linked the PRIDGE towers to the Radionic Quantic system and began re-balancing the pond. Within six months, February to August of 2000, the oxygen supply in the pond stabilized and fish mortality was eliminated. Independent analysis confirmed that pollutants, including heavy metals had fallen significantly. Stucki added, "Quite remarkable are the falls in chrome concentration from 2.38 mg/l to 0.0015 mg/l and lead concentration from 11.1 mg/l to 0.005 mg/l.

"For the time being, the pond has returned to its biological balance. It would of course be desirable that no new factors of encumbrance continue to be conveyed on the water drainage from the roads, but this would imply a steady change in the environmental conditions. Hence it is more astonishing to see the lake recovering so fast in spite of the continuing encumbrance that led to its poor condition in the first place. It appears here that we obviously now have a method at our disposal that can begin a process of recovery in a sustainable way. This result has been made possible by combining precision analysis with information through the use of the Quantec system, and by creating vital energy through the use of the PRIGE technology.

"The result shows us that in all purification it would be best to work in two ways:

Fig 20-5. PRIGE tower in Dreipfuhl pond

by producing energy for the process, and by directing this process with the help of precise information.

"This also opens up economically affordable, gentle and radical possibilities for restoration in agriculture, forests, and in all types of waters. The Dreipfuhl pond contains pure, healthy and clear water. Even in hot weather its water is cool, and its oxygen level high. The pond's surroundings have changed in such a way that in wet weather pure, healthy and clear water flows in. The waterside residents now take great care of their environment and avoid for instance the excessive use of fertilizers and toxic products for their gardening and car washing and pollution caused by oil, gas, varnish, etc."

For many of us, successes of this kind seem beyond miraculous. If in fact these environmental cures work, they need confirmation by impartial scientists outside the belief envelope of those employing the technology. Many people today wonder how our world will overcome generations of environmental neglect. The expense and the work involve seem completely out of proportion to the assets available for the task. Perhaps, radionic tools like those utilized by these European companies will provide some hope in this task. Where's the harm in finding out?

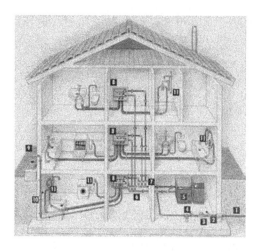

Fig 20-6. Quantec in Water Conditioning

Other Quantec applications for treatments of various household environmental contaminants exist, such as water purification, suppressing mobile phone radiation, and the effects of smog. However, by far the most outrageous (and timely) claim made for the beneficial virtues of Quantec radiation are increased fuel efficiency in motor vehicles. According to M-Tec, a combination of radiation of the fuel tank and motor with the information "oxygen," coupled with an appropriate affirmation, results in more efficient fuel combustion and less toxic emissions from the exhaust.

According to von Buengner, some years ago a building biologist from Hof, Bavaria demonstrated this fuel saving process to his satisfaction in his Renault Espace diesel. Documentation (in German) is available on the M-Tec website. More recently, another German conducted his own test on a GMC SUV he purchased in Canada and drove throughout the North American continent. Using the Quantic system to enhance the overall performance of his SUV, he reported an overall increase of fuel consumption from 17 to 21 mpg. He also conducted the same experiment

on his Harley Davidson Roadking 1550 cc motorcycle, which produced a mileage increase from 35 to 50 mpg.

For most readers unfamiliar with the potential radionics holds for addressing the more intractable problems of life, the assertions of M-Tec and its associates must seem the height of delusion in a world of crackpots. Yet, individuals and businesses from around the world continue to try these methods and obtain favorable results.

Artistically, the Quantec system would seem to hold great promise. Employed in the Dreipfuhl Pond Project was a truly unusual object, the PRIGE tower. The tower was floated in the pond with the intent of supplying an increase of life energy to the environment. From my vantage point, the PRIGE tower is a uniquely designed sculpture. I am aware of no mechanical or electrical technology that can transfer life energy into a compromised ecosystem, so I must assume the tower either functions in some unknown radionics fashion or is a complete fraud. If the PRIGE tower works as claimed, we are looking at a very great opportunity for artists to create sculptures that also foster environmental rehabilitation.

One could also view the whole process of linking intent to an object through radionics software as a type of conceptual process art. One application could include the staging of such an artwork simply as an experiment. For instance could the artist measure intent by devising a means of weighing its effects through experiment?

On a more philosophical note, given the fact that mainstream science abhors the careful research conducted at Princeton by PEAR, and would certainly require life-support before entertaining von Buengner's ideas, why not drop any pretension of calling Quantec

    The Secret Art

"scientific" and just call it and these other radionic tools "art," with a potential for utilitarian application in design? It's more honest and more to the point. Von Buengner is appropriating scientific language and data to explain radionic events, something almost every inventor has done before with disastrous consequences. Mimicking science would be unnecessary if radionics was presented purely as art, especially as a modern interpretation of the healing arts practiced by indigenous peoples throughout the world. In eliminating science from the discussion, von Buengner and other innovators would in no way diminish the fact they have developed marketable radionics systems. At the same time, they would circumvent many of the legal and public relations pitfalls.

Modern radionic devices and training do not come cheap, and Quantec is one of the most expensive systems I have encountered to date. However, von Buengner has made every effort to make the investment worthwhile by continuing to publish the many applications and instances where his technology has met with success. Only time will tell if he can avoid the pitfalls encountered by other successful radionics practitioners, including the inevitable smear campaign by science that radionics can't possibly work.

Artistically speaking, radionics devices have already proved wildly successful in circumventing cultural limitations imposed on creativity, albeit mainly within the healing arts. Today radionics is morphing into a cultural de-conditioning tool. (Better we free ourselves than seek to control others, right?) When the global reach of an individual computer combines with the cosmic reach of a radionics device, the potential for serious creativity expands exponentially. We are witnessing this now, as the European radionics labs apply their computerized radionics skills to health, business, agriculture, and the environment. One can only guess what comes next.

Wait, we can guess: how about radionics with no device at all?

The Paper Doctor

It's 1992. The institutional witch-hunt on radionic practitioners is decades old; nobody even knows what the word "Radionic" means anymore. But hold on, science isn't done with radionics quite yet.

The place is somewhere in Texas at the home of 52-year-old Don Gerrard. The authorities have entered his home and seized all copies of his book, *The Paper Doctor*, which he published the year before. Health food stores carrying it are ransacked and his books confiscated. Later we hear rumors that all copies are brought to a military base and burned. Gerrard then receives a threatening letter from the attorney general of Texas, warning him never to try selling his book in that state again.

What was in this book?

The year before, veterinary doctor, Walter A. McCall, described *The Paper Doctor* in one of his clinic handouts as "Possibly the most important book to appear in many years. Every person should own and study this book. If the AMA had any idea of the power that this one book gives to people to take back their health they would have the FDA outlaw the book and someone would have a contract on Don Gerrard's life. Buy one before it becomes illegal to own."

McCall's words were prescient. Gerrard would eventually be forced to mail a disclaimer to every registered book-owner stating that no cures in the book would work and please ignore everything in it. Even today, Gerrard has refused to let the book be republished, even on the web. He went as far recently as informing Jerry Decker at KeeleyNet that downloaded patterns from the book would "reproduce inaccurately and give indifferent results."

By his own reckoning, Gerrard had spent fifteen years researching *The Paper Doctor* before he published it in 1991. Gerrard began as an author, publisher, and bookseller; then, in 1976 he withdrew from publishing to study alternative health care. Later, he began to develop a theory about how to enhance health through the selective use of remedies for stimulating natural healing. The problem was, at that time, there weren't many natural remedies to be had. Gradually, the idea emerged that one could produce one's own remedies through charging water with magnets and geometric patterns. Like the radionic rate cards of Malcolm Rae before him, Gerrard's healing patterns are simple geometric drawings.

The way *The Paper Doctor* works is very ingenious. The book contains numerous treatments in the form of simple line drawings of irregular shapes. Instructions for how to select a treatment are very simple. In the back of the

Fig 20-7. Radionic Multiplier

book was stored a thin board that contained a magnet in the center. Each drawing has a dot inside the shape. You put the dot of the drawing over the center of the magnet and then cover the drawing with a piece of clear plastic. On that diagram is placed a small round glass with a thin, flat bottom. Into the glass is placed one teaspoon of water. The glass is centered over the dot on the drawing. It takes five minutes for the energy in the pattern to charge the water, and you drink it right away, or following directions in the book. There are other instructions on how to evaluate the results. If it works, according to Gerrard, you will feel it quite soon. If it doesn't, there are further instructions to follow.

The basis Gerrard uses for composing each of his drawings are natural substances with well-documented healing properties. These "parent" remedies exist originally in liquid form. Gerrard has translated 58 different liquid remedies into the 58 magnetic patterns (drawings) used in the book. Each pattern corresponds to the healing signature of the remedy. The magnet's function is to "copy" the pattern from the drawing into the water. It is also used to orient the field around the drawing to magnetic north as the copy is made. This form of treatment falls into a methodology called micro-dose pharmacology.

Normal chemical medicine is taken in by the bloodstream from the stomach, via pill or solution or by injection. By contrast, microdose pharmacology directly affects the nervous system, the information conduit for the body. The mechanism by which this transpires has been described as "resonance," that semiotic pool of biological communications that can be demonstrated far better than explained.

In medical science, "message" based healing is referred to as psychoneuroimmunology, or PNI, which is the study of how a personal belief can influence an illness. The study of PNI began because the spontaneous remission of fatal disease is a well-observed medical fact. Some subjective factor(s), it was thought, perhaps informational, must trigger this extraordinary phenomenon. Today, the study of PNI has demonstrated that not only can the nervous and autoimmune systems learn, but they can also transfer information along their pathways in a nonchemical fashion.

In the "How it Works" section of his book, Gerrard discusses an interesting study of the placebo effect, which occurs when a patient experiences the benefit of a drug from taking only a sugar pill. He states that according to his research, "comprehensive studies over the past 20 years have demonstrated that 55% of the therapeutic benefit of all drugs is due to the placebo effect. This means that more than half of the people who took placebo, but thought they were taking some powerful drug, received a beneficial effect similar to those who actually took the drug. This holds true even for morphine – a powerful pain-killer used to ameliorate intense pain."

Gerrard credits radionic and radesthesia researchers in England and France for his inspiration, especially Malcolm Rae. Gerrard carefully replicated Rae's experiments, which took him several years. It is in fact the radionic rate, or emanation of a substance, that is represented by the drawing and transferred from the drawing into the water, though no numerical identification is required. The drawing takes the place of the numerical rate.

How the drawing is constructed is interesting for students of radionics. First, the original "parent" liquid in a vial is placed over a circular grid oriented to magnetic north. (Any reckoning more than one degree off magnetic

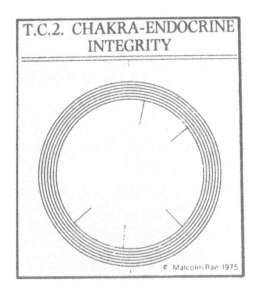

Fig 20-8. Rae Chakra-Endocrine Integrity card

north can compromise the effectiveness of the remedy.) Measurements are made of how far the energy of the substance extends from the center of the substance across the grid. A minimum of eight points, based upon the compass, are plotted and then marked on the grid. Lines forming the drawing connect the ring of points. This shape now depicts the boundary of the energetic field of the liquid in the vial. Most drawings of these fields are irregular in shape. Exactly how the measurements are surveyed is not stated in the text, but likely they are dowsed or determined by kinesiology. Researchers seeking to duplicate Gerrard's efforts are encouraged to study the techniques he learned from Rae's book *Dimensions of Radionics*, as well as Aubery Westlake's *The Pattern of Health*.

To address the question of how the magnet effects the water, Gerrard referenced the work of Bernard Grad at McGill University in the 1960s, showing that magnetized water stimulates the growth of plant seedlings. He also discusses the unusual properties of water and how it contributes to the success of the process. At every turn Gerrard proposes experiments and makes drawings to further clarify for the reader exactly how and why these techniques work. Tips, cautions, what to do if something doesn't work, how to get started, how to select a remedy, what to do here, and what to do there, all are voiced in simple, accessible terms. The clarity of his writing and the purity of his intent come through the text like a shining light.

In conclusion, Gerrard states that successful treatment from *The Paper Doctor* all comes down to five basic ingredients:

"1. The all-pervasive but invisible power of magnetism.

"2. The ability of water to store patterns of energy.

"3. The ability of geometric patterns to store healing potential.

"4. The essentially energetic nature of all matter, including the human body.

"5. The body's ability to transfer information by non-chemical means."

The method of radionics espoused by *The Paper Doctor* has also been called "geometric healing." Post-Paper Doctor practitioners of this methodology often dispense with the water remedy altogether, preferring to just touch the drawing. (Who can miss the artistic potential in this technique?) Others simply write the name of a remedy or affirmation in ink on a piece of paper, then set a glass (clear bottom, with no words) filled with an inch of water on top of it. Next, they swing a pendulum over the top of it for some time, and then leave the water to charge for ten minutes, at which point it is swallowed. Numerous other variations of charging water exist in many traditions, some of which are extremely ancient.

Is it any wonder that mainstream medicine had a fit when it grasped that a simple, non-invasive, simplified form of radionics had been re-born, which anyone could use in their own home, virtually free of charge? Gone were the black box and the blood samples. Gone was the goofy electronics. No longer need the radionics practitioner be a lonely figure working in constant fear of entrapment. Gerrard had dispensed with all that, leaving only nature and intelligence to work with each individual for their own benefit. No wonder they burned his books.

Fig 20-9. Radionic Sock Design

    The Secret Art

CHAPTER 21
RADIONIC/ART OVERLAY:
A PERSONAL NOTE

The case for using radionics in art is complicated by the many ways that people experience art and the expectations they bring to the art forms. No doubt much of what I term "radionics" is already intuitively understood and applied in all forms of art, and is really nothing new to those familiar with following their own inner vision. What I'd like to add is my perspective on radionics as an artist, over and above whatever it is as a technology.

The first question that comes to mind is whether some type of energy exists in the world that could account for the type of effects seen in radionics. If so, what other forms would it take in practical experience? How would it appear to an artist?

When I first began the training to become a sculptor I was a graduate student in the Fine Arts Department of the University of Pennsylvania. I had little knowledge of art, and less of the world of subtle energy. The year was 1970. I was amazed and delighted to discover a post graduate degree could be obtained

from a major university simply by working with tools and materials, with only the intent of turning that experience into "art." My particular orientation in sculpture soon became carving. I spent week after week, month after month, simply hitting wood or stone with chisels and then finishing the surface with rasps, files, and sandpaper. The methodology I was being taught did not require much intellectual debate or any profound knowledge of the history of sculpture. Rather, I was guided to learn from the materials themselves – to focus on their particular characteristics and how to shape them with tools. The idea was that when you shape a particular form, it would provide enough working questions that a series of new forms would be necessary to supply the answers. As each new form again raised its own set of questions, a series of objects derived from earlier creations emerged exponentially to expand the parameters of the sculptural experience.

The questions that prompted carving

were not necessarily verbal. When working in the round, one can never fully visualize the surfaces of the sculpture hidden by its mass, especially in abstract forms. The feel of one's hands upon the surfaces replaces sight. After working in sculpture for a while I realized I didn't comprehend the third dimension as well as I should as a sculptor.

An intuitive process drove my explorations of three-dimensional form, and in return mysteries of sculptural relationships became apparent through touch. The relationship to radionics lies in the discovery of added dimensionality hidden within normal experience. Sculptural awareness, discovered by practical application, of tools to materials with the intent of studying formal relationships led directly to a specific state of awareness one could think of as a precursor condition to making art.

In a different context, consider the surface texturing of the old wooden sailors trunk in my studio. The marred surface has provided the trunk with added dimensions of meaning. As an object, it continues to deliver fresh impressions seen from different angles and in different light. It has also stored on its surface aspects of all the places it has been and the things it has come in contact with. With age, the trunk has become something of a bas-relief sculpture. Time and experience has added surface textures impossible to fully assess without moving around it, hidden dimensions of meaning that remain at most, vague impressions. The sum total of visible and subtle impressions carried by an object could be considered its radionics provenance.

The means to opening the radionics provenance to full inspection is sealed shut to our normal consciousness. It is only felt or perceived by our aesthetic awareness, in large part

a non-verbal response. Radionic perceptions are not limited to aesthetics and beauty, but are felt in other ways, such as communication with nature, animals, or the unknown. There are countless ways we interpret the meaning of form and intent through the radiations they impart to our physical and subtle senses.

Subtle radiations speak to us in a different language than the voices in our head. More often, they are squelched by the louder voices of need and desire. The subtle stream of impressions that guide creative activity are to me comparable to the impressions that guide a radionics practitioner to turn dials and look for a sticky sensation on his or her fingers while dowsing a rate. As in the radionics process, moving my hands around the surface of a sculpture I was carving became a completely new way of understanding reality.

While carving, my mind was free to entertain any type of thought. It didn't matter what I was thinking at all, as long as I kept carving away and watching how the sculpture emerged. It didn't even matter "who" I was, as the redundant work process gradually eclipsed even identity. To force a concept onto the rock, such as "carve a head," or any other preconceived idea, began to seem very unnatural. If art work can proceed on such an intuitive and non-verbal basis, then why not healing work through tools like radionic devices?

The work process I was being taught was designed to orient me away from external art influences and onto an internal set of coordinates. I would describe this transition in radionic terms as re-calibrating, in the same sense that radionics dowsers had to go from listening to and interpreting the sounds percussed on the patient's stomach to understanding and mastering the stick plate and the rates to diagnose and treat the patient.

In graduate school, the success of one's internal orientation process in making art was publicly judged by ones' peers and instructors. Juries were a feedback process with no purpose beyond training potential artists to navigate and qualify an internally generated set of coordinates.

The question arises whether in following these guidelines the student actually makes contact with an actual energy or intelligence outside of his own brain. If so, does it guide the experience of learning to be an artist? In radionics, the implication is certainly that the practitioner guides a curative energy or information signal into the patient, facilitating a cure. But, does this take place in art? The argument will not be resolved here, but in favor of the hypothesis is the durable power of great art to stir emotions in people, regardless of race, color, creed, and time; plus the value culture places on these objects, words, music, and performances. Certainly the semiotics of the art can be said to convey energy, intelligence, inspiration, and meaning across space and time to the mind of the viewer.

My art program lasted three years. At the end of the program I was awarded a bachelor's and a master's degree in fine art that certified me to teach sculpture at the collegiate level. In essence, it was a degree in Artistic Radionics, with some drawing and tool training added in. The fine artists who were my teachers understood the nature of this education; their influence transcended individual styles and aesthetic proclivities.

There was also another energetic component to the learning experience.

When I began carving, my hand to eye coordination was very poor, resulting in many bruised knuckles and skin abrasions. In time, my coordination improved along with my concentration, but on some days, I would push beyond my limits and keep carving. At that point I found myself lifted from the tedium of the process to a higher level of functioning. Exhaustion would temporarily dissipate. My hands would become spontaneously coordinated and fly across the surface of the stone. Some force applied the perfect angulations and pressure to the chisel to get the job done. Inertia would take flight at the ease of it all; I felt seized by a process that trumped my inexperience and gave unusual balance and harmony to my movements and state of mind. The experience would usually last as long as I continued to carve. Nevertheless, at the beginning of a new day it was back to the old ineptitude.

At first, I believed it to be an intoxication born of weariness. Later I learned scientists attributed the experience to natural opiates released by the brain. Dopamine, serotonin, and adrenalin released by the brain through physical exertion, excitement, or danger can provide a sudden relief from exhaustion, a sharper mental focus and even tranquility. However, I never heard a claim that automatically translated that experience into enhanced creativity. By contrast, the experience of creative exhilaration feels like the universe is pumping one full of energy and concentration over long periods of time. One feels released from the inertia of normal functioning. Ego awareness is eclipsed by a wider bandwidth of perception. The experience becomes cognitive, a state of awareness filled with insight as well as energy.

Today, I identify this experience as feeling guided by an intelligence within nature. The experience superimposes itself over normal functioning in a very gentle and seamless way, smoothing out the wrinkles of ego driven behavior. The experience is not invasive; there is an immense purity to it. In time, however regrettably, the inertia of daily life resumes, the experience dissolves, and the sense of grace has to be fought for and won all over again.

What does this experience have to do with healing people with odd devices? Actually, everything: the alternative healing experience implies that some factor or force in nature, which we are not thoroughly cognizant of, is summoned to heal under certain mysterious conditions. Is it an actual physical energy, or is it a semiotic system of information transfer from one domain to another? Does it come from outside the body or from within? The process of creating art contains this very same mystery and no one knows for sure where it comes from.

I do know that today a small cottage industry has emerged selling radionically inspired devices that claim to assist the healing process. Most derive their methodology from one or another radionics or dowsing techniques described in this book. In some cases, the manufacturers present their tools as aids to a process of internalization, of looking within oneself for new abilities, knowledge, and faith. They present radionics as a natural extension of the human potential movement. The true radionics pioneers present their technology as a prompting of the mind/body relationship, which historically has been described as placebo cures or spontaneous remission of disease in countless instances, both in scientific and alternative settings.

Increasingly, the potential of radionics to inform a more profound aspect of human functioning is being re-packaged as a device driven technology. In the old mechanistic sense, it is the tool you buy that is doing the work. This interpretation allows the manufacturer to ascribe an inflated value to the cost of producing the technology. The assumption

being, the mysterious radionic forces inherent in the design must command an astounding premium over the components. Such assertions provide grist for the skeptics' mill. In these instances, the skeptics are doing the consumer a great favor in identifying these fraudulent devices.

The damaging consequence for radionics is that the skeptics, being confirmed mechanists, cannot possibly imagine or credit nature with any means of providing human healers or artists with energetic support that is outside the realm of acceptable scientific discourse. Never mind that each new generation of scientists basically overturns the findings of the last, as newly discovered facts lead to revised theories, different conclusions and ultimately, improved technology.

A case in point is the November 18, 2007, *Seattle Times* investigation, "Miracle Machines: The 21st-Century Snake Oil," which states: "They cure cancer, reduce cholesterol, and even eliminate AIDS. Their operators say these 'energy medicine' devices work by transmitting radio frequencies or electromagnetic waves through the body, identifying problems, then 'zapping' them. Their claims are a fraud. *The Seattle Times* has found that thousands of these unproven devices — many of them illegal or dangerous — are used in hundreds of venues nationwide."

The Seattle Times investigation specifically took issue with specific individuals and their devices. One, William Nelson, operating out of Budapest, Hungary, sells a computerized device called the EPFX that purports to diagnose and heal disease with radio frequencies. Reputedly, Nelson has made millions of dollars with it. EPFX executives and operators claim that Tour de France champion Lance Armstrong was treated with EPFX during his 2003 victory, a claim Armstrong has denounced. In the case of the EPFX, the story gets even darker. Slick graphics and exaggerated claims convinced a dying cancer patient named Karen McBeth of Seattle, the newspaper reports, to spend $17,000 on one of Nelson's machines, while JoAnn Burggraf of Oklahoma died of undiagnosed leukemia while being diagnosed and treated for joint pain with the EPFX.

Another Utah-based energy device company, Vantage, the newspaper claims, gave false information to Washington state regulators about clinical studies in prestigious institutions to get their product approved for chiropractors. In language reminiscent of radionics, the Vantage made claims to "detect and treat 'imbalances' in the heart, lungs and other organs"; when in actuality it was designed only to relieve stress. As to the true function of the device, the newspaper reports that "in its written materials, BioMeridian says practitioners can boost office revenues by $100,000 a year by using the Vantage to detect any imbalances and selling supplements to correct them." *The Seattle Times* research also found that Washington state's chiropractic board had already approved over 100 devices and procedures with little or no research to support their conclusions.

Today, a plethora of devices based in whole or in part upon radionics are sold in every corner of the world. The skeptics are having a field day reporting how gullible individuals fall for these techniques due to mistrust of the medical establishment or the inability to pay for adequate health care. Not only do false hope and deceptive advertising victimize sick individuals, but families also suffer as the people they love squander valuable resources and time pursuing products with no proven efficacy. Worse in some ways than the perpetration of false hope, is the implication that all alternative methodologies are hoaxes, frauds, and pure exploitation. Little mention is made in these skeptical critiques of the many genuine, world-transforming discoveries that were initially labeled fraudulent, impossible, or untrue. The sad fact of the matter is that throughout history, and even among respectable scientifically based institutions today, false cures and dubious practices are routinely promoted as effective.

By contrast, when we are healed because a mysterious intelligence or energy restores balance within the body and dissipates the disease, we look for an explanation. One is that human radionics systems and nature act together in concert. The operator of the device calibrates the precise need, place, and time for nature to enter the diseased condition and restore balance, if appropriate. It becomes appropriate whenever it works. It is not always our place to know when that is so.

If nature can enter a landscape of frozen biological entities and reanimate them each spring, couldn't it also reanimate human tissue, organs, or electro/chemical processes? Consideration of nature as an operational intelligence along side human intelligence has been seriously undervalued and under-utilized. Why? Perhaps we cannot accept what we perceive to be random and chaotic acts of nature as having an intelligent origin. We also have been taught by science that the physical world is in large part a huge mechanism defined by mathematical laws. Life force is an unknown that circulates endlessly until inertial forces and entropy gradually wear it down and absorb it back into an incomprehensible subatomic state. Nowhere does science provide a complete understanding of consciousness or its linkage to nature. The common excuse is the problem of bias and observer contamination in doing the science.

As a consequence, we take for granted a huge part of reality that we scarcely comprehend at all. Then, along come the radionic inventors and practitioners. They suggest we can employ consciousness in our scientific methodologies. For their trouble, they go broke trying. Often they are arrested and occasionally jailed for their trouble. Science declares their discoveries fraudulent and then people think they are all just clever con artists.

Art and Faith can't be defined scientifically either, yet they seem to work just fine.

In art, there is no such thing as ignoring consciousness; there is no ridding art of "bias" or "observer contamination." Artists are fused with the outcome of their work. Furthermore, many feel indebted to nature, animated by the mysterious muse of inspiration. Science has

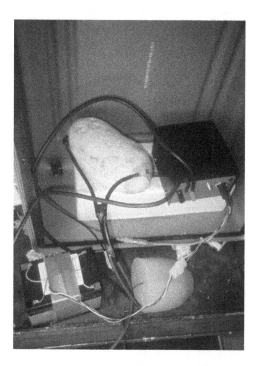

Fig 21-1. Quartz rock in a Faraday Cage

demonstrated that we are imbedded in an energy matrix of countless fields and potentials; it is what nature consists of in the world beyond human sense organs. When great artists reach us emotionally with their work, they move something inside of us, something we cannot define scientifically. We feel it in our heart, in our feet, in our consciousness.

Radionics uses a very artistic methodology to heal. It doesn't always work. A potter doesn't always throw a perfect pot. Some pots are even poor, while others, done only a short while later, hit the ball out of the park. In spite of the inconsistency, people since the beginning of time have been viscerally moved by art. The energy within the art form does not need the consent of the observer to penetrate to the deepest levels of their being. Since it is not necessarily so in art, why should it be so in radionics? Why can't skilled radionics practitioners target disease with "bullets" made of pure intent, as artists target emotions and cultural pre-conceptions with their metaphors?

Flash forward nearly 30 years from my early experiences carving stone and wood in school. Half a lifetime of making art and studying subtle energy and mysticism has lead to working with an electrical engineer, Gordon Salisbury. We are studying in-depth radionics, subtle energy, and nature intelligence from the combined platform of art and scientific observation.

We collected a large number of old radionics devices and tested them to see if they broadcast any energy. We detected nothing coming out of them that could explain their reputed historical capacity to cure disease. This observation led us to conclude that the curative process is imbedded in how consciousness is employed in the task. There are questions to be answered. How can we isolate this force and render it visible? How to describe it? And what is nature intelligence, how do we define and isolate it?

We perform experiments. Gordon builds devices to isolate and capture the small milli-voltages emanating from plants and rocks. We turn the voltage gradients into pitch shifts and use computers and software to process the pitch shifts into sonic forms and music. This study takes us years. Slowly, we discover something interesting in the process. We became convinced that the plants and rocks can occasionally generate beautiful melodies under the correct circumstances. We cannot force a plant or rock to produce a tune; it is a spontaneous process. Occurring when we are happy and having fun, and it all but disappears when we try to engineer it into being.

Preposterous as it sounds, we feel that we are making contact with something mysterious imbedded in even the humblest signals of nature. Do we question this supposition? Absolutely. We wonder if we are insane. There is some unusual evidence; a rock that delivers up to ½ a volt output, day in and day out, for weeks, months, and possibly for years. Other rocks have been producing strong signals on brainwave analysis software in the region of human mental activity, 1–30 Hz. These rocks have consistently displayed activity at around 7–8Hz, the region of the Earth's resonant frequency, the Schumann resonance.

There are other odd and beautiful things we witness: plants that respond individually to people touching them and plants that respond to rocks being touched or visa versa. We see enough to know it represents artistic investigation, one filled with wonder and discovery. We imagine singing orchestras of plants and rocks. There is one problem: we have not isolated a specific energy or scientifically quantifiable output that can explain our observations. Nor have we drawn any closer to a theory about how a radionics device heals, beyond crediting a nature intelligence that works through man and instrument.

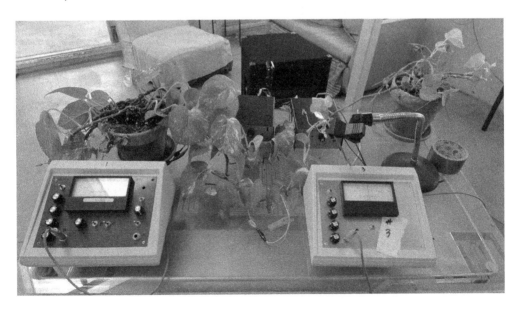

Fig 21-2. Measuring devices attached to plants

We have witnessed on our graphs and instruments, a plant responding to a friend humming Buddhist chants, playfully following the rise and fall of his melody. We have recorded a Venus flytrap happily playing along with Cajun Zydeco music, adjusting almost instantly to abrupt changes in melody and beat as songs are suddenly changed. We have seen our plants and rocks go numb and mute to ourselves and twenty or thirty adult guests, only to respond vividly and wildly to a friendly adolescent.

The impression left by these experiences is of a greater, more mysterious nature presence concealed within familiar, mundane forms. In a similar sense, art forms contain subtle emotional information and meaning. Sometimes that information seems unique to each person – the way a song can – and sometimes that information remains essentially non-verbal. Because of these qualities, we believe art represents the human spirit or the spirit of an age. There is no scientific standard that can verify this commonly held assumption. Yet, we place such value on the highest of artistic achievements as to term them "priceless."

Thanks to Todd Thille, who joined us in 2007, there is now a sampling of this work on the internet at: www.duncanlaurie.com. While it has been frustrating to make sense of the questions raised by radionics and subtle energy, the connection to art has grown stronger. We have begun to make contact with other artists with similar interests throughout the world. As a result, even more questions and observations have been raised about the connection of subtle energy to creativity.

As this manuscript was being honed and polished into a finished book, we had an interesting development. Two artist friends, Terry Golob and Michele Darling, of the group Aerostatic, asked if we would be interested in hosting a healer, Larry Banks, for a weekend project at the studio. Terry wanted to film Larry performing a healing session. The way Larry heals does not require any physical contact. He simply opens up a connection between himself and the subject, usually through conversation and meditation, and the healing energy passes through him directly to the condition being treated. Gordon jumped at the possibility of using our equipment to try and detect an energetic signature around the healing procedure.

Larry, it turned out, was also a filmmaker as well as the Chair of the Media Arts Department of Long Island University in Brooklyn, New York. In the course of working for Larry, Michelle had herself discovered his aptitude for healing, and later Terry did as well. This was getting interesting; here was an artist that was also a healer.

In the course of the weekend, we all watched Larry use his energy to control the amplitude spikes on a waterfall graph of an instrument we use, the IBVA (Interactive Brainwave Visual Analyzer), which at the time was attached to a rock, from 10 ft across a room. Using directed intent only, Larry affected the low end, 0-10Hz, of the stone's EM millevoltage output. Gordon, Terry , Michelle and I were present.

Before the experiment started and without our knowledge, Gordon had set up along the wall another 10 feet behind the rock and display, an ultrasonic transmitter and receiver. The ultrasonic device remains silent unless something enters its frequency range, at which point you hear a pitch shift. In other words, it acts as a microphone in the 40 kHz band. When Larry began to focus intent on the IBVA and the rock, we wanted to see if the same intent that moved the IBVA graph would in some way distort the ultrasonic field.

During the last ten years that Gordon and I have experimented with radionics and sonified plants and rocks, the question we kept returning to was whether subtle energy activity took place in the physical world as a measurable force or was instead a feature of consciousness, i.e., informational, non-physical, semiotic, etc. Gordon put it another way: "We would be looking for a physical pressure exerted by a focused intent on a field in the physical world."

Thus far, we had been unable to detect the presence of any physical process through direct measurement of any radionics instrument in our collection. However, while designing bio-sensors and working with plants and rocks, we did see physical evidence of something unusual taking place. We began to focus on the response to touch, noticing, for instance, that an untouched plant responded to the touch of another plant nearby, suggesting the radio part of radionics or some other mechanism connected the plants.

Being difficult to interpret, our experiences quickly moved into the realm of art. Gordon's scientific curiosity was not so easily ignored. When we had the opportunity to work with Larry, a person capable of directing a healing force into another, the opportunity presented itself to test whether the experience was indeed manifested physically, as experienced by the healing subject, or if it was psychological.

In fact, in Gordon's makeshift use of an ultrasonic detector, we not only saw Larry move the graphs of the IBVA which he was asked to do, but concurrently, he also modulated the ultrasound, which he was unaware of doing. I remember asking Gordon to turn down the interfering sound, not being aware of its significance.

The fact that Larry moved two physical detectors, one consciously and one unconsciously, lends credence to the possibility that focused intent becomes a measurable event in the correct circumstances.

Larry is totally involved in the manifestation and direction that his healing energy takes, to the extent that he tunes out much of the external world. This concentration was even more evident during the healing sessions that Gordon and I received from Larry later that weekend. They more than confirmed for us that Larry did indeed project a type of energy into our bodies. From Larry's perspective, he acts like a conduit for the energy. When asked about it, Larry indicated that it was the energy that evaluated the condition being healed and decided what and how to effect it. He feels that his job is to essentially hold open a conduit between himself and his subject, to sustain a corridor through which the energy passes of its own free will. Questioned as to whether he felt this energy was intelligent, his response was "Absolutely."

Was any energy apparent during the healing session?

Gordon's stated: "During a healing session, Larry remains available for conversation and input. When he was working with me, maybe a foot apart, Larry would talk and mutter to himself, and there was no physical impact on me until I got the sensation of heat in the middle of my back, that quickly became damp. He was treating my lungs. I stopped him and asked him to feel the hot, wet spot for himself. My t-shirt was actually damp. Following my interruption, the heat went away, only to return about half an hour later in the session. In looking at him during the session, Larry seemed very relaxed during the whole process. Up to this event, I might add, I have been among the more skeptical toward any type of energetic healing style."

The overall impression we received from working with Larry, who up to this time was a complete stranger, was that he was a completely genuine healer, quite modest about it actually, in that he had no idea how the mechanism of the healing took place within the subject. The fact that he manifested the energy successfully both in tests and in substance suggests he became the radionics device itself, acting as a conduit and tuner for the recipient. Larry provides the focused intent, acting as it does, to filter and direct the energy toward what the subject identifies and agrees to be healed. Larry makes no attempt to convince the subject of the merits of his process.

In a sense, as a healer, Larry is acting not only like a radionics device, but is also analogous to a radionics doctor working with a device, but with more cognition about how the energy is impacting the condition. In a sense, as a healer, his function can be compared to Leon Corte, de la Warr's assistant, without whose touch a radionic emulsion would not become a photograph. Gordon and I suspect that the truth regarding radionics is that it is a way for nature intelligence to work with human intent to heal, when appropriate. Any device serves the primary purpose of getting the operators ego out of the way, and the secondary purpose of tuning in the parameters of the condition being treated.

As to the relationship of radionics healing to art, Larry left us with this thought: "Think of 'energy' as a symbolic-information-matrix that can be tuned into, which opens new pathways of 'energy.' If shared between people, this energy can release blockages and energetic bindings, which subjectively are experienced within as freedom and creativity.

This experience is sometimes called healing. Naturally, it also leads to expression that can manifest as art. I see my role in this process as one of attunement and integration."

Consider the role of radionics as a technological metaphor capable of illuminating and bridging the worlds of consciousness. When the consciousness of an intelligent nature works with human expression and activity, "healing" becomes possible in any sphere of life.

AFTERWORD

This abridged history of radionics has shown that over the last 100 years a number of individuals assembled a wide range of purportedly workable devices. Each inventor produced practical results according to their varied professional experience and expectations. The common denominator throughout all designs was neither mechanism nor electricity; it was the fact that each inventor learned to use the power of applied intention to do work in the material world. We call this capacity: Information to Energy (I > E).

Dr. Abrams believed human disease could be detected in the form of electrical resistance, and he designed instruments that did just that, and much more. Guyon Richards wanted to prove that Abram's rates were scientifically valid, and soon discovered they corresponded to atomic numbers. Ruth Drown didn't understand the science, so her devices did away with electricity. Instead, she wanted to see her radionics device produce photographs, which she achieved (along with a British Patent for her camera).

Curtis P. Upton and his associates weren't concerned with pictorial proof; they wanted farmers to use their devices to replace fertilizer and pesticides, and that's exactly what they did. Galen Hieronymus helped in that effort, but he was a respected electrical engineer and wanted to see his device patented and used in industry, which it was. His friend, John Campbell, the editor of *Astounding Magazine* wanted something to bait science with. He demonstrated that the Hieronymus patent would work right from the schematic, without even being constructed. Malcolm Rae didn't want to use electricity either, so he designed a whole radionics system around diagrams, names, and numbers. Darrell Butcher couldn't work a pendulum or a stick plate, so he designed devices that worked automatically, without electricity, rubbing plates, or rates.

Bill and Marjorie de la Warr wanted to expand the design parameters of radionics and to explore its potential in new areas. They designed devices that operated on a theory of resonance, thereby elevating the discussion of radionics into a more subjective, artistic domain. Nevertheless, they made radionic cameras, detectors, and treatment instruments and produced thousands of experiments that expanded the field in many directions. Decades after the fact, researchers found holographic images imbedded in their radionics glass plate negatives before holography was even discovered.

Lutie Larsen demonstrated that radionics was a subtle and beautiful way to interact with nature at home or on the farm, with family, animals, and in the garden. She followed the artistic radionics direction of de la Warr and Darrell Butcher by making colored radionics cards that appeared to be miniature paintings but worked as practical devices.

In the 1980s, when computer technology was re-shaping society, Willard Frank designed the first computerized radionics device. Frank wanted more diagnostic and treatment capacity from his instruments, and soon they were treating patients faster and with more capacity than ever before. Society was becoming environmentally conscious, and so organizations like the Institute for Resonant Therapy in Germany applied computerized radionics to treat and re-certify large forests damaged by pollution.

Other German radionics pioneers, like Peter von Buengner, discovered design inspiration in world-class scientific experimentation conducted at Princeton on consciousness. From the effect of thought and intention on probability machines, von Buengner designed radionic software to optimize existing computers for radionics functioning in the home, farm, environment, and clinic.

Each of these individuals created a working radionics technology from their intellectual and aesthetic design preferences. There appears to be no underlying commonality guiding each personal effort beyond that of human consciousness guiding intent into instrumentation or design. Maybe a different perspective could help to interpret the whole field of radionics as intelligent design guiding the human creative process into a more natural and harmonious technological orientation.

If one can accept nature intelligence as a parallel consciousness interacting with human free will, the implication of a joint nature/human technology, actualized through consciousness, is possible. The history of radionics and naturopathic healing may well be a demonstration of that potential. Could these inventor/healers, each developing their own unique tools and techniques, in fact have established a connection with nature that remains an unacknowledged factor in their success? What is clear is that each inventor used human consciousness as an applied natural force on the tasks they confronted.

It is unlikely that the long record of cures among all the radionic systems utilized is either delusional or criminal, as has been claimed. The inventors sometimes faced court or prison rather than admit wrongdoing. In the process, many patients helped by radionics testified in their defense, as did notable scientists, doctors, and engineers.

But what do we mean by nature? For most people nature is the word beyond our homes, cars, offices, and the environments man has created – it is the world not governed by man; space, distance, time, rock, fire, light, electricity, sky, moon, stars, galaxies, and so much more. To a quantum physicist, nature has another interpretation altogether. For them, nature is composed of particles, or quanta, discrete little units that behave in very strange ways, appearing and disappearing from physical reality. Sometimes they behave like particles of matter, but other times they are mass free, like waves of energy. Even more peculiar, quanta will interact with each other over incredible distances.

When Abrams invented radionics the electron had only been discovered a few decades before. Nineteenth century physicists were only starting to comprehend that invisible energy such as light, electricity, and magnetism flowed in waves. When physicists discovered that light shining on a metal plate produced an electric current, the notion of energy being a continuous wave composed of individual units, or quanta, was established. Einstein called the particles produced in the photoelectric effect "photons." Soon quantum particles became the basis for understanding the core of all matter and energy. In spite of its strange behavior, quantum theory was mathematically confirmed over and over again, to the point that now quantum mechanics is engineered into many scientific inventions.

The problem remained that quantum theory was so weird even the scientists who invented it had to admit they couldn't completely comprehend it. One element of the puzzle is how, on the quantum level, perception determines the outcome of events. Strangely, for most of the last century, a theory was produced and engineered, but all the while what it was saying about the world was not fully understood.

Perhaps the deeper the level of nature, the more consciousness and physical reality intertwine. In this sense, there are parallels to radionics. Here we find certain devices that claim to do work with energy, in the form of particles or waves that travel along wires or light and interact with electricity and magnetism. Yet, in other circumstances, radionic activity appears only as a manifestation of consciousness, a psychic ability, working through a symbolic apparatus. This design dichotomy has not been resolved.

Radionics defies rational explanation or intellectual analysis. It is an experiential process, an empirical methodology, that links mind to matter through intent. What radionics has yet to become is a system of self-reflection. A self-reflective radionics won't be a device or a design, a science or a philosophy, but a relentless anarchy experienced as art.

In that freedom of expression, perhaps nature intelligence will assume the guise of a technology to initiate a dialogue.

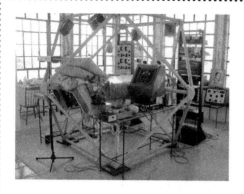

Fig a-1. Purr Generator

Fig a-2. Purr Generator controls

The Purr Generator

An experimental sonic radionic device designed by Gordon Salisbury and Duncan Laurie as a bridge mechanism linking radionics to art.

(See duncanlaurie.com for more information.)

Fig a-3. Radionic Amplifying Pattern

ACKNOWLEDGMENTS

The origins of *The Secret Art* and the idea that radionic technology may prove useful to artists began with bull sessions that took place in a special loft at the intersection of Soho, Chinatown, and Little Italy in Manhattan, and in my small row house and backyard in Long Island City, N.Y. Contributing valuable insights to those early raps, were Daffi Nathanson, Sue Skinner, Jim Brawley, Alix Toland, Michael Bradford, Jerry Vassilatos, Bjorn von Schlebrugge, Bokara Legende, Chris Haile, Ira Bauer, Ingo Swann, John Keel, Eldon Byrd, Peter Kelly, Heather Foxhall, and Jane Morgan.

Later, the topic developed momentum with Josh Reynolds at his family home, "Devotion" in Dobson, N.C., adding Aymon de Roussy de Sales, Eric Dollard, Lorenzo Catlett, Andre Puharich, and others to the discussion.

When designing the Dragonline Studio in Jamestown, R.I. along radionic principles, the advice of Michael Helius, John Michell and Gerry Vassilatos proved invaluable. Adding enthusiasm and diva energy to that process was Kim, Lena, Oona and Bryn Laurie.

In linking radionics to art, the advice and friendship of Peter Rittmaster, John Norseen, Remy Chevalier, Tom Brown, Michael Brennan, Mike Theroux, Steve and Kay Geller, Richard Metzger, Will Wadsworth, and Paul Laffoley proved valuable.

Without the professional expertise of Gordon Salisbury, the top floor sonic lab and ten years of experimentation would not have been possible. Radionics applied to performance and time-based media was first explored by Daffi and later on by Carly Ptak and Twig Harper. Their efforts were followed by Todd Thille, Steve Nalepa, David Last, Michele Darling, Terry Golob, Richard Devine, Josh Kay, Justin Boreta, Brian Kane, Sariah Storm, and Brendan Angelides.

Special thanks to Steve Nalepa who first fronted the idea of the book and later brought his group of friends together in

Rhode Island to play with the technology. The process of transforming my notes and draft manuscripts into book form would have been impossible without the help of Liisu Carlson, Todd Thille, Mike Bossick, Jessica Paulk, and Patrick Huyghe. Special credit belongs to Todd Thille, whose graphic skills and enthusiasm for the book and website duncanlaurie.com made them into reality.

SOURCES

01 Ancient Radionics

Bednarik, Robert. G. [PDF] "Cupules: The Oldest Surviving Rock Art" mc2.vicnet.net.au/home/cognit/shared_files/cupules.pdf – *International Federation of Rock Art Organisations* (IFRAO), P.O. Box 216, Caulfield South, Vic. 3162, Australia. Web Publication.

Bednarik, Robert. G. [PDF] "The Earliest Evidence of Palaeoart" *Art Research 2003* – Volume 20, Number 2, pp. 89-135.

03 The Origins of Radionics in Dowsing

Bird, Christopher. "Applications of Dowsing, An Ancient Biophysical Art." *Future Science: Life Energies and the Physics of Paranormal Phenomena.* Ed. John White and Stanley Krippner. Anchor Press edition, 1977. 347-365, 394, 399-400.

Callahan, Philip S. *Exploring the Spectrum.* Acres USA, 1994.

Young, Arthur D., *Nested Time: An Astrological Autobiography.* Anodos Publications, 2004.

04 Science and Scientism

Carey, Benedict, "PEAR & Dr. Robtert Jahn": *The New York Times*, 2/10/2007.

Jahn, Robert G. and Brenda J. Dunne. *Margins of Reality: The Role of Consciousness in the Physical World*, San Diego: Harcourt Brace Jovanovich, 1987.

Mizrach, Steve: "Alternative Medicine and the Appropriation of Scientific Discourse: The Cases for Homeopathy and Radionics" Internet Publication: http://www.fiu.edu/~mizrachs/altern-med.html.

05 The Divided Legacy of Medicine

Coulter, Harris L. *Divided Legacy: A History of the Schism in Medical Thought; Vol IV, Twentieth-*

Century Medicine, The Bacteriological Era. North Atlantic Books, Berkeley, California. 1994.

Mizrach, Steve. "Alternative Medicine and the Appropriation of Scientific Discourse: The Cases for Homeopathy and Radionics." Website: http://fiu.edu/~mizrachs/altern-med.html.

Vassilatos, Gerry. *Lost Science*. Borderland Science Research Foundation: La Canada, 1997.

06 The Father of Radionics

Barr, James, ed. *Abrams Methods of Diagnosis and Treatment*. William Heinmann Medical Books LTD: London, 1925.

Barr, James. "Sir James Barr on Dr. Abrams." *Pearsons Magazine*: August 1922. Reprinted in *ERA: The Electronic Reactions of Abrams*. Borderland Sciences. Bayside, California. p.21.

Colson, Thomas. "Abrams' Contribution to Electronic Medicine." *The Electronic Medical Digest Special Edition*, 1960. Reprinted in *ERA: The Electronic Reactions of Abrams*. Borderland Sciences. Bayside, California. p.33-44.

---- "Effects on Living Tissue of Chopped or Pulsed Energy." EMD Fourth Quarter, 1951. Reprinted in *ERA: The Electronic Reactions of Abrams*. Borderland Sciences. Bayside, California. p. 73-76.

---- "The Electronic Test." Reprinted in *ERA: The Electronic Reactions of Abrams*. Borderland Sciences. Bayside, California. p.59-68.

Russell, Edward W. *Design For Destiny*. Ballantine Books Inc: New York, 1971.

Russell, Edward W. *Report on Radionics: The Science Which Can Cure Where Orthodox Medicine Fails*. Random House UK, 1996.

07 The Oscilloclast

"Abrams Oscilloclast Rates Freqency Characteristics." Reprinted in *ERA: The Electronic Reactions of Abrams*. Borderland Sciences. Bayside, California. p.45-52.

Barr, James, ed. *Abrams Methods of Diagnosis and Treatment*. William Heinmann Medical Books LTD: London, 1925.

Cave, Francis A. DO MD. "The Electronic Reactions of Abrams." *Pearsons Magazine*: July 1992. Reprinted in *ERA: The Electronic Reactions of Abrams*. Borderland Sciences. Bayside, California. p. 17-20.

Colson, Thomas. "Oscilloclast Energies." Reprinted in *ERA: The Electronic Reactions of Abrams*. Borderland Sciences. Bayside, California. p.53-58.

--- "Effects on Living Tissue of Chopped or Pulsed Energy." EMD Fourth Quarter, 1951. Reprinted in *ERA: The Electronic Reactions of Abrams*. Borderland Sciences. Bayside, California. p. 73-76.

Russell, Edward W. *Report on Radionics: The Science Which Can Cure Where Orthodox Medicine Fails*. Random House UK, 1996.

08 Inside Dr. Abrams' Clinic

Sinclair, Upton. "The House of Wonder." *Pearsons Magazine*: June 1922. Reprinted in *ERA: The Electronic Reactions of Abrams*. Bor-

derland Sciences. Bayside, California.

09 Psychical Physics

Blum, Deborah, "The Ghost in the Machine" *The New York Times*, Op Ed section, 2006

Tiller, William A. *Science and Human Transformation: Subtle Energies, Intentionality and Consciousness.* Pavior Publishing, 1997.

10 From Agricultural Radionics to Prehistoric Art

Russell, Edward W. *Report on Radionics: The Science Which Can Cure Where Orthodox Medicine Fails.* Random House UK, 1996

11 Prana, Kundalini and Occult Technology

Krishna, Gopi. *Kundalini: The Evolutionary Energy in Man.* Shambhala: Boulder, Colorado, 1971.

Mermet, Abbe'. *Principles and Practice of Radiesthesia.* Thomas Nelson and Sons: New York, 1959.

Paijmans, Theo. *Free Energy Pioneer: John Worrell Keely.* IllumiNet; Lilburn, Ga, 1998.

Tromp, S. W. *Psychical Physics.* Elsevier Publishing Company, Inc., 1949.

Vassilatos, Gerry. *Lost Science.* Borderland Sciences Research, 1997.

Vassilatos, Gerry. *The Vril Compendium.* Borderland Sciences Research, 1992.

12 Radionics: Occult or Electronic?

International Hahnemannian Association. Certain Body Reflexes in Their Relation to Certain Radiant Energies. International Hahnemannian Association, 1926.

The Journal of the Universal Society of Pathometrists, Vol. 12, Section 4, May 1940.

Russell, Edward W. *Report on Radionics: The Science Which Can Cure Where Orthodox Medicine Fails.* Random House UK, 1996.

Tansley, David V. *Dimensions of Radionics.* Health Science Press, 1977.

Tiller, William A. *Science and Human Transformation: Subtle Energies, Intentionality and Consciousness.* Pavior Publishing, 1997.

13 Ruth Drown

Constable, Trevor James. *The Cosmic Pulse of Life.* Borderland Sciences: 1976. P. 259, 260, 262.

Drown, Ruth B. *The Drown Homo-Vibra Ray & Radio Vision Instruments.* Borderland Sciences Research.

Mathers, MacGregor S.L. *The Kabbalah Unveiled.* Weiser, 1989.

Russell, Edward W. *Report on Radionics: The Science Which Can Cure Where Orthodox Medicine Fails.* Random House UK, 1996.

Tiller, William A. *Science and Human Transformation: Subtle Energies, Intentionality and Consciousness.* Pavior Publishing, 1997.

Young, Arthur D. *Nested Time: An Astrological Autobiography*. Anodos Publications, 2004.

14 Profiles in British Radionics

Baerlein, E. Dower, A. L. G. *Healing with Radionics - The Science of Healing Energy*. Thorsons, 1980.

Burr, Harold Saxton. *The Neural Basis Of Human Behavior*. Charles C. Thomas, 1960.

Denning, Murray R. *My Search For Radionic Truths*. Borderland Sciences Research Foundation: Garberville, California, 1981, 1988.

Ganot, Adolphe. *Elementary Treaties On Physics*. 5th Edition, translated by E. Atkinson, Ph.D., 1872.

Henderson, Linda D. *Duchamp In Context*. Princeton University Press, 1998.

Lawlor, Robert. *Sacred Geometry: Philosophy and Practice*. Thames & Hudson, 1989.

Resines, Jorge. *Automated Detecting Devices*. Borderland Sciences Research, 1989.

Richards, W. Guyon. *The Chain Of Life*. The C. W. Daniel Company, Ltd., Essex, England, 1954.

Russell, Edward W. *Report on Radionics*. The C.W. Daniel Company Limited: Saffron Walden Essex, 1973 (Quotations P.93).

15 George and Majorie De La Warr

Adcock, Craig. "Marcel Duchamp's Gap Music: Operations In The Space Between Art And Noise." *Wireless Imagination Sound Radio and The Avant-Garde*. Ed. Douglas Kahn and Gregory Whitehead. The MIT Press: Cambridge, Massachusetts, 1992. 105, 131.

Day, Gerald William Langston and George de la Warr. *Matter in the Making*. Vincent Stuart Publishers, 1966.

Day, Gerald William Langston, and George Walter De La Warr. *New Worlds Beyond the Atom*. Vincent Stuart: London, 1956.

Emoto, Masaru. *Messages From Water*. Vol. 1 & 2, HADO Kyoikusha Co., Ltd. Japan. 2001.

Gordon, Mel. "Songs from the Museum of the Future" *Wireless Imagination Sound Radio and The Avant-Garde*. Ed. Douglas Kahn and Gregory Whitehead. The MIT Press: Cambridge, Massachusetts, 1992. 208, 218-219.

Hallmon, Henry and Carl Hollingsworth. "The Geometry of the Naked Singularity." *Nexus*. Nov./Dec. 2002.

Henderson, Linda D. *Duchamp In Context*. Princeton University Press, 1998.

Kandinsky, Wassily. *Concerning the Spiritual in Art*. Adrian Glew, ed. Trans. M. T. Sadler. New York: MFA Publications, 2001.

Lawlor, Robert. *Sacred Geometry: Philosophy and Practice*. Thames & Hudson, 1989.

Russell, Edward W. *Report on Radionics: The Science Which Can Cure Where Orthodox Medicine Fails*. Random House UK, 1996.

Vassilatos, Gerry. *Lost Science*. Borderland Sciences Research, 1997.

16 T. Galen Hieronymus

Bearden, Col. Thomas Website: http://www.cheniere.org/toc.html

Beautlich, Robert, Personal Conversation, 2001.

Goodavage, Joseph F. "The Incredible Hieronymus Machine." *Future Science: Life Energies and the Physics of Paranormal Phenomena.* Ed. John White and Stanley Krippner. Anchor Books, 1977. 394.

Hieronymus, Dr. Sarah W. *The Story of Eloptic Energy, The Autobiography of an Advanced Scientist Dr. T. Galen Hieronymus.* The Institute of Advanced Sciences, 1988.

Jensen, William D. "Preliminary Report on the Patented Hieronymus Machine." Website. http://wdjensen123.com/hieronymus/Report1.htm

Russell, Edward W. *Report on Radionics: The Science Which Can Cure Where Orthodox Medicine Fails.* Random House UK, 1996.

Tromp, S.W. *Psychical Physics.* Elsevier Publishing Company, Inc., 1949.

U.S. Patent Office, #2,482,773, 1949.

Vasiliev, L.L. *Experiments in mental suggestion.* Institute for the Study of Mental Images, 1963.

Young, Arthur D., *Nested Time: An Astrological Autobiography.* Anodos Publications, 2004.

Young, Arthur D. Website. http://www.arthuryoung.com/ntexc.html.

17 Radionics Meets Popular Culture

Curtis, Adam. dir. *The Century of the Self.* BBC 2002.

Hieronymus, Dr. Sarah W. *The Story of Eloptic Energy, The Autobiography of an Advanced Scientist Dr. T. Galen Hieronymus.* The Institute of Advanced Sciences, 1988.

White, John, and Stanley Krippner. *Future Science: Life energies and the Physics of Paranormal Phenomena.* Anchor Books, 1977.

18 Agricultural Radionics Today

Diver, Steve, and George Kuepper "Radionics in Agriculture" Website. http://home.earthlink.net/~gkuepper/index/Radionics.htm 1997.

Larsen, Lutie. http://littlefarmresearch.com.

Larsen, Lutie, et al. "The Radionic Homestead Report" http://www.littlefarmresearch.com/productCat44814.ctlg.

Larsen, Lutie. Interview. "Lutie tests MZ Alchemist Oils" Marie Allizon. Jan. 2001.

19 Radionic Photography Today

Benford, M. Sue, "Empirical Evidence Supporting Macro-Scale Quantum Holography in Non-Local Effects" *Journal of Theoretics,* 1999.

Benford, M. Sue, Mitchell, Edgar, Marcer, Peter, Moscow, Peter "QuantaGraphy: Images From the Quantum Hologram," *Fifth International Conference on Computing Anticipatory*

Systems (CASYS '01), Liege, Belgium, 2001. http://newvistas.homestead.com/CASYS.html

Burr, Harold Saxton. *The Neural Basis Of Human Behavior*. Charles C. Thomas, 1960.

Day, Langston, and George De La Warr. *Matter in the Making*. Vincent Stuart Publishers: London, 1966.

Gordon, Mel. "Songs from the Museum of the Future" *Wireless Imagination Sound Radio and The Avant-Garde*. Ed. Douglas Kahn and Gregory Whitehead. The MIT Press: Cambridge, Massachusetts, 1992. 208, 219. Lawlor, Robert. *Sacred Geometry: Philosophy and Practice*. Thames & Hudson, 1989.

Mitchell, Edgar, "Nature's Mind: The Quantum Hologram" *International Journal of Computing Anticipatory Systems*, Volume 7, "Fuzzy Systems, Genetic and Neural Algorithms, Quantum Neural Information Processing: New Technology? New Biology?" 1999.

Online Oxford Dictionary

Russell, Edward W. *Report on Radionics: The Science Which Can Cure Where Orthodox Medicine Fails*. Random House UK, 1996. (149-150).

Young, Arthur D., *Nested Time: An Astrological Autobiography*. Anodos Publications, 2004.

20 From Computerized Radionics to Radionics Without Devices

Cieslar, "Saving Fuel with QUANTEC," http://www.quantec.ch/english/areas_ap-plication/areas_application_environment_gas.html.

Cross, Matthew, Lutz, Franz "Resonance Therapy." Institute for Resonance Therapy (IRT), Cappenberg, Am Struckmansberg 32, D-44534 Lünen, Germany. http://web.archive.org/web/20020808192638/www.irt-cappenberg.de/kpl_e/irt-1.htm.

Gerrard, Don. *The Paper Doctor, A Vibrational Medicine Cabinet*. The Bookworks, 1991.

Heuvelop, Sabine, "Health Management of Show Horses Using Instrumental Biocommunication" M-Tec Website: http://www.quantec.ch/english/

Jahn, Robert G. and Brenda J. Dunne. *Margins of Reality: The Role of Consciousness in the Physical World*. San Diego: Harcourt Brace Jovanovich, 1987.

Koehne, Peter "Radionics, The Healing Method of the Future" Raum & Zeit, July/Aug 1993. Reprinted in *Regaining Wholeness Through the Subtle Dimensions* by Don Paris. Living from Vision 1993.

M-Tec Website: http://remotehealingonline.com/english/white_noise/white_noise.html.

McCall, Walter A. Website. http://nrgvet.com.

Paris, Don. *Regaining Wholeness Through the Subtle Dimensions*. Living from Vision 1993.

Peoc'h, Rene, "Psychokinetic Action of Young Chicks on the Path of An Illuminated Source," *The Journal of Scientific Exploration*, Vol. 9, #2, pg. 223-229, in 1995.

Stucki, Anton, "The Dreipfuhl Pond Project In Berlin" M-Tec Website, http://web.archive.org/web/20071026212235/www.m-tec.ag/1_3_1_1.asp?lang=eng.

Von Buengner, Peter, M TEC AG INSTRU-MENTAL BIOCOMMUNICATION website: http://www.quantec.ch/english/.

Von Buengner, Peter. *Physics and Dreamtime*. Altkirchen, Germany: Privately published, 2001.

Von Buengner, Peter. *Biocommunication With Quantec*. Altkirchen, Germany: M-TEC AG, 2003.

21 Radionic/Art Overlay: A Personal Note

Berens, Michael J. and Christine Willmsen "Miracle Machines: The 21st-Century Snake Oil." Seattle Times, 18 November 2007. http://seattletimes.nwsource.com/html/medicaldevices/

ILLUSTRATION CREDITS

artwork by Jessica Paulk

14-10. Induction Furnace CD jacket
by Michael Brennan and Rafael Attias

14-11. Butcher — Meter III
from "My Search For Radionic Truths"
Denning - http://www.borderlands.com

15 George and Majorie De La Warr

15-1. De la Warr Diagnostic Instrument with
Oscillator
artwork by Jessica Paulk

15-2. Nodal point diagram
artwork by Jessica Paulk

15-3. Thomas Wilfred playing the Clavilux
from Wilfred, Thomas, Pps Manuscripts &
Archives, Yale University

15-4. Mark I De la Warr Camera
from "Matter in the Making" Day and
de la Warr

15-5. Thought photograph of Pen Knife with
Mark I Camera
from "Matter in the Making" Day and
de la Warr

15-6. Photograph of Nodal Point in Space of
Copper Sulfate Crystal
from "Matter in the Making" Day and
de la Warr

15-7. George de la Warr
courtesy of Leonardo Olazabal Amaral
Center of Radionic "Darjeeling" in SPAIN.
www.shambala-roerich.com

16 T. Galen Hieronymus

16-1. T. Galen Hieronymus
courtesy of Leonardo Olazabal Amaral
Center of Radionic "Darjeeling" in SPAIN.
www.shambala-roerich.com

16-2. Pathoclast
artwork by Jessica Paulk

16-3. US Patent #2,482,773
from US Patent Office

16-4. Three Bank Hieronymus Radionics
device
photo by Todd Thille

16-5. Three Bank Hieronymus Radionics
device
artwork by Jessica Paulk

17 Radionics Meets Popular Culture

17-1. THE HIERONYMUSBOX
Paul Laffoley 1982
collection of Duncan Laurie

17-2. Radionic T-Shirt design
by Duncan Laurie

17-3. Tony Malone's Hieronymus Circuit
artwork by Tony Malone

17-4. 13th Century Geomantic Device - front
artwork by Jessica Paulk

17-5. 13th Century Geomantic Device - reverse
artwork by Jessica Paulk

17-6. Butcher Upright Diagnostic Instrument
artwork by Jessica Paulk

Visit Duncan Laurie's website at:

http://www.duncanlaurie.com

For supplemental material and discussion
on radionics.

CPSIA information can be obtained
at www.ICGtesting.com
Printed in the USA
BVHW07s1926240518
517269BV00005B/38/P